Advance Praise for *The Spirit of Vatican II*

"Written in an inviting and accessible style, McDannell's work captures the important movements in the church and American society that preceded (and prepared the way for) Vatican II, the details of the Council, and its unique effects on various parishes. The book underscores the contributions of women whose roles may not have been as public as those of male clerics but which were influential at the local level. Catholics who lived in this era will recognize the history and younger generations will learn the nuances of the history that has shaped contemporary religious experience."

—Chester Gillis, Professor of Theology at
Georgetown University and author of *Roman Catholicism in America*

"Part social history, part family memoir, Colleen McDannell's *The Spirit of Vatican II* beautifully evokes the dramatic transformation of Catholicism in the middle decades of the twentieth century. The way she entwines her stories of family and church is a breath of fresh air all its own."

—Leigh E. Schmidt, Charles Warren Professor of
American Religious History at Harvard University

"In this engaging and compelling text McDannell uses her mother's story to trace the impact of Vatican II's reforms on the everyday lives of American Catholics. Through the lens of family history we come to understand not only the theological, liturgical, and cultural changes the Council set in motion, but gain insight into broader issues such as immigration, family history, gender, class, region, and popular culture. McDannell's accessible narrative makes important contributions to the history of religion in America."

—Judith Weisenfeld, Professor of Religion at Princeton University

The Spirit of

VATICAN II

ALSO BY COLLEEN McDANNELL

Catholics in the Movies, editor
Picturing Faith: Photography and the Great Depression
The Religions of the United States in Practice, editor
Material Christianity: Religion and Popular Culture in America
Heaven: A History (co-authored with Bernhard Lang)
The Christian Home in Victorian America, 1840–1900

The Spirit of

VATICAN II

A History of
Catholic Reform in America

\\|//

Colleen McDannell

BASIC
BOOKS
A Member of the Perseus Books Group
New York

Published by Basic Books,
A Member of the Perseus Books Group

Books published by Basic Books are available at special discounts for bulk purchases in the United States by corporations, institutions, and other organizations. For more information, please contact the Special Markets Department at the Perseus Books Group, 2300 Chestnut Street, Suite 200, Philadelphia, PA 19103, or call (800) 810-4145, ext. 5000, or e-mail special.markets@perseusbooks.com.

Designed by Jeff Williams
Set in 11-point Kepler Light by the Perseus Books Group

Library of Congress Cataloging-in-Publication Data
McDannell, Colleen.
    The spirit of Vatican II : a history of Catholic reform in America / Colleen McDannell.
        p. cm.
    Includes bibliographical references (p.   ) and index.
    ISBN 978-0-465-04480-1 (hardcover : alk. paper)—ISBN 978-0-465-02338-7 (e-book)
1. Catholics—United States—Case studies. 2. Church renewal—Catholic Church—History—20th century. 3. Catholic Church—United States—History—20th century.
4. United States—Church history—20th century. 5. Church renewal—Catholic Church—History—21st century. 6. Catholic Church—United States–History—21st century.
7. United States—Church history–21st century. 8. Vatican Council (2nd : 1962–1965) I. Title.

BX1406.3.M34 2011
282'.7309045—dc22
                                                                                    2010051633

E-book ISBN: 978-0-465-02338-7

10 9 8 7 6 5 4 3 2 1

For Linda Jansen, Lillian Wondrack,
Dianne Ashton, and Margaret Toscano,
always there

CONTENTS

First Holy Communion, April 1962.
Margaret McDannell with
daughter Colleen and son Kevin.

INTRODUCTION

I am the last of a generation. In April of 1962 I received my First Holy Communion. That fall, the Catholic bishops of the world traveled to Rome to spend four years debating changes that would alter Catholicism forever.

As an eight-year-old, I was dressed like a bride but wearing white, lace-edged socks. I eagerly awaited receiving the body and blood of Christ. The Holy Names Sisters who taught me at St. Stephen's school did their best to explain the meaning of the Mass. Patiently they translated its Latin texts and deciphered the ritualized gestures. Earlier in the week, I had confessed my sins to our parish priest. Those of us who would receive Communion that day had dutifully fasted for three hours. That the girl kneeling beside me fainted under the stress of the event only heightened the emotional intensity of the ceremony. It was a heady week for a second grader.

That fall would also begin four heady years for the world's Catholic leaders. By early October 1962 over two thousand "Council Fathers" had traveled to Rome to attend the Second Vatican Council. The prominence of this meeting of Catholic leaders also attracted an even larger assembly of journalists, pilgrims, theological advisors, and curiosity seekers.

Dressed in their finest clerical garb, 2,540 men processed into St. Peter's Basilica on the Feast of the Maternity of the Virgin Mary. These Council Fathers came from seventy-nine different countries, with the number of Americans almost equaling the number of Europeans. That total would be matched by those who came from Asia, Oceania, and Africa. The French bishops brought four tons of baggage, but the 239 Council Fathers from the United States traveled far lighter.[1]

All had arrived in response to Pope John XXIII's call to "open a window and let in a little fresh air" to the Catholic Church. The pope and many of the leaders of the world's Catholics had decided that the Holy Spirit now required the renewal of her people. Four years had already gone into the preparation for such a discussion. Now there would be another four autumns of intense reflection on how to make the gospel of Christ relevant in a modern world.

M Y FAVORITE PICTURE from the day of my First Holy Communion has me posing with my mother and brother in our California backyard. Even though I got to wear a veil and my brother sported a natty plaid jacket, it is my mother, Margaret, who steals the show. For this major rite of passage in her daughter's life, she is wearing a feathered hat she made in a "how-to" class, fake pearls, and a mink stole—just the outfit for a southern California spring day.

My mother is also the last of a generation. In 1962 she was in full adulthood, aged thirty-six, having been born just before the Great Depression and marrying during the Second World War. Unlike hers, my generation was too young to notice the end of a particular kind of Catholicism. I grew up after the Second Vatican Council, playing guitar music at English-language Masses. I can remember my father crying in 1963 at the funeral of John F. Kennedy, but I have no memory of the day when priests turned around and faced their congregations. My mother and her generation do.

My parents are now in their eighties. Their generation flourished in spite of the profound challenges of the times, motivating some journalists to anoint them the "Greatest Generation." Theirs is the last generation of Catholics to live half their lives before the Second Vatican Council and half after the Council. My parents hold their religion close to their hearts. Only a serious illness could keep them from going to Mass every Sunday. For the Catholics of the Greatest Generation—those who lived through the Depression, World War II, the sixties, and the terrorist attacks of 9/11—the Second Vatican Council looms large.

"Vatican Two" conjures up the spirit of a defining religious moment. Catholics still talk about what things were like "before Vatican II" or "after Vatican II." Even those who have little understanding of the specific documents of the Council can remember the excitement and turmoil of the period between 1959, when Pope John XXIII announced his plan to convene a worldwide meeting of bishops, and 1978, when Pope Paul VI died. The phrase "the spirit of Vatican II" refers to a constellation of changes that Catholics experienced in their homes, churches, and schools.

For Margaret, the Second Vatican Council stimulated changes that brought her more intimately in contact with the ritual and theological life of her church. Like millions of other Catholics, she was the granddaughter of immigrants. Until she left home, she had attended Mass in a highly decorated church and went to a school taught by nuns who wore equally elaborate habits. After World War II, Margaret's husband took advantage of the GI Bill, and the young couple eventually moved into a newly built suburb in Toledo, Ohio. There they joined a fast-growing parish that relied heavily on the involvement of young families. Suburban Catholicism prepared many Catholics for the changes that would come from Rome in the sixties. However, when Margaret moved to Los Angeles, her California parish had a pastor who showed no interest in altering how Catholicism was practiced. Only after Margaret and her husband moved to Denver, Colorado, did they experience the full implications of the Second Vatican Council. Margaret enthusiastically embraced the "Spirit of Vatican II" at her new "exurban" parish. She joined with other men and women to distribute Communion at Mass, sing folk songs, and call their pastor by his first name. Now retired and living in central Florida, the couple no longer go to a Mass with guitars, but Margaret still enjoys her women's Bible-study group and supports the church's sister parish in Uganda.

Margaret's Catholic life is not unusual, but it has received little attention. In the past ten years, what has stood out in the American Catholic Church has been the sex abuse scandals. Priests preying on boys and young men along with the reluctance of bishops to end this behavior have rightfully grabbed the attention of both Catholics and non-Catholics. This attention, however, plays into an enduring misunderstanding of Catholicism: that the Catholic Church is energized, defined, and determined by the actions of men. Most of the written Catholic history has revolved around men because it is the story of priests, theologians, and popes. Too often women drop out of this history.

Charting the changes of the Second Vatican Council through Margaret (the one in the feathered hat) helps shift the focus away from priests, men, and boys and instead toward nuns, women, and girls. Women's continual commitment to Catholicism—a commitment that, nevertheless, has always had its limits—has been grossly underacknowledged. My mother and her friends welcomed the changes of Vatican II. As for those parts of Catholicism that did not change, like the prohibition of divorce and birth control, they thought about them deeply and then ignored them. This rejection of certain Catholic norms was not invented in the rebellious sixties; parish life has always been constructed out of conflict and compromise. The changes of the Second Vatican Council, however, both amplified and acknowledged lay participation in Catholicism.

Although Catholics are as diverse as America itself, my mother's story is typical of much of her generation. Born into a European immigrant family in the urban Northeast, she quit college to get married to a man who was going off to war; she raised children in the suburbs while her husband worked at a profession made possible by the GI Bill; and when he retired, they moved south. Although she lived near cities, she had little interest in them. Hers was a mobile life, lived mostly in the western United States.

Margaret's Catholic life mirrors many of the changes the nation experienced after World War II. The very iconic character of my mother's life makes her an ideal lens through which to narrate the religious reforms that we call the spirit of Vatican II.

chapter one

CATHOLIC NEIGHBORHOODS

Before the epoch-defining Vatican Council of the sixties, the Catholic Church was a very different institution. Since the Enlightenment era, European rulers, politicians, and philosophers had struggled against religious control. Catholic leaders fought to hold on to political power while simultaneously reinforcing religious influence in the affairs of home and family. Rejecting innovations in philosophy that stressed individualism and in science that promoted rationalism, Catholic theologians portrayed a world based on fixed truths defined by supernatural realities. In order to understand the Catholic reforms that culminated in the *second* Vatican Council, we must get a feel for the Catholic culture of the era of the *first* Vatican Council that took place in 1870. This Catholicism—defined by the Council of Trent and upheld by Vatican I—was to be renewed and updated at the Second Vatican Council.

In the United States, European immigrant families and their American-born children defined American Catholicism during this period. Their piety was shaped both by experiences in the old world and the realities of the new world. The religion of Margaret's grandmother and mother, as well as that of her own childhood, was a volatile mix of the hopes of immigrants and the fears of their religious leaders. It is the Catholicism of the immigrant church and not the suburban church of the fifties that was most altered by the reforms of the sixties.

After World War II, the Catholicism of the long nineteenth century began to slowly change under theological, ritual, and artistic reforms. Margaret was one of the millions of grandchildren of immigrants who would leave the ethnic neighborhoods of their families and move to the growing postwar suburbs. She would marry a non-Catholic. Regardless, however, her commitment to and knowledge of Catholicism was formed in the neighborhoods of her youth.

W HEN WE IMAGINE Catholic immigrants settling in America's cities, we see Irish and Italian faces. Movies and television shows have told us time and again that Catholics are Irish and Italian. From James Cagney in *Angels with Dirty Faces* to Martin Scorsese's *Gangs of New York* and *The Departed*, Irish American men have always defined ethnic Catholicism for Americans—and the primacy of the Irish is challenged only by the Italian representation of the same story. Even the recognition of the Spanish-speaking Catholic in the contemporary Church is only slowly changing the widespread assumption that urban Catholics are either of Irish or Italian heritage.

Although the Irish did dominate the Catholic hierarchy and the Italians cultivated a lively popular piety, German Catholics are the ones who filled the church pews. In 1866 more than 50,000 German immigrants had entered the United States through New York harbor alone. A few years later the number grew to over 117,500 migrants from the various states that became Germany in 1871. Although determining religious commitments is difficult, scholars estimate that after 1860 approximately 35 percent of German immigrants were Catholic.[1] Between 1865 and 1900 over 700,000 German Catholics arrived in the United States. Not long after this mass movement began, the number of Germans equaled the number of Irish who had arrived a generation earlier. It was not until the turn-of-the-century's influx of large numbers of Italian Catholics that Germans no longer comprised the majority of the Catholic foreign-born.

Although many German Catholics moved to the farming regions that lay within a triangle defined by St. Louis, Milwaukee, and Cincinnati, others moved to the country's growing cities. Germans settled in Pennsylvania and all along the shores of the Ohio River and the Great Lakes.

Such was the case with Margaret's grandmother and grandfather. In 1879 Angelika (nicknamed "Annie") Froess, along with her sisters Anna and Katie and their brother Joseph, emigrated from the village of Bechenheim. Census enumerators noted on their forms that they were all born in the Grand Duchy of Darmstadt-Hesse, not far from the city of Mainz. The siblings ended up in Erie, Pennsylvania, a well-established manufacturing city on an active waterfront. Single and eighteen when she arrived, Annie was twenty-one when she married Louis Liebel, a local butcher. Louis was also from southern Germany, his family bringing him to America from Leimersheim in 1866 when he was six. Annie and Louis would do what immigrants have done since the settling of the United States: They brought over the rest of their family and supported them.

As an old woman, long after the death of her husband, Annie Liebel developed a special relationship with her granddaughter Margaret. Annie lived with her daughter's family, and Margaret helped her cook and keep house. When Margaret asked her why her family came from Germany to the United States, the answer was not for the good jobs in a growing industrial city. Annie explained to her granddaughter that her father, Margaret's great-grandfather, wanted to keep his sons from being drafted.

The Froess's family concern was a real one.

Although the state of Prussia was powerful, until 1871 there was no central German state: Germany as a country did not exist. The bulk of the Catholic population lived in two areas, the southern region of Bavaria and the lands to the west of the Rhine River. Both the Froess and the Liebel families made their homes near the Rhine. Although Bavaria was relatively secure because of Austria's protection, Catholics with homes bordering the Rhine had the misfortune of living in a highly contested territory. Because France had historically sought to extend its borders to one of Europe's greatest waterways, those living by its west bank often found themselves caught between warring states.

In the spring of 1793, under the enthusiasm of the French Revolution, the lands to the west of the Rhine fell under French rule. The French then plundered villages to support the troops. They also brought their revolutionary reforms into the area: Serfdom was outlawed, civil records were kept, and new technologies were introduced. The French also came with the innovation that every citizen should be a soldier and every soldier a citizen. After the Revolution died, Napoleon embraced the idea of universal conscription, and eventually other European rulers saw the potential of a national draft. As a result, the state of Prussia required military duty from every citizen (only reinforcing the notion that women were not citizens). This enabled Prussia to mobilize a large number of relatively well-trained men for their successful 1870 war against France. Five men from Louis Liebel's village of Leimersheim died in that war.

The next year, Prussian Count Otto von Bismarck became chancellor of a new, unified Germany. Bismarck was determined to make Germany a strong military and industrial state. The draft continued, and higher taxes were instituted to support the army. Bismarck's government hoped that a stint in the army would instill in the farmer from the provinces an orderly, disciplined, obedient, and patriotic life geared toward the good of the whole nation. In 1903 a German official noted that men leaving for America were "mostly strong, healthy persons, with habits of cleanliness, which they derived from their service in the army."[2] On a practical level, avoiding the draft made sense for the safety of the family's sons. On a symbolic level, avoiding the draft meant trying to preserve a modicum of self-sufficiency and independence in a rapidly changing Europe.

For rural families like Annie's, modernization brought many problems during the last decades of the nineteenth century. As competition stiffened, agricultural prices fell. Cheap, mass-produced goods threatened the livelihoods of village artisans. German immigrants looked to the United States as a place where they might maintain their connections to the land, their trades, and their families.

However, Catholic families had additional worries. When Bismarck came into power, he started what was called the *Kulturkampf*—the "struggle for true culture." The new government sought to ensure that Germany's fragile national unity would not fragment into competing regional or religious loyalties. The state had to be the people's highest authority, and the Catholic Church couldn't be allowed to compete.

Many European thinkers and politicians of the time were trying to promote an Enlightenment model of life. They hoped to restrain religion within a limited, private sphere of personal piety and morality while insisting that the public sphere fall under the control of the state. European leaders, who historically had to negotiate power arrangements with Catholic bishops and the pope, wanted to strip religious organizations of their public influence.

The Catholic Church resisted, and doing so placed it on a collision course with both politicians and philosophers. From the French Revolution onward, Catholic leaders struggled to maintain their political authority, and Bismarck made matters no easier. Believing that the Vatican would stand in the way of German nationalism, Bismarck and the Reichstag, the general assembly of the German empire, enacted a series of laws in 1873 to limit the educational and ecclesiastical power of Catholicism. These "May Laws" prohibited papal authority over German Catholics and abolished religious orders. They stipulated that the education of Catholic clergy was to be overseen by the state and that bishops could not discipline their priests or appoint pastors without the government's approval. Church property was to be handed over to lay trustees, and religious instruction in elementary schools was to be conducted by teachers acceptable to the state. Bishops who resisted were put in prison, and some Catholics soon found that no priests remained to say Mass nor nuns to teach school.

The Kulturkampf backfired. A fledging German bureaucracy failed at enforcing its mandates, and Vatican ecclesiastical authorities were able to work around problematic state officials. Most importantly, rank-and-file Catholics refused to abandon their religious leaders. Rather than cultivating fear of the state, the Kulturkampf caused anger and resentment that frequently broke out into stubborn resistance and informal dissent. Some families emigrated, whereas others stayed home and became more aggressively Catholic. Catholic newspapers flourished, and parishes learned how to survive without state funds by charging for religious rituals. Lay men and women created societies to promote a Catholic community life that excluded Protestants. Because German nationalism appeared to abandon Catholics, Catholics looked to the institution of the Church to defend their religious traditions.

The Kulturkampf's ramifications would be enduring. The importance of being a Catholic was passed on to the children of German immigrants—children like Margaret. This was not the case for all Catholic immigrant groups who traveled to America. Southern Italians, for instance, were very skeptical about their parishes' priests because in Italy the priest often sided with landowners against the peasants. Thus, immigrant Catholics saw their religion through the lens of what they had experienced in the Old Country. For many German Catholics this meant commitment to parish life.

C ATHOLICS WHO SETTLED IN America's growing industrial cities tried to create neighborhoods that resembled European villages. When Annie and her family arrived in Erie, it was a patchwork quilt of various ethnic and religious communities. The Scots-Irish attended several Presbyterian churches. Episcopalians built a brick church in 1834 and opened a much larger Gothic edifice in 1866. A third, "The Church of the Cross and the Crown," became a parish in 1872. There were three Methodist churches for whites and one for blacks. German Protestants had their choice of attending either a Baptist or a Lutheran congregation, and German Jews founded Anschai Chesed Reform Congregation, which met in each other's homes until they built a synagogue in 1882. The Universalists had a church whose land was donated by one of the city's prominent judges. Unlike in Europe, where nationalists ridiculed religion as superstitious and challenged the authority of the clergy, patriotic Americans supported their houses of worship. All of the proper citizens in the town went to church.

In the United States after the Civil War, religious tensions were more pronounced *within* the churches rather than between denominations or the state. This was particularly the case with Catholics because different immigrant communities had unique worship styles and attitudes toward the clergy. Catholics brought their local saints, healing traditions, and ways of celebrating along with them when they came from Europe. At times those practices came into conflict with Church leaders. Immigrant Catholics, many of whom had left their own homelands because they felt they could not practice their religion as they wanted, resented such interference.

In 1868, two years after Louis Liebel arrived in America, Tobias Mullen became the bishop of the Erie diocese. Mullen had come to the United States from Ireland as a young seminarian, initially settling in Pittsburgh. He was one of the many Irish men who dominated the Catholic hierarchy in the United States. Mullen's appointment as the Catholic "prince" of Erie would span thirty-one years. However, almost immediately after his installation, a crisis erupted: The Irish bishop would have a run-in with the German parishioners of St. Joseph's over the construction of a cemetery.[3] The family of Louis Liebel went to this parish, and fourteen years later, the young butcher would marry Annie in St. Joseph's Church.

Whereas priests provide the sacrament of the Last Rites to Catholics, burial is under the auspices of the laity. Finding a proper place for the dead is not easy. During the wet season in Erie, the graves of one Catholic churchyard filled up with water, so occasionally the coffins had to be weighed down by stones piled on top of them. When Bishop Mullen arrived, he decided to address this problem by buying land outside of the city for a cemetery to be used by all of the parishes in his diocese. In addition, the bishop intended to charge burial fees to pay for a new cathedral.

From Bishop Mullen's perspective, both the cemetery and the cathedral would reflect the unity of the city's Catholics—bringing together all ethnic groups under the banner of faith and thus demonstrating the enduring truth of Catholicism. Throughout the nation, bishops were proclaiming the permanence and authority of Catholicism by making their churches grand spaces of prayer. Mullen was carrying out the wishes of the Vatican in its desire to strengthen the international church by ensuring that local or national customs never interfered with Catholic unity.

The German parishioners of St. Joseph's Church thought differently. The cemetery would be five miles from their church and it would take at least an hour and a half to walk there. Hiring wagons to transport the dead and their families was costly. Back where they came from, even the smallest town had its own cemetery tended by local women. They reasoned that if they were working hard to build their own church, why should they have to support the building of a cathedral? Consequently, even though some men had voted for the new cemetery, a group of women from the St. Joseph's rosary society bought a plot of land for their own burial ground. Their pastor, Father Joseph Stumpe, approved of the idea because the revenues raised from burial fees would go back into his church. A cemetery, not unlike a church supper, could provide a steady stream of income to the parish. Father Stumpe and the rosary society women were thinking in terms of local parish needs.

"But alas," a parish historian wrote in 1918, "how little they knew of the determination and firmness of Bishop Mullen," how little they knew of "the power over priests and people vested in any Catholic bishop." In 1869, on a sultry July Sunday, Bishop Mullen walked unannounced into St. Joseph's church and, after Mass, told the parishioners not to set up a separate cemetery. He warned them "most earnestly" not to resist authority, and then asked them to follow the saintly model of their patron St. Joseph, who was humble and obedient. As he left the church, he must have realized that he had failed in his mission. A number of men "did not as much as tip their hats" as he walked through the dispersing crowd.[4]

Lay Catholics in nineteenth-century Erie were not cowed by their bishop, especially an Irish one. Father Stumpe either sided with the parishioners or failed to convince them of the bishop's power. Soon the congregation began burying their dead in their own parish cemetery. First two children and then a respectable matron who was a member of the rosary society were buried there. Father Stumpe followed his bishop's orders, and so the internments took place without the services of a priest and without the sound of the bell announcing another soul committed to eternity.

At first Bishop Mullen ignored the rebellious parishioners. He might have concluded that a group of women could not possibly maintain their dissent if he transferred their pastor. Father Stumpe was given the choice of either leaving the diocese or taking charge of the mission in Brookville—a tiny outpost in the forest, thirty miles from the nearest railroad station. Stumpe went off in exile. Bishop Mullen then appointed Father John Kuehn as pastor, a thirty-year-old member of the predominately German order of the Redemptorists. But Bishop Mullen overlooked the fact that it was the women of the parish who cleaned and prepared bodies for burial, coordinated funeral suppers, comforted families as they walked to the graveyard, and kept the cemetery in order. In the days before funeral parlors and undertakers, women were experts in the dead, and they did not want to turn over any of their duties to the diocese. The alternate cemetery continued.

Father Kuehn also failed to bring the crisis to an end. St. Joseph's parishioners split into two factions: those who supported the parish cemetery and those who cast their lot with Bishop Mullen. The conflict had caused division not simply between the parishioners and the bishop but also among parishioners. For almost six months, the two sets of parishioners would not speak to each other. The disputing factions sat on separate pews and insisted that separate collections be taken up so as not to support the wrong cause. Income into the parish declined. In order to maintain the church and school, Father Kuehn had to borrow money (at 10 percent interest) from the diocese. In the upstairs part of the school, two nuns were brought in to teach the children of those who supported the bishop's cemetery, whereas downstairs the "new cemetery party" children were taught by Father Stumpe's brother-in-law. On Christmas morning there were even two choirs singing simultaneously upstairs and downstairs.

Naturally, both sides claimed the right to ring the bell at funerals. That issue was solved when someone cut the bell rope, causing an unsuspecting bell ringer to fall sprawling to the floor. Bricks and stones were tossed into the living area of Father Kuehn, who "repeatedly lost his temper." Now that the cemetery had become so important, the parish's men took it out of the hands of the rosary society women and organized their own St. Joseph's Cemetery Society, obtaining a charter of incorporation from the Court of Erie. All this must have surely irritated the young bishop, who did what many a politician does when faced with an ugly domestic episode: He took a trip overseas.

In October of 1869 Bishop Mullen, along with several other bishops and cardinals, boarded the sailing ship *Baltimore* and left to attend the First Vatican Council. For Tobias Mullen, attending to the factious St. Joseph's parish would have to wait. There were larger Church matters to consider.

Tobias Mullen had been called to an ecumenical council to be held at the Vatican within the city of Rome. An ecumenical council was an assembly of representatives from the whole Church who met for consultation and to make decisions. The meeting took place in St. Peter's Basilica and involved cardinals, bishops, and the heads of the male religious orders from all over the world. Because this was an ecumenical council, the patriarchs of the Eastern rite Catholic Church joined with their Latin brethren. They came to the Council from places like Jerusalem or Antioch in Syria. These Eastern patriarchs, even as they paid allegiance to the pope, oversaw churches with distinct rituals, theologies, and traditions from those of the Latin West. Within their communities, for instance, married men could be ordained priests and the language of their Mass was not Latin.

This "first" Vatican Council actually was the twentieth such meeting but the first held at the Vatican. The first Council had been held in Nicaea in 325. The 318 Council fathers who assembled there argued about key questions in Christianity: Who was Jesus? Was he only divine, or was he fully divine and fully human? The leaders then voted on a set of religious definitions called "doctrines," which then were to be considered final and binding. Some bishops went away unhappy but still submitted to the rule of the majority and upheld the Council's decisions. Others rejected the decisions, broke with Rome, and formed new Christian communities. The doctrines decided upon at Nicaea became the "Nicene Creed." A version of this statement of faith is recited each Sunday by many Protestants as well as all Catholics. Councils can also decide on practical matters. At Nicaea, for instance, a date was established for when Easter would be celebrated.

For Catholics living in the nineteenth century, the Council of Trent (1545 to 1563) defined their religious lives. This nineteenth ecumenical council had been held three hundred years earlier in Trent, Italy. The Council had been called to clarify Catholic doctrine, strengthen the boundaries between Protestant and Catholic thought, and address abuses that were damaging the Church from within. Held in the northern Italian city of Trent, three separate sessions of meetings were the culmination of many reforming trends that had gone on for generations in the Church. The decrees provided sharp criticism of the Protestant Reformation.

The effects of the Council of Trent were wide-ranging. In 1570 the Vatican published the *Missale Romanum*, laying out the proper structure and prayers of the Mass. This text remained basically unchanged for the next four hundred years. Latin acquired a sacral character, and popular devotions were encouraged as a means to enliven the faithful and defeat those in error. Preaching, clerical literacy, and seminary training were made a high priority. Priests were to be set apart from their congregations. Church organization became more hierarchical and centralized. The power of the pope expanded, as he was understood to be the only figure who could curb the misbehavior of priests and bishops. Heretical corruption was countered by the careful definition of Catholic belief and ritual as well as the establishment of an Index of Forbidden Books. The Roman Inquisition was also expanded.

After the Council of Trent, Catholics had a complete and clear statement of doctrines—something that had not occurred during the Middle Ages. The flavor of Catholicism that emerged out of the Council of Trent (often called "Tridentine Catholicism") became the standard for matters of faith and Church discipline.

JUST AS THE COUNCIL IN TRENT was designed as a response to the Protestant Reformation, Vatican I was itself a response to the Enlightenment and the changing political situation of Europe. Catholic leaders had watched as political and philosophical revolutionaries in France, Italy, and Germany had taken property away from monastic orders, killed and humiliated priests, ordered religious instruction out of schools, denied the existence of miracles, and turned Christ into a philosophical teacher rather than a supernatural savior. Enlightenment thinkers argued that *some* individuals (not slaves, for instance) had rights *not* connected to specific religious beliefs. For them, religion belonged in the private sphere of the home not the public space of government and economics. Vatican I was called at the very time when politicians like Otto von Bismarck were curtailing Catholic influence on European society. By the time Bishop Mullen arrived in Italy, the lands the pope ruled over had dwindled to almost nothing and a unified Italy was about to be born.

Just two days before the conference, on December 4, 1864, Pope Pius IX published the encyclical *Quanta Cura* with its attached "Syllabus of Errors." The language of *Quanta Cura* was sharp and dramatic, setting a confrontational tone for Vatican I. In his encyclical, Pope Pius IX referred to modern thought as "the nefarious enterprises of wicked men," whose words and deeds were like the "raging waves of the sea foaming out their own confusion, and promising liberty whereas they are slaves of corruption." The pope saw nothing good in the new world created by these men and women because they had "striven by their deceptive opinions and most pernicious writings to raze the foundations of the Catholic religion and of civil society."[5] He called on Catholic bishops to defend the faithful—so as to save them from perdition—by understanding exactly what were the modern errors spread by the enemies of the Catholic Church.

All of the ideas condemned in *Quanta Cura* concern the notion that the natural order was higher than the supernatural order—that human thought could supersede the Church. The encyclical reflected the tensions that existed between Catholics like the pope—who wanted to maintain the medieval synthesis between religion, society, science, and culture—and those who wanted to define reality without reference to the supernatural. Enlightenment thinkers had reversed the proper ordering of reality by stressing the innate strength of human reason over divine revelation.

In *Quanta Cura* the Church stood by its conviction that it alone held the keys to truth and salvation. Not only was the supernatural real, but it was also eternally true and unchanging. Condemned was the belief that God revealed his intentions slowly and that true religion could be altered or be improved. More specifically, the bishops rejected any sense that Catholic doctrine, institutions, or political philosophy were equal to any other religion or system of thought. Protestants did not please God. In Catholic countries, non-Catholics had no right to worship in public. Pope Pius IX condemned in no uncertain terms many innovations in philosophy and politics that we now take for granted.

Political movements in Europe that sought to curb the political power of the Church were now to be defined as "false sects." The Church was within its rights to have dominion over both temporal and spiritual affairs because only through a faithful society could goodness prevail in the world. When government and Church law conflicted, to assume that civil law rather than religious law should triumph was incorrect. Likewise, it was wrong to think that schools should concentrate on profane knowledge and vocational training. The mandate that public schooling should be open to all and freed from ecclesiastical authority was condemned as an error. Governments had also wrongly taken over the Church's role in legitimating marriages. Some nations even permitted divorce. Notions of religious liberty corrupted the morals and minds of people, leading them to think that all beliefs were the same.

In the 1860s, when Catholic leaders looked around at the industrializing world, they did not see a utopia of free individuals helping each other actualize their highest potentials; instead they saw factory owners exploiting their workers, women reduced to prostitution to feed their children, and squalid cities. By separating the civil state from religion and morality, modern thinkers—socialists, liberal Catholics, even Masons—had let loose a torrent of greed and exploitation. What, if not religion, would keep people from merely single-mindedly amassing riches and pursuing the "unchastened desire of ministering to [their] own pleasure and interests"?[6]

The pope who called Catholic leaders to the Vatican believed that an ecumenical council would make an even stronger statement than *Quanta Cura* did against liberal nationalists and those Catholics who indulged in modern thought. For him, only by returning to a society based on Catholic principles could true freedom and salvation be guaranteed. Consequently, the men he chose to prepare the schemas, or "proposed decrees," that would be debated when the bishops arrived in Rome reflected the antimodern stance of Pius IX and other European conservatives. The schemas of Vatican I ranged from citing the errors that sprang from rationalism to condemnations of dueling to defining the mission of religious orders. The point of calling Vatican I was to clarify timeless truths and to confront those who had gone astray. Very little in the proposed documents recommended the modern world of the nineteenth century.

MOST OF THE MEN who attended the Council had the problems of Europe on their mind. That Catholics in America were flourishing in a modern environment was not considered. Of the approximately seven hundred Council fathers who attended the opening session on December 8, 1869, two-thirds were Europeans, and of those, one third was from Italy. Most of the bishops coming from missionary lands were also Europeans. Forty-eight American bishops and one abbot arrived from the United States. All of the Council's discussions were conducted in Latin and in secret. No reporters or observers were permitted in the sessions, although Council gossip was printed in every European newspaper and summarized in the U.S. press. The debates moved slowly, and American bishops wrote home about being exceedingly bored. The sound in St. Peter's was so poor that a sail had to be rigged over the hall so the men could hear each other.

Casting its shadow over all the discussions was the issue of papal infallibility. Would the Council shore up the pope's declining temporal influence by according him the power, at certain times, to speak on morals and faith without the possibility of error? Would the world's bishops support intensifying the authority of the pope and his administrators, the Roman Curia? What would be the impact of those decisions on the larger world of Christianity? On governments?

By the end of April 1870, after considering almost three hundred proposed amendments to the original schemas, the Council Fathers approved *Dei Filius*. Although its language was more controlled than in *Quanta Cura*, this dogmatic constitution also taught that God's direction utterly surpassed the understanding of the human mind, that God authored the books of the Bible, and that Scriptures needed to be interpreted by the Church. Faith was a supernatural virtue not because it accorded with reason but because it came from God. "To the Catholic Church alone," *Dei Filius* explained, "belong all those things, so many and so marvelous, which have been divinely ordained to make for the manifest credibility of the Christian faith."[7] If one accepted Catholicism, there would never be a reason for changing or calling one's faith into question. Continuing in the spirit of *Quanta Cura* and of all the Councils since Nicaea, the constitution ended in a list of ideas that were to be condemned.

Not all of the world's bishops agreed with the antimodern stance of Pius IX and other conservatives. Most American bishops recognized that Catholicism was thriving in the United States in spite of the separation of church and state. True, there were anti-Catholic Protestants who, a generation earlier, had burned convents and churches, but American Catholics had not experienced the same level of anticlerical fervor as Europeans. Protestants in the United States viewed ethnic parishes with suspicion, but they were also drawn to Catholicism's romantic character and theological precision. A Catholic had signed the Declaration of Independence, Catholics fought alongside Protestants on both sides in the Civil War, and immigrant Catholics were, for the most part, paying for their church.

American Council Fathers also had varying views on the issue of papal infallibility. Several American bishops argued that papal infallibility was not evident in the Bible or in past Council decisions. They believed that the definition of "infallibility" was unclear and that there was too much debate over when an infallible statement could be legitimately pronounced. Council Fathers worried that approval of papal infallibility would accelerate the shift of theological and institutional power away from their control. They feared the heightened involvement of Italian bishops working in the Curia who would interpret and enforce papal decrees. Not only would this involvement threaten the American bishop's ability to set policy in their own diocese, but the expansion of Vatican authority would also alienate Protestants. Although only a few of the bishops at Vatican I opposed infallibility entirely, a healthy number felt that this was not the right time to assert such a doctrine. The moment, they argued, was inopportune. Bishop Mullen of Erie was one of twenty bishops and archbishops who signed a petition asking for the withdrawal of the discussion of infallibility.

The dissenters did not have the required vote to overrule the infallibility language. When it became clear that infallibility would be approved, eight bishops received permission to leave Rome before a final vote was taken. Bishop Mullen stayed, voting along with 433 Council Fathers to assent to the constitution *Pastor Aeternus*. One of the only two dissenting votes was cast by an American. On July 18, in the middle of a torrential rain storm, the statement on infallibility was read aloud to the world's Catholics. The Council was then adjourned and set to reconvene in November. The rest of the schemas would be debated then.

The next day, on July 19, 1870, war erupted between France and Prussia. Previously, France had stationed troops in Rome to protect the Papal States from those Italians who wanted to craft a unified, secular Italian state. After a long struggle, Rome was the last piece in their unification puzzle. So when French troops moved out of Rome to fight the Prussians, Italian forces entered and secured Rome. Italian republicans proclaimed Rome the capital of the new nation of Italy. Angered at being robbed of his temporal kingdom and the ascendance of liberal nationalists, Pope Pius IX withdrew into his quarters. He declared himself a prisoner of the Vatican and excommunicated the leaders of the new Italy. Vatican Council I was suspended, never to be reconvened. Hostility between the pope and the Italian government would not be resolved until 1929, when Pope Pius XI and Benito Mussolini approved the Lateran Treaty.

Like *Quanta Cura* and its Syllabus of Errors, the mood of Vatican I had been confrontational. It extended the spiritual power of the pope at a time when he had all but lost his secular power. Later papal writings would reject modern trends in theology and political theory again and again. In 1907 Pius X issued another list of condemned theological errors along with his encyclical *Pascendi*. The Vatican was particularly concerned about the precedent for religious pluralism and free thinking in the United States. Even though bishops and theologians consistently reassured Europeans that they misunderstood what was happening in the New World, the American hierarchy did not hesitate to restrict Catholic theological inquiry.

Attitudes that had been cultivated in the Vatican as well as among conservative Europeans had practical effects in American parishes. The doctrine on the infallibility of the pope reinforced the power dynamics in American Catholic community: the husband over the family, the nun over her students, the priest over his parishioners, and the bishop over all. Although American bishops did not share Vatican pessimism about religious pluralism, they did use the Vatican's antimodernism as a springboard to rail against everything from jazz to the length of women's skirts. At their own meetings in Baltimore in 1884, they agreed that Catholics were required to send their children to parochial schools, which should be free and supported by parishes. Catholics who were married by a Protestant minister or those who remarried after a divorce were excommunicated.[8] Such decrees were designed to keep Catholics within their own worlds, separated from modern innovations ranging from divorce to public schools.

P ERHAPS ERIE'S BISHOP was encouraged by the discussions he heard at the Vatican. The conversation certainly leaned toward asserting ecclesiastical power and limiting the influence of the individual. While in Rome, Bishop Mullen exercised his spiritual power over those who disobeyed him when they buried their dead in their own cemetery by placing an interdict on St. Joseph's parish and locking the doors of the church. This interdict meant that there would be no Mass or sacraments conducted in the parish. Priests at other churches were told not to minister to the members of St. Joseph's nor even baptize their children. Only the dying who truly repented and renounced their allegiance to the "new cemetery party" would be allowed to receive the Last Rites.

Catholics during the era of Vatican I could—and did—disagree with their pastors or bishops. However, ordinary Catholics had little formal power and no theological justification for dissent. Just as a father had control over his children, so did the bishop over his congregations. Dissenters at St. Joseph's, if they wanted to remain Catholic, had no alternative. They petitioned the bishop to lift the interdict and reopen the church. Eight months after its closing, Bishop Mullen reopened the church with a mission (a Catholic revival meeting) led by a team of Jesuits. "At its close," the parish's historian concluded, "the bulk of the congregation had been reconciled to the Church, to God, to the Bishop."[9]

The experience of the Germans at St. Joseph's was indicative of a larger trend occurring in the country. Like the American bishops who reconciled themselves to the doctrine of papal infallibility even if they thought it inopportune, the parishioners of St. Joseph's submitted to the authority of their bishop. Parishes in America would not look like the village churches of their European hometowns. The Irish and American-born bishops who sought a strong, unified, and prominent Catholicism were succeeding in building powerful parishes. If the people of a parish had problems with a priest or with each other, they would have to be very cagey in how they pursued change. Layers of authority were clearly defined, and challenges could be easily condemned as evidence of modern impudence.

City churches of the Vatican I era reflected both the politics and the theology of international Catholicism. To look at the altar of a Catholic church was to see into heaven. There resided the Trinity—God the Father, the Son, and Holy Spirit—attended to by the community of saints and angels. People came to the church to look upon this heavenly community—not to be a part of it. The priest and the altar boys were attendants at that throne. As with the people, they faced the tabernacle and directed their prayers toward the divine center. Just as no one would dare turn their back on a king, so all faced Christ as he appeared in the guise of bread and wine.

The focal point of attention was the tabernacle, where the consecrated hosts were stored. A golden crucifix stood in a niche above the tabernacle. This holy area was surrounded by various niches holding statues and platforms for the placement of banks of candelabras for candles. Each time they crossed in front of the tabernacle, Catholics genuflected, making one of their knees touch the floor. Because the altar area represented God on his throne in heaven, statues of Catholic saints and even marble angels were placed on either side to indicate worship of the divine presence. Both the side altars and the main altar were dressed with white, laced linens. The sanctuary displayed an array of flowers and living green plants; palms were especially popular.

Areas for the clergy and for the people were carefully delineated. To preach, the priest accessed the pulpit (known as the "ambo") by mounting a set of stairs that raised him above the congregation. A short railing separated the altar area from the nave, and this was where Catholics knelt when they received Holy Communion. This railing was also dressed with a white linen cloth. Opulent stained glass windows—the more detailed in their telling of biblical stories or the lives of the saints the better—filtered the outside light. Underneath the stained glass, along the side walls, painted Stations of the Cross illustrated the drama of Christ's passion and death.

Entering the sacred space of the altar area was restricted during services to men—priests and altar boys. But women made the space *look* special and holy. When services were not being held, women scrubbed and polished all the altar brass. Any ornate woodwork on the main altar or the long altar rail had to be dusted. Candle wax stuck to the red vigil lights needed to be scraped off. Women also made sure that the array of vestments that the priests wore was in good order. They pressed the albs, the long, white linen garb worn by the priests at Mass, taking care that the lace on the bottom was treated properly. In the days before steam irons, this meant ironing on a wet bath towel and putting the altar cloths on special rollers so that no creases would appear. In a world without air conditioners or even large fans, women had to keep towels handy to prevent their sweat from dripping on the fresh linens.

The church was a glimpse into heaven, but it also replicated a formal, Victorian home. Catholic churches of the immigrant era reflected late Romantic aesthetic styles: opulent, meticulously decorated, colorful, and formal. Catholics layered their churches with images, textures, colors, and even smells. Empty spaces were to be filled because they signaled a lack of concern, a lack of abundance, a lack of expansiveness. Churches symbolized the richness of religion just as an overstuffed parlor indicated that a family had taste and wealth. Watching the drama of the Mass performed within a monumental and highly decorated building connected Catholics to the power of God—a God who determined one's life and fate.

Royalty—even divine royalty—does not come cheap. With no government willing to fund church upkeep, construction, or salaries, lay people had to raise the money needed to support their parish. Immigrants and their children could not provide large endowments, as wealthy Protestants might, but they could be convinced to give whatever extra cash they had to the church. Priests relied on women to organize a constant succession of festivals, parties, suppers, and dances to generate the funds needed to run the parish. In Erie, women convinced breweries to donate beer for church suppers and coordinated their families to gather for the cheap meal. When there were leftovers, they served them up the next night at half-price. Catholics raised as much money through such events as they did through pew rents or church collections.

Immigrant men and women spent their free time in different ways. In the German American community, men joined singing societies and fraternal organizations. For instance, Annie's uncle, who was president of a singing society in Germany, continued to be active in one like it in Erie. In these societies, Catholic men might socialize with Protestants and freethinkers. A general sense of German American identity—not attached to region and often expressed in English—was cultivated by men. For men, such nonreligious associations provided a place for political discussions rather than religious ones.

Excluded from the male-oriented ethnic societies, women looked to the church as a place for socializing outside the home. In parish life women like Annie Liebel found a spiritual and social atmosphere that was meaningful amidst a growing industrial city. Before the arrival of radio and the movies, most entertainment—particularly for women—came from religion. Consequently, in Margaret's family, women cultivated a Catholic, rather than German American, identity. Parish life provided a mixture of socializing, gossiping, prayer, and education that many women found fulfilling.

Immigration continued at full force in the United States until World War I, when antiforeign sentiments in the twenties cut off the flow of

European settlers. In 1895 Annie and her family stopped going to St. Joseph's Church because population increases motivated new parishes to be established. The new Sacred Heart Church was built literally around the corner. Annie's daughter Angelica and her granddaughter Margaret were both baptized in Sacred Heart parish. In 1900 the city of 52,733 had eleven Catholic parishes. Increasingly these new parishes were "national parishes" set up to serve the new immigrants who were arriving in Erie. By 1920 the city's population had almost doubled to 93,372, and parishes had been established for the Slovaks (Holy Family, 1908), Poles (St. Casimir, 1916), Hungarians (St. Stephen, 1917), and Romanians (St. George, 1918). By the time Angelica married in 1922, there were seventeen Catholic churches in Erie.

After World War I there were more Catholic churches across the country, but there was also more competition for the attention of the children of the immigrants. Churches were no longer the sole purveyors of entertainment in Erie. Although Annie felt the most comfortable with her German-speaking relatives, her daughter Angelica had a wider circle of acquaintances and distractions. Friends went together to the movies, cheap food could be bought at the baseball stadium, and the production value of a vaudeville act was much higher than any parish play. Even though immigrant neighborhoods had never been hermetically sealed, by the twenties, expanding leisure and time at school brought more ethnic groups in contact with each other than ever before. In Erie, young people met each other at work, in downtown department stores, while picnicking at the lake, or when riding the trolley. The German American Angelica could have met her Swedish American boyfriend, Karl Johnston, at the movies, the roller-skating rink, the public park, or even at a dance hall.

Angelica was not supposed to marry the non-Catholic Karl. Catholics were forbidden by Canon Law from marrying non-Catholics. Nevertheless, love often intervened. Significantly, Angelica met with no hostility from her parents about the marriage. Karl was a "good boy," and Swedish Lutherans had values not unlike German Catholics. All agreed, however, that the engaged couple would have to get a dispensation from the rule that Catholics could not marry Protestants. There would be forms to fill out.

Even a quick foray through the archives kept by America's bishops reveals that Catholicism was as much a religion of dispensation as it was a religion of rules. To receive that dispensation, Karl had to sign a paper agreeing never to impede Angelica's Catholic activities. He had to let her be buried in a Catholic cemetery, from which he would be excluded unless an additional dispensation was granted. Angelica had to promise to try to convert Karl by her prayers and good example. All of their children had to be raised as Catholics, even if Angelica died and Karl remarried a non-Catholic. Angelica must not attend Karl's church even "just for the sake of peace" as to do so would be a tacit admission that all Christian communities were equal in God's eyes. The Church clearly insisted they were not. If Karl refused to agree to any of these strictures or if the couple was married by a Protestant minister, Angelica was to be automatically excommunicated. Her marriage would be null and void; she would be living in sin, banned from receiving any sacraments, and forbidden from burial in a Catholic cemetery. Only a bishop could revoke the excommunication.

Fortunately, Angelica and Karl secured the dispensation that allowed them to marry. Excluded from the sacred space of the church, they had to be married in the parish rectory, where the priest wore none of his customary Mass vestments. Because to be in church was to be in the presence of the divine, to be excluded from church was a powerful gesture.

Such weddings were meant to be bleak. In 1917 a priest-writer described such a wedding "as cold and soulless as agnosticism and Protestantism can make it; it looks more like a funeral service or an ordinary business transaction than a marriage ceremony."[10] Angelica and Karl, however, understood both their wedding and marriage to be proper and fulfilling. Karl did not chafe under the requirement to send his children to Catholic school. As Annie aged, Karl dutifully walked her each day to early-morning Mass. While waiting for her, he smoked a cigar at the drugstore across the street and chatted with his buddies. Then he walked her home.

Catholic devotional life after World War I was complex and theatrical. Erie Catholics walked to church for Sunday and daily Mass, but not as family groups. Children who went to parish school were required to attend their own Mass, typically at nine in the morning. They would sit together, in the order of their classes, and with their teachers. Mothers and grandmothers would go to early morning "low Masses" that had no singing. The priest would read the texts of the Mass from the missal on the altar and the altar boys would give the responses.

The main Sunday Mass was the sung "High Mass." At this Mass a choir would sing the parts of the Mass. In 1903 the encyclical *Tra le Sollecitudini* tried to eliminate dramatic church music from High Masses and reinstitute Gregorian Chant. Because the choir was considered to be a part of the liturgical office, women were to be excluded. The encyclical explained that boys should sing the soprano parts. This effort failed miserably at Sacred Heart, where Florence Messmer played the organ and led the choir for almost fifty years. Angelica became just as well known in the parish for her singing.

Attending Mass was the central but not sole religious practice of parish life. Along with the Sacred Heart choir, Angelica sang at funerals, weddings, Christmas celebrations, and church novenas, which were services that included a blessing of the sick and the recitation of prayers to the Virgin Mary or a saint. They typically ended in Benediction, the exposition of the host in a golden container called a monstrance. Because novenas took place outside of Mass, they were more personal. They encouraged Catholics to create intimate relationships with Jesus, Mary, and the saints. Flourishing during the thirties and forties, when families were struck by the troubles of the Depression and World War II, novenas always included a "petition box," where people wrote on slips of paper the things that they needed from God. Novena prayers were dramatic and formal: "Look down with a mother's tenderness and pity on me, who kneel before you to venerate your Dolors," Catholics called upon the Virgin of Sorrows, "and place my requests, with filial confidence, in the sanctuary of your wounded Heart."[11] Whereas only Latin hymns were to be sung at Mass, at novenas congregations sang popular hymns in English, which were as florid as their prayers.

Using Latin contributed to creating a religious environment not easily accessible to outsiders. It would be incorrect to conclude, however, that Catholics were mesmerized into ritual compliance, so they had no understanding of what they were doing. The movements and rhythms of Catholic life were repeated to a point at which they were inscribed on the body and became a natural way of moving, acting, and participating.

Ritual participation, specifically in the sacraments, mattered more than believing in a collection of ideas. Being Catholic meant mastering a set of practices until they became second nature. Through those practices, Christ, Mary, and the saints became as familiar as family members. Catholics cultivated involved relationships with these holy characters much like they did with their own kin. Although the process of learning practices, relationships, and meanings could come from growing up in Catholic neighborhoods and homes, increasingly, Catholics learned them at the parish school.

T HE MOST ENDURING LEGACY of the nineteenth century for the average American Catholic was *not* the doctrine of infallibility of Vatican I; rather, it was the construction of a nationwide, parish-based school system. As European governments threatened the autonomy of Catholic schools, the Church denounced the growing public school movement. The Syllabus of Errors attached to *Quanta Cura* condemned educational systems free from ecclesiastical control, unconnected with Catholic faith, and under the authority of the civil state. The Vatican warned American bishops in 1875 that public schools were fraught with danger and hostile to Catholicism. In 1884 the country's bishops required all Catholics to send their children to parochial schools.[12] At a parish school, students would learn that the main goal of education was to enable them to move toward salvation. The spirit of Vatican I expected that education would support and articulate specific Catholic doctrines and practices.

For the most part, Erie Catholics tried to cultivate in their schools the unification of faith and knowledge. By 1926, the year that Angelica's daughter Margaret was born, almost 15,000 children went to parish schools in the diocese. Within the city, German American parishes maintained schools of about 400 pupils; the Irish parish of St. Patrick managed 500 children. The Poles, however, beat them both. The Sisters of the Holy Family of Nazareth taught 1,012 students at St. Stanislaus Parish and the Felician Sisters had 721 pupils at Holy Trinity and 369 at St. Hedwig's. Only the Italians at St. Paul's and the Hungarians at St. Stephen's did not have parish schools, although St. Paul's did begin one in 1966 The number of children in Erie's Catholic schools remained high well into the 1960s.

At Sacred Heart both Margaret and her mother Angelica had the same first grade teacher, Sister Francis Joseph, who taught at the parish from 1903 to 1934. By 1936 she would be among the fifteen nuns who taught seven hundred children, coping with an average class size of forty-six. Sister Francis Joseph belonged to a religious order of nuns called the Sisters of St. Joseph, and they dominated both the Catholic schools and social services in Erie. Of the fifteen parishes with schools in 1936, nine were taught by Sisters of St. Joseph. Although the schools of the Poles and Slovaks included recent immigrant nuns who spoke those languages, the majority of Erie's Catholics were taught by local, American-born women. Sister Francis Joseph was born in Erie in 1879 as Edith Kress. Like Margaret and her mother, she was a German American who did not speak any German. Because the Sisters of St. Joseph recruited women from the multiethnic area of northwest Pennsylvania to teach and do social work, they relied on English as their common language of communication.

Throughout their schools, the Sisters of St. Joseph instilled a sense of order and hierarchy that reflected the ideals of the nineteenth-century Church, the sisters' ethnic traditions, and working-class American values. Each morning children arrived at school by 8:30. At the ringing of a bell, they fell silent and assembled into their classes. The classes entered the school building in order of rank, with the oldest classes going first. At Sacred Heart, this procession was accompanied by a student playing a march on a piano. Students sat one behind the other at wooden desks in their classrooms. There, they studied in spaces as elaborately decorated as their church: Among statues of Mary and the saints, there was an American flag and colorful educational prints. Respect for authority was assumed and enforced. Pupils stood when a sister, priest, or any adult entered the classroom. Children learned the priorities, proprieties, and protocols of a disciplined, Catholic life.

Sisters were taught to be reasonable with their students. "When a child observes in the teacher a tendency to be tyrannical or too exacting," a Sisters of St. Joseph's teaching manual explained, the "desire to please her is proportionally lessened and the teacher's authority is impaired." Likewise, the sisters were expected to be pleasant and encouraging: "Never speak in a scolding, fretful manner" the manual warned, "and try to cultivate a pleasant countenance. Do not wound the sensibilities of the duller pupils by making comparisons of one child with another."[13]

At the same time, however, children were constantly reminded of where they were on each sister's scale. At Sacred Heart School, every other month a report card was issued that gave the pupil's rank in his or her class and a percentage grade. At the top of the card were listed conduct, application (effort), and neatness. Then came Christian Doctrine, arithmetic, reading, spelling, grammar, geography, U.S. history, penmanship, composition, and, lastly, drawing. "Christian doctrine" included a weekly Bible history lesson and memorizing a core set of prayers: the Lord's Prayer; Hail Mary; the Creed; Confiteor from the Mass; the Acts of Faith, Hope, and Charity; and the Act of Contrition (said during Confession); the Memorare; Angelus; and Grace before and after each meal. American Catholics were learning how to be Catholic at school even more than at home.

Although the Catholic school composed of overly strict nuns has entered into American folklore, Catholics themselves—especially Catholic women—often tell a different story. Even as work opportunities were expanding for women in the twenties and thirties, Catholic women entered religious orders to become teachers, nurses, and social workers. Their experiences as schoolchildren did not keep girls from the convent but rather presented them with an acceptable alternative to motherhood. As a nun, a girl might integrate her spiritual and professional desires. Sisters, who in Erie moved between teaching and social service activities, modeled lives of intellectual and professional engagement. Some boys may have chafed under the classroom discipline of teaching sisters, but for many girls the order and academics of school dovetailed well with cultural codes of feminine behavior. Fine penmanship, quiet study, facility with memorization, a curiosity about religious matters— these were Catholic school values that were also middle-class feminine values.

In addition, every day girls saw women exert piety, professionalism, and authority. "We were taught that the sisters were the Brides of Christ and that they served God," Margaret recalled. "You didn't talk nasty to the sisters because they were holier than we were." Adults might criticize the priest "because he was the boss." They would say, "Why does he want

more money? He has a big car. But the sisters? They didn't have anything, they didn't even drive."

Although sisters certainly showed deference to the parish priests and
had far less independence then their clerical counterparts, they commanded the respect of parents and children. Only the most foolish priest
would interfere with a Mother Superior when it came to running a school.
With the Sisters of St. Joseph dominating the schools as well as running
the city's hospital, orphanage, day care center, and training school for
boys, even bishops had to respect the sphere of influence of nuns.

Increasingly, Americans were sending their children to high school
and even on to college. Sometime during the twenties the idea of the
teenager was born: a grown-up child who did not have to work, who
went to school, and whose parents gave him or her freedom to enjoy the
burgeoning entertainment culture of movies, dances, and radio. When
Margaret finished at Sacred Heart elementary school in 1940, she went
to Villa Maria Academy, also run by the Sisters of St. Joseph. Her mother,
Angelica, did not want her daughter to have to work in a silk mill as she
had. When Angelica was young, she had had to convince her former
teacher, Sister Eleanora, to help with her career plans. The nun supported Angelica's ruse that she was taking music lessons at the convent
while she actually attended Erie Business College in order to get an ac-
counting certificate. Angelica knew that there was a world beyond the
parish, the neighborhood, and the silk mill. Making sure that her daughter, as well as her son, was exposed to that world meant assuring that
Margaret would go on to high school.

Although most Catholic youth went on to public high schools, increasingly they had the option of attending religious schools. In 1892 the
Sisters of St. Joseph had already established an academy for older girls.
They opened a college in 1925. By 1920 another Erie order, the Sisters of
St. Benedict, added to their private elementary school a three-year commercial course for women. In 1923 they introduced a four-year high
school. Their sisters started to take college courses, and their facilities
included three science laboratories. The Sisters of Mercy moved to Erie
in 1926, buying seventy-five acres of farmland to begin Mercyhurst Academy. By 1931 their educational complex also included a fully accredited
college with 104 women students. In Erie, Catholic boys had fewer
choices: They could go to Cathedral Preparatory (founded 1921) for high

school and then on to Cathedral College (founded in 1925, later called Gannon College).

To enter Villa Maria in 1940 was to learn how to be both a lady and a scholar. Students were taught how to live by both nineteenth- and twentieth-century norms. On the one hand, sisters chided their charges to speak with a low voice and to practice the habits of good living: punctuality, regularity, and good character. On the other hand, they taught chemistry labs where girls experimented with hydrochloric acid. Students wore white starched collars on their dark dresses, but they also formed the Erie Chapter of the National Association of Cost Accountants. Girls took Latin and algebra but also signed up for typewriting and public speaking. There was a club created to promote the appreciation of the works of Virgil and also a basketball team. Good posture was stressed more than anything else in gym class, but Villa Maria also had its own swimming pool.

When the graduating class of 1930 imagined what they would be doing as grown women in 1940, the future they saw was fully situated in the twentieth century: They would be novelists and book critics, stenographers and newspaper reporters; lawyers, nurses, and dentists. Bea would have her pictures shown at an art exhibition ("which had caused quite a sensation") and Rose Calabrese would be a historian. There was no mention of being housewives, but Eva turned out to be a beauty specialist, Helen a governess, and Mary a seamstress. The graduating class predicted that only one fellow classmate would enter the convent.[14] To be a professional, however, did not mean that a woman would forget who she was. "We girls, we didn't want to have a bad reputation," Margaret remembers. "When I asked, 'why couldn't I do it?' the answer was always the same: 'Because I said so, and because you're a lady and ladies do not do things like that.'"

Increasingly, however, formal convent education was looking more and more like that of the public high schools. Margaret received a scholarship to Mercyhurst Academy for her senior year. Although the academics continued to be strong, the Mercy Sisters were more in tune with the needs of modern teenagers. Mixed dances were held in the auditorium with the sisters watching from the balcony. Senior girls who secured their parents' permission could light up cigarettes in their own smoking room.

In both schools, girls learned religion in both theory and practice. A priest taught Bible and Church history, basic theology, and ethics. They made yearly retreats with visiting clergymen that included sermons on modern living and time for silent prayer. Mass was said in the academy chapel, and the bishop came once a year to visit. Students had free days from class on the feast days of St. Patrick and St. Joseph. In May they crowned a statue of Mary in the school's garden.

Religious life, like academic life, was spoken of and experienced in the ideal. Villa Maria and Mercyhurst were places detached from the realities of the Depression, which had sent industrial Erie into a tailspin. The Catholic school, in the same way as the space of the church, was expected to reflect a divinely ordered perfect society and, thus, to inculcate eternal, heavenly values.

SHORTLY BEFORE MARGARET and the other sophomore girls at Villa Maria stopped for Christmas break in 1941, the Japanese attacked Pearl Harbor. From that point until they graduated in 1944, life in the cloistered world of the girl's academy seemed particularly unreal. Margaret received a scholarship to continue as a college student at Mercyhurst, but her mind was not on her studies. The war made the future look bleak.

In 1943, before he even graduated from high school, her boyfriend, Ken, was drafted into the Army. Wouldn't it be better if they married before he left to fight? Margaret knew her mother did not approve and that she wanted her daughter to finish college, but both the nation and her heart were calling. It was, Margaret explained later, "my patriotic duty to get married."

When Ken came home on an Army furlough, she got engaged. The couple filled out the paperwork to secure the dispensation needed for Catholic Margaret to marry Protestant Ken; the groom memorized the catechism while training to be a soldier (so he could be "good enough" to marry a Catholic); and on December 20, 1944, they married in the rectory of Sacred Heart Church.

Catholics throughout the country were leaving their neighborhoods and joining the military. They were seeing new parts of the nation and meeting new people. Women started working in the war industry. Higher education would soon become more available. The world of Vatican I was ending.

chapter two

POSTWAR SUBURBS

For the generation of Catholics who came of age during World War II, it was the fifties—not the sixties—that were revolutionary. Catholics were leaving their urban neighborhoods and venturing out into America's growing suburbs. In addition, the difference between how they practiced their faith and how their parents did was significant. The suburban fifties introduced Catholics like Margaret to new ideas that Council Fathers at the Second Vatican Council would legitimize and institutionalize.

When President Roosevelt declared war on Germany and Japan, he marshaled the full force of the American government to convince and motivate the country to participate in the war effort. Given the brutality of the Axis powers, this was not difficult to accomplish. From saving scrap metal and rubber for the war effort to mourning with families whose sons had been killed, no one could forget that the country was at war.

Margaret was eighteen when she married a soldier. At that point in her life, she had barely ever left her hometown of Erie. A vacation to nearby Buffalo, New York, was a bold undertaking. When Ken shipped out for training to Oregon and later to Nebraska and Texas, the young bride traveled for days on crowded trains to be with her husband for a few hours on the weekends. "It was exciting but scary," she remembers. "What if you missed a connection?" Looking at the world outside the train window, she learned the same thing that many formerly provincial young

Americans were learning for the first time: The United States was an immense country full of all kinds of people.

While Ken went to war, Margaret stayed in Erie and waited. For almost two years, she followed her husband's movements across the South Pacific—to Guam, to Okinawa, then to Korea. Geography had been a favorite school subject for her, but now it took on a terrible relevance. Whenever she had time off from her job making generators at Burke Electric Company, she went to the movies to watch newsreels discussing the upcoming assault on Japan. Margaret worried that the invasion could make her a widow. To note that war makes men out of boys is a cliché; saying that war makes women out of girls is an overlooked truism.

THE GENERATION who were children during the Depression and young adults during World War II came to embrace religion differently from either their parents or their children. Eighty percent of the men born in the twenties were veterans of military service, and their wives, girlfriends, sisters, and mothers intimately felt the reality of war. Wartime sacrifices pared life down to the essentials; the closeness of death led them to listen more carefully to the promises of their religious traditions. At the same time, war gave that generation a confidence that made them wary of churchy paternalism. As Catholic men formed platoons and women talked during breaks from their factory work, they discovered that Protestants and Jews and even atheists shared their fears and aspirations.

During the war years, powerful media images brought Catholics into the mainstream of American culture. At the movies, Catholic characters often represented the very values that the Allies were struggling to defend. In 1944 Jennifer Jones won an Academy Award for her portrayal of a nineteenth-century Catholic visionary. *The Song of Bernadette* (nominated for twelve Oscars with four wins) was an uplifting tale of a French peasant girl who stuck to her assertion that she saw the Virgin Mary even when her family, her neighbors, her priest, and her government challenged her.

In *The Song of Bernadette*, Hollywood used miracles, visions, virginity, and suffering not to divide Catholics from others but to celebrate the value of everyone standing firm in their convictions. Bernadette died a

painful death at the end of the film but not before her adversaries became convinced that the Virgin Mary *did* appear to the teen. Wartime
patriotism motivated Hollywood to use an innocent yet supernatural
and unbending Catholic faith as an example of how the good and the
true eventually triumphs over adversity.

Movies also encouraged Americans to think differently about ethnicity. Unlike during World War I, when European immigrants were expected to give up their language and customs in order to demonstrate
their Americanism, World War II government propaganda was multicultural. Pamphlets and posters represented European ethnic groups and
even African Americans as having freedom and opportunity in the
United States. After all, it was Hitler, not democratic Americans, who
could not tolerate difference. Following this lead, Hollywood made
movies in which, in the crucible of war, the multi-ethnic Army platoon
evolved from an argumentative group of individuals to a fighting brotherhood of Americans. Ethnic differences were not erased; they were har-
nessed for the common good.

The year after St. Bernadette appeared on the silver screen, *Going My
Way* swept the Academy Awards with ten nominations and seven wins.
As with *The Song of Bernadette*, Catholic characters were used to express
both religious difference and general American values simultaneously.

Going My Way centers around two priests: one Irish and one American. The Irish-born Father Fitzgibbon is charming in his Old World ways,
but he cannot hold a candle to Bing Crosby's Father Chuck. Audiences,
sick of the misery of war, fell in love with the priest's comforting smile,
jaunty straw hat, and athletic ease. Father Chuck's care of the parish's old
Irish pastor as well as his ability to transform jazz into crooning, neighborhood hoodlums into choir boys, and the unrealistic dreams of youth
into the appropriate behaviors of adults pointed to an accepting, more
modern Catholicism.

People flocked to see *Going My Way*. At times, real Catholics might
seem ethnic and exotic, but in the movie theater they were always de-
lightfully American. An informal Father Chuck wore sweatshirts, played
golf, smoked a pipe, and used subtle persuasion rather than theological
arguments to motivate change. He brought his parishioners together
and gently led them. Similar themes occurred in the sequel, *The Bells of
St. Mary* (1945). In the movies, the unique religious characteristics of

Catholicism never undermined the American values of progress, individ-ualism, and personal fulfillment.

Wartime violence also motivated Catholic leaders to stress the com-mon humanity of those who struggled against evil. The realities of the war demonstrated that something existed that was fundamentally more malevolent than the split between Catholics and Protestants. In his 1941 Christmas radio address, Pope Pius XII called for all Christians to work together for peace and rebuild society, even if they were not Catholics. Catholic thinkers in the United States, like Jesuit priest Wilfred Parsons, argued that "our first duty is not, as unfortunately many still seem to think, to win the recognition of the spiritual authority of the Church," but instead that we need "to arouse the torpid world to a sense of the Divine life that exists within it."[1] In 1943 at their annual meeting, American bish-ops approved of individual Catholics cooperating with non-Catholic groups if the organizations were like the Red Cross and had no religious affiliation. Thus, an openness to other faiths was evolving that would continue to develop in the next decades.

THE END OF THE WAR brought about sweeping social changes for many Americans. In March 1946 Ken arrived back home after fighting in the battle for Okinawa and spending seven months as a part of American occupational forces in Asia. Wartime propaganda and the reality of vic-tory helped empower veterans and their families, but it was the hard cash of a federal entitlement program that altered postwar America in the long term. President Roosevelt had signed into law what came to be known as the GI Bill of Rights. The government worried that the combi-nation of the homecoming of 15 million men and women serving in the armed services and the end of war production would cause massive un-employment. To facilitate the veterans' transition and avoid a recession, the government pumped money into the economy.

The GI Bill was designed to provide veterans with unemployment compensation, health care, funding for education and training, and sup-port for the purchase of homes and businesses. The monetary cost would be high, but the government wagered it would get a strong return on its investment. Earlier, Roosevelt had predicted that America's wartime sacrifices would secure Four Freedoms, one of which was "freedom from want." With the GI Bill, he ensured that he would be right.

"I took advantage of the 52/20 club right away," Ken remembered. The GI Bill paid unemployed veterans $20 a week for fifty-two weeks to help them reestablish their lives. The returning soldiers were eager to get back to work, and they were successful in their efforts: In the end, only about 20 percent of the funds set aside for the 52/20 club were paid out. Ken first went to work at a zipper factory, but because he had been trained as a welder in the Army, he eventually got a job at the Westinghouse plant in Erie.

All over the country, men and women were joyfully settling back into domestic life and having babies. For some, this wasn't so simple. After finally finding an apartment, Margaret and Ken's postwar optimism was tested by two miscarriages in the space of a few years. Everywhere Margaret turned she saw cheery ads promoting the latest baby gear or articles on the proper afternoon snacks for children. She wondered how something so "natural" could be so painful and difficult.

The traditional Catholic response to suffering was to "offer it up." Pain became meaningful when it was translated into sacrifice. Devotional literature as well as the advice of priests and nuns elaborated on the Passion narrative: Out of the crucifixion of Jesus came the glorious resurrection and promise of eternal life. The clergy particularly addressed this message to women. By intimately connecting their pain with the suffering of Jesus, they became spiritual exemplars to others. Catholic authors never tired of reminding their readers that the Virgin Mary herself watched helplessly as her son was tortured and killed. Artists depicted her as a "Sorrowful Mother" whose heart was pierced with many swords.

The message was clear: Women had to be stoic. To articulate one's unhappiness to friends and family would be to ignore the example of Jesus who quietly accepted his fate on the cross.

To a certain extent Margaret accepted the wisdom of "offer it up." She followed the lead of the Virgin Mary who, according to the account in Luke, "kept all these words in her heart." Like her husband who did not speak of his war years, Margaret also accepted her childlessness in silence. She prayed to her name saint, St. Margaret Mary Alacoque, to help her get through those difficult days. Like Catholic women before her, she struggled with grace and without complaint.

But this was not her only response. Margaret prayed not simply that God grant her patience and courage. She also expected Jesus, Mary, and the saints to guide her and her family toward making correct decisions. Hers was an active rather than passive devotion. Prayer helped her take appropriate action in a complicated world of expanding possibilities. Somehow the prayers of the novenas, with their flowery language and messages about women submitting to pain, did not seem quite right. Margaret preferred prayer to be intimate, personal, and private.

Margaret was not alone in rejecting the sentiments of the previous generation's piety. Although Catholics continued to join together in large groups to say the rosary or petition the saints, many like Margaret were moving away from such public displays of their faith. In Pittsburgh, for example, attendance at novenas to Our Lady of Perpetual Help declined after the war. Women were finding other ways to meet life's challenges.

The "can do" ethic of the war years was moderating the "offer it up" philosophy of traditional Catholicism. Margaret did not retreat into the reassuring comfort of her family and friends, and she refused to resign herself to an unhappy life. Instead, the sting of her miscarriages sharpened the couple's awareness of their marital relationship and their future.

Postwar America seemed giddy with possibilities. Ken and Margaret wondered how they could best take advantage of them. The couple began to see life in Erie as limited. Ken's welding job paid well, but the knowledge that his work was going nowhere remained an unspoken presence between the two of them. So even though Margaret was the more bookish of the two and had put in her time in the Defense industry, she knew that only Ken was eligible for the benefits of the GI Bill. Echoing her mother's and the nuns' stress on education, Margaret convinced Ken to go to college.

The GI Bill paid $500 a year for tuition, fees, books, and supplies for college or vocational training. Because no university in the country charged more than that for tuition and a couple could scrape by on the $105 monthly allowance, Uncle Sam was in effect passing out free tickets to higher education. In Pennsylvania, Penn State University promised to save 75 percent of its seats for returning veterans. When it quickly ran out of space on its main campus, it asked 3,500 first-year students to start college at centers around the state. So in 1947 Ken began his studies in Erie, and the next year he and Margaret moved to the main campus in the center of the state.

The tidal wave of students that crashed into America's colleges and universities came with wives and children. Ken and Margaret were not alone in complaining about the 350 secondhand trailers and old army barracks set up for them downwind from the poultry barns at Penn State. The university charged the families $25 a month and threw in utilities for free. Margaret supplemented the government checks by working as a secretary in the School of Agriculture. Ken finished a degree in sociology and started graduate studies in social work, but he stopped short of a master's degree because "I was just sick and tired of going to school at my age." The GI Bill gave a generation of men the tools to build a more secure future. By 1956, when the original program ended, 7.8 million World War II veterans had participated in either educational or vocational training programs. The government's bet paid off: Veterans eased into the labor pool as better-educated workers, and they were now making more money and paying more taxes.

The experience of going to college, like the experience of going to war, boosted many Americans' self-confidence. Ken and Margaret were no exception. As Ken was pursuing his degree, Margaret read along in his textbooks and contributed to his term papers. Studying together with those outside the neighborhood continued the trend that began with Margaret's mother marrying a Swedish Lutheran and Margaret marrying a Scots-Irish Methodist. A rise in their educational level, deeper interactions with non-Catholics, and openness to new ideas prepared these Catholics for the innovations that would come with the Second Vatican Council.

THE OPENING OF THE Second Vatican Council in 1962 came on the heels of a decade awash in religious pop culture and tentative ecumenical overtures. During the fifties, as the population of the United States grew by 19 percent, church and synagogue attendance went up 30 percent. Those who claimed a religious affiliation rose from 59 percent of the population to 65 percent.[2] Such membership growth accompanied a wide-ranging fascination with all things religious. The country flocked to movies with biblical themes, read novels with religious characters, and bought inspirational literature. A Catholic bishop had a popular television show. Even works that criticized religion, like Paul Blanshard's anti-Catholic books, became best sellers.

Not to be outdone by popular culture, the government also joined the religion craze. In 1954 Congress decided to add the phrase "under God" to the Pledge of Allegiance. Written in 1892, the Pledge became a popular schoolyard ritual after World War I, but it contained no religious references. During the fifties, the Knights of Columbus (a fraternal order of Catholic lay men) decided that the threat of communism and the rise of secular culture required that the Pledge explicitly place the nation under God's care and rule. They first added "under God" to the Pledge they recited at meetings and then convinced President Eisenhower and the Congress to make the change official. In 1956 another bill was approved to replace the long-standing national motto of *E pluribus unum* ("one from many") to "In God We Trust," which had been appearing on coins since the Civil War.

In a nation eager to define itself as God-fearing and against godless communism, religious leaders assumed a more public presence. Catholic priests were asked to join with Protestant ministers and Jewish rabbis on civic committees or to preside at city events. Some Americans claimed a "Judeo-Christian" rather than "Protestant" heritage. A generic form of religion that supported civic (and civil) society emerged.

AFTER KEN GRADUATED, he became a professional social worker and took a job as a probation officer in Toledo, Ohio. Like many men of his generation, he saw that his small Pennsylvania hometown of Meadville and even the larger city of Erie did not hold real professional opportunity. With a degree, he wanted a career that was challenging and interesting. Staying in Erie would condemn him to mindlessly "sitting on the front stoop in a T-shirt with a beer in my hand."

Toledo was the seat of Lucas County and was experiencing a postwar boom. As late as 1940, half of the town was unemployed or paid by the government to do public work. Two decades later there was almost full employment and the average wage had risen by 30 percent. This Ohio city was diversifying its economy, was proud of its Jeep plant, had a new airport, and had renovated its train station. Margaret quickly got a job as a secretary at the local newspaper, the *Toledo Blade*. Contrary to what we might think, women did not immediately quit their jobs when the soldiers came home. In Toledo more women worked immediately after the war than during the war years. In 1953 they comprised 30 percent of the workforce, and during the 1950s the number of working women increased by 50 percent. Toledo working women were like Margaret; 70 percent of them worked in white (or perhaps, better, "pink") collar jobs.

At the *Blade* offices, Margaret soon made new friends. Jackie was a Protestant who had moved from Michigan with her husband Bill. The couple became Margaret and Ken's neighbors. Harriet was a Catholic who, like Margaret, had gone to an all-girls Catholic high school. These women maintained friendships with each other for the rest of their lives. Among Margaret's friends, religion was often a topic of conversation. It seemed that after the war, the whole nation had "got religion."

Although individual Catholics had non-Protestant friends and joined multireligious civic organizations, they were still required to keep their distance from non-Catholic religious practices. Without their bishops' permission, Catholics were forbidden to attend the religious services of their relatives and neighbors, including weddings and funerals. They could join the Red Cross, but they were forbidden to cooperate with non-Catholic groups like the Salvation Army or the YWCA. Parish bulletins warned Catholics not to buy lots in non-Catholic cemeteries. Some bishops prohibited their priests from participating in graduation ceremonies or Thanksgiving services along with ministers and rabbis.

The Vatican wanted to maintain distance between Protestants and Catholics, but many American bishops preferred to cultivate religious cooperation. In 1947 Archbishop Samuel Stritch of Chicago voiced his concern over the Vatican's mistrust in a letter to Archbishop John T. McNicholas of Cincinnati: "How in a mixed country is it possible to fight secularism," Bishop Stritch wondered, "if in civic affairs we abstain from saying a prayer simply because there is some Protestant minister who also says a prayer?"[3]

Church laws designed to keep Catholics away from Protestants were only partially successful. Catholics routinely went to the weddings and funerals of their non-Catholic friends and neighbors. In spite of continual preaching against mixed marriages, Catholics married outside their faith. Margaret was not alone in falling in love with and marrying a Protestant. The apartment the couple moved into was in an older part of Toledo, in the parish of St. Agnes. A parish census from 1954 reported that 23 percent of the married couples at St. Agnes contained a member who was not Catholic. In addition to these, there were also seventy-five "invalid" marriages—unions in which the Catholic partner had not received permission to marry the non-Catholic. Of the thirty-six marriages that took place that year, eleven were to non-Catholics. These numbers were typical of Toledo and the rest of the country. Catholics were supposed to maintain a distinct religious community, but increasingly their hearts were not in it.

Margaret NEVER ASKED Ken to convert after they married. She knew that her Church expected her to gently lead her mate into the fold, but she was reluctant. Her father had never converted. What one believed, she thought, was a private choice. In any case, nagging never got anyone anywhere. Ken often accompanied her to Mass at St. Agnes, which was much better than going to Mass by herself as she had at Penn State. So on a sunny spring day in March of 1954, when Ken tagged along with her to church, she thought nothing of it. Father Ignatius Felley was saying Mass that Sunday, and just as Margaret was getting ready to leave her pew to walk up to the altar to receive Holy Communion, he stopped the Mass. In surprise, the congregation listened to him announce that Ken McDannell had been baptized earlier in the day and for the first time would be receiving the body and blood of Christ. Margaret held on to the back of the pew to steady herself; she didn't know her husband had been going to St. Agnes during his lunch hour to take instructions in the history and beliefs of Catholicism. Ken had decided to become a Catholic.

Margaret came up to the altar with her husband, and it was only then that she noticed their many acquaintances at the Mass. Catholics and non-Catholic friends had come for the event. Ken knelt at the Communion rail with his wife and the other parishioners of St. Agnes. "*Corpus Domini nostri Jesu Christi*," the priest said, making the Sign of the Cross with the small round host, "*custodiat animam tuam in vitam aeternam. Amen.*"

Then he placed the host on the tongues of the waiting people while the altar boy held a platelike paten under their chins. "May the Body of our Lord Jesus Christ," Father Felley had said in Latin, "preserve your soul unto life everlasting. Amen."

The rate of conversion into Catholicism more than doubled between 1930 and 1950. Although Ken wanted his decision to be a private one and so he kept it a secret even from his wife, other conversion stories became the stuff of public discussion. In 1938 a graduate student named Thomas Merton was baptized into the Catholic Church. A few years later he not only decided to become a priest, but he also entered a Trappist monastery where prayer began two hours before dawn and most talk was prohibited. *Seven Storey Mountain* (1948), his memoir of conversion and life in a monastic community, became a national best seller. When Henry Ford II wanted to marry a Catholic in 1940, he converted; five years later he took over as president of Ford Motor Company. In 1945 Louis Budenz, an editor of the American communist newspaper the *Daily Worker*, became a Catholic. In 1946 Clare Booth Luce, the wife of the owner-founder of *Time* and *Life* magazines, converted. These high-profile conversions drew media attention to the lure of Catholicism.

One element of Catholicism that attracted converts was the enduring consistency of the Mass. Throughout most of the Catholic world, priests said the same words and made the same movements day after day, Sunday after Sunday, year after year. Catholics watched as the priest, clothed in elaborate vestments, entered the sanctuary with his young male assistants and walked up the three steps to the church's main altar. "*Introibo ad altare Dei*," the priest recited in Latin—"I will go to the altar of God." "*Ad Deum qui laetificat juventutem meam*," the altar boys responded on behalf of the congregation—"To God, the joy of my youth." After the Council of Trent, Pope Pius V named a group of scholars to establish a standard set of texts and gestures for the Mass. This "Tridentine Mass" was made official in 1570. Any revisions would have to come from the Pope himself.

Although the texts of the Mass had not changed for generations, the environment in which people heard the Mass changed continually. The altar that Ken looked at when he received Communion in 1954 reflected a modernization that many American churches had undertaken long before the Second Vatican Council. As Catholic parishes grew, churches renovated their interiors. St. Agnes, for instance, expanded the nave of its church in 1924, but it was only in 1939 that the parish raised enough money to complete the renovations. By then both the Liturgical Movement and modernist trends in art would alter the appearance of the church interior.

The Liturgical Movement began in the early twentieth century when monks in France and Germany sought a deeper connection to God through a more serious participation in Catholic rituals. They wanted to make the Mass a vital thing in the life of the faithful, and their efforts toward renewal comprised this movement. Whereas earlier ritual experts had looked to the Middle Ages as the primary resource for Catholic life, by the twenties, reformers were studying historical documents from the earliest years of Christianity. They were searching for clues about communal worship. Scholars in France then published translations of ancient texts that shed light on what Christians were doing when they were just a small religious group within the Roman Empire. European specialists on the liturgy came to conclude that power had corrupted the purity and authenticity of worship.

By the forties, "Vernacular Societies" in Europe and the United States argued that the language of the early Church was what people spoke, not some sacred tongue. Conferences on the liturgy held throughout the United States encouraged parish priests to explore the deeper, supernatural meanings of the sacraments with their congregations. Americans—like Benedictine Virgil Michel, Jesuit Gerald Ellard, diocesan priest Martin Hellriegel, and musical educator Justine Ward—translated, interpreted, and spread European writings through the journals they founded, like *Orate Fratres* and *Liturgical Arts*. They argued that the liturgy belonged to the entire Church, not just those monks and clergy who were skilled in its performance and understood its language.

Participants in the Liturgical Movement asked significant questions about their faith: What was the point of going to church? Was it to consecrate the host so that Christ could be adored like a king by loyal and obedient servants in a court ceremony? Was attending Mass to be a private time to communicate with the saints in heaven? Or should the Mass be a communal time of sharing faith, joy, and happiness? The Liturgical Movement stressed the importance of congregations concentrating on the primacy of Christ's sacrifice and his mystical appearance in the bread and wine of the Mass. Writers warned that the Catholic devotion to the saints had overshadowed the importance of the Eucharist. Although a fuller answer to these questions would be forcefully given by the documents of the Second Vatican Council, the Liturgical Movement began the conversation.

For the average Catholic, the impact of the Liturgical Movement could be best seen in the renovations of their sanctuaries. Catholic design companies of the thirties combined the renewed focus on the Mass with new, more modern styles of art. At St. Agnes, for instance, the Daprato company removed the late-nineteenth century Gothic altarpiece that towered over the altar. In its place they added a baldachin, which is a type of canopy, from which they draped a green velvet backdrop. The new altar had the clear, straight lines of a common table. Where a life-size statue of St. Agnes once stood on top of the tabernacle, Draprato hung a large metallic crucifix over a new cylindrical tabernacle of wrought aluminum. On the wall behind the altar, the old painted designs were removed and a multicolor mural of abstract designs added. Two angels presenting the Eucharist to the congregation were painted on either side. Only two statues, one of St. Joseph holding the child Jesus and a new statue of the Sacred Heart, remained in the renovated sanctuary.

Church design companies like Daprato kept up with artistic and theological changes, so many Catholics experienced changes in their worship space as their parishes grew or new sanctuaries were built. Nevertheless, change was slow. By the mid-fifties, clerical supporters of the Liturgical Movement and progressive lay leaders painted a bleak picture of the state of Catholic worship. In order to illustrate the dire need for reform, they focused on the ritual illiteracy of the average Catholic. In 1958 a *Commonweal* article reported that at a recent Good Friday service some of the congregation was following the priest's Latin in English translation, but the majority "might as well have been listening to readings from the Tokyo phone book." In spite of their Mass missals, they were "bored and restless." The ones who recited the rosary did so just as they did at "weddings, funerals, Baptisms, ordinations, confirmations or Sunday Mass." Nobody understood the importance of the day. The disappointed author speculated that from what he saw, "it might as well have been Christmas as Good Friday."[4]

Critics complained that Catholics had little understanding of the deeper meanings of their religious life, in spite of any change in sanctuary design. The use of Latin had only managed to unify the whole Church in mystification because so few had mastered the ancient language. Because parishioners did not understand the spiritual dimension of their faith, they saw the Church as little more than a legal institution set up to enforce a complicated set of moral and ritual laws. Catholics said their rosaries mindlessly at Mass because worship had become highly individualistic and inwardly focused. For many critics, American Catholics acted like passive and threatened sheep performing their religious duties in a stupor.

If America's Catholics had been as mystified by and subservient to the Church, as critics asserted, then the innovations of the Second Vatican Council would have failed. As educational levels rose after the war, Catholics became more interested in learning about their religion. Some went to Catholic colleges on the GI Bill and learned much from the required theology courses. Interactions with non-Catholics stimulated discussions about the various interpretations of Christianity as well as the validity other faiths. A handful of parishes experimented with *Missa Recitata*, a "Dialog Mass" that had become popular in parts of northern Europe. In the Dialog Mass, the congregation and the altar boys together said the Latin parts of the Mass. At times they recited in unison the longer prayers of the Mass—the Gloria, Creed, Sanctus, and Agnus Dei. Most American parishes, however, were not so adventurous.

One popular innovation of the thirties that accompanied modernized church interiors was the replacement of prayer books by missals. Up until the turn of the century, Catholics were not permitted to translate the Latin of the Mass into vernacular languages. Then in 1905 Pope Pius X approved an Italian translation for use by the laity of Rome. The move spurred other translations, and in 1932 a Brooklyn priest published a translation of the Mass as *My Sunday Missal*, which had Latin on one side of the page and English on the other. "We loved our missals," said one Toledo Catholic woman. "You never went without your missal," explained another. Three million copies of *My Sunday Missal* were sent to the Armed Services during World War II. By the early fifties there were millions of missals in circulation. A study of one parish reported that 35 percent of people at Mass used a missal, whereas 22 percent continued to say prayers from a prayer book and 21 percent recited the "Hail Marys" and "Our Fathers" of the rosary. "The remaining persons simply stare into space," the reporting sociologist observed, "although several men in the last pews read a copy of *Our Sunday Visitor* during Mass."⁵

Throughout the fifties the Vatican itself changed Catholic religious practices. For instance, in 1955 Pope Pius XII permitted the translation of the Latin word *perfidies* from "perfidious" to "unbelieving." This word had been used to describe the Jews in the Good Friday liturgy—the only day of the year when the Mass was not offered. For generations, Catholics had assumed that perfidious meant "treacherous," and so this new, more accurate translation addressed the anti-Semitism that continued to plague Catholicism. In 1959 Pope John XXIII removed the word entirely, although he maintained in the prayer the requirement for the conversion of the Jews.

There were other changes as well. Pope Pius XII altered the Easter celebrations in 1951 and included the new translation at a time when the Holy Week liturgy was being revised. Pius XII also liberalized the Communion fast, which had previously required fasting from food and drink from midnight. In 1953 he permitted drinking water during fasting, and in 1957 he reduced the fasting time from solid food to three hours. During the fifties, certain liturgical rubrics were simplified. English was permitted at times during the sacraments of Baptism, Extreme Unction, and Matrimony as well as at funerals. Thus, changes were occurring both in the minds of theologians and ritual specialists as well as in the daily lives of Catholics.

S OON AFTER Ken became a Catholic, Margaret became pregnant again. The couple had already begun procedures with Catholic Charities to adopt a baby when they received the good news. When Margaret went to withdraw the adoption paperwork because she would be giving birth in November, the sister at the downtown office asked her to reconsider. "Why not wait?" the nun suggested. "You can always withdraw the application after the birth." That November, Margaret miscarried for a third time. A few days later the sister called to tell the couple that a baby girl had been born in Detroit and that they should ready their home for a new arrival. Just before Christmas, Margaret became a mother.

Now new parents, Margaret and Ken wanted a place free from the intrusions of family and neighbors. Other veterans thought the same. A key provision of the GI Bill was the loan guarantee program that enabled them to buy homes at low interest rates. The veterans would buy 4.3 million homes, and by 1955 nearly one of every three new houses built owed their financial backing to the Veterans Administration. Homeownership went from 44 percent of the nation in 1940 to 62 percent in 1960.

In Toledo, like in the rest of the country, the best housing for the lowest price was in the suburbs. In 1955 Ken and Margaret bought a three-bedroom, one-bathroom home within a fifteen-minute car commute from downtown Toledo. Tiny by today's standards, the 1,000-square-foot home in a treeless neighborhood was a symbol of safety and security after decades of personal and social strain.

Many other young families also moved to the suburbs during this era. For the men and women who moved out of the cities, the suburbs were an adventure. Creaky wooden floors were exchanged for "rec" rooms, built-in appliances, and backyard barbeques. New social networks replaced confining ethnic customs. Families customized their tract houses with additions, landscaping, paint, and handmade yard ornaments. The fifties saw a confluence of social desires: Couples wanted independence and domesticity while companies (and the government) wanted to sell these things to them.

After three decades of social disruption, Americans were marrying earlier and having more children. By the end of the fifties, 70 percent of all women were married by the age of twenty-four. If Margaret felt that it was her patriotic duty to marry a soldier in 1944, by 1954 she knew it was her patriotic duty to raise children and improve America's economy by spending and consuming.

American women were also consenting to stay home. Both Margaret and Jackie quit their jobs at the newspaper after their babies arrived. Their husbands made enough money to pay the bills, and they wanted their wives to be full-time mothers. Margaret, who had been working for ten years, agreed it was time to raise children. Harriet, who was having a difficult time getting pregnant, continued to work. The nation's population boomed: a growth of 12 million between the end of the war and 1950 followed by an additional 30 million between 1950 and 1960.

Furthermore, the Cold War created an atmosphere that encouraged Americans to hunker down in their homes. The family was to be a bulwark against communist subversion and the suburban home a safe place in the advent of a nuclear war. The militant language of Catholicism, once hurled at heretics and schismatics, certainly contributed to this atmosphere of fear. In 1949 Pope Pius XII decreed that anyone who joined the Communist party or supported communism in any way would be excommunicated. Article headlines in the Toledo diocesan newspaper the *Chronicle* resounded with the evil of communism: "China Reds Kill 24 Priests, Oust 1,046 Missionaries in '52"; "What Can You Do About Reds in the US?"; "England Fetes Tito, Killer of Christians"; "There Are Plenty of Reds in Our Schools." In Europe, Catholic political parties faced strong opposition from communist and socialist organizations. The Vatican watched as Italians voted for communist mayors and legislative representatives. As the Cold War progressed, Catholic bishops in Eastern Europe and parts of Asia found their priests and people persecuted by hostile secular governments.

Accompanying this anxiety over communism was the shrill promotion of Catholic motherhood and families. The Toledo Catholic newspaper reprinted stories about a Rhode Island woman—"a slender, blue-eyed blonde who looks decades younger"—who had had ten caesarean sections. "My goal is to be a good mother and bring my children up to God," she explained. "That's what keeps me happy."

On the political front, the newspaper described how the National Catholic Family Life Conference was calling for the passage of a national "Family Allowance Act" in order to "get mothers out of factories and help parents rear good families." The Conference called for the rejection of all divorce and appealed to fathers to take up their positions as the "divinely ordained head of the family."[6] Catholic writers believed that the disruptive social elements of the thirties and forties (increases in the divorce rate, women working, rebellious offspring) would be contained by rearing children in proper homes.

Margaret and Ken's new house on Croydon Avenue was in Christ the King parish, which had recently been carved out of existing parishes. In the first decade of the twentieth century, eleven new churches had opened in Toledo, but during the Depression, parish building came to a standstill. Then a flurry of new churches were begun in the fifties, when Bishop George J. Rehring established eight new parishes in the diocese. In 1952 he appointed Basil Goes to be the first pastor of Christ the King Church.

Father Goes was a typical suburban priest of the era. Born in 1908 in rural Ohio, he went to a preparatory seminary immediately after finishing elementary school. For the next twelve years he lived and studied with a community of boys and men isolated both from their families and American popular culture. Although the monastic character of seminary life limited the life experiences of boys, it also meant that they would be the most educated of all of America's clergymen. Even a dull boy had to pass tests in Latin, theology, and Bible history.

Basil Goes was ordained in 1934, at a time when more men were entering the priesthood than at any other time in American history. Until the Depression hit, dioceses had built sprawling seminary complexes for men eager to develop their religious vocations and enter into a well-respected occupation. The economic instability of the twenties simultaneously reduced the numbers of churches being built and increased the number of priests working in parishes. By 1942 there was one priest for every 617 Catholics. There were so many priests that they taught high school, staffed Catholic colleges, and worked in hospitals and social service agencies. They also spent many years as assistants to older priests. After serving as a curate for almost ten years, Father Goes was appointed pastor of the newly established Christ the King when he was forty-four.

By the time he became pastor, the situation of priests in America had begun to change. Between 1940 and 1960, the Catholic population almost doubled. Americans in general were having more babies, and the Catholic birth rate was even higher. At the same time, the number of men being ordained had increased by only 52 percent.[7] The GI Bill lured Catholic men away from the seminary just as it had lured them away from factories and farms. The general prosperity of the country captured the attention of Catholic boys as dreams of professional careers became more realistic. The very same television shows and magazine advertisements that glorified family life made it difficult for vocational directors to convince young men that having a surrogate "parish family" was the highest good. The number of men entering the seminary could not keep up with the booming Catholic growth. A decade before the turmoil of the sixties, a priest shortage had begun.

As the ratio of people to priests increased, so did the pressures on Father Goes. The year that Ken and his new daughter were baptized, Father Goes baptized sixty babies. The year the family joined the parish, a census counted 1,152 adults at Sunday Masses. Two years later in October of 1957, Father Goes said five Masses per Sunday, with the occasional help of a priest from a religious order. A full-time assistant priest arrived that summer because Christ the King had grown by five hundred families in four years. Throughout the fifties only two priests served this growing suburban parish. Father Goes remained as pastor at Christ the King for over twenty-five years until his retirement in 1978.

W HEN A CATHOLIC SOCIOLOGIST surveyed parish priests at the end of the fifties and asked them what took up most of their time, the priests responded clearly: schoolchildren. They told researchers that they spent most of their time on finances, schools, and administration, and they liked those tasks the least.[8] Since 1884, American bishops had required Catholics to send their children to their parish schools, and many Catholics had ignored the command. It was only in the mid twentieth century, after unions increased factory wages, laws required children to attend school, and education became the ticket to affluence, that Catholics enthusiastically embraced parochial education.

Between 1945 and 1962 Catholic school enrollment increased by 129 percent while the general public school population rose by only 69 percent. During the fifties, Cardinal Francis Spellman built more than 200 new elementary schools in the New York archdiocese, and in Philadelphia 133 elementary and 20 diocesan high schools were built. Catholics spent $175 million in 1958 on new elementary and high school construction, most of which was raised by individual parishes. Across the country, Catholics were educating about one of every eight students enrolled in school.[9]

In spite of a flurry of building, no Catholic classroom stood empty. After years of cajoling pastors to build or expand their schools and then pleading with parents to send their children to them, the Church was suddenly experiencing a "crisis of success."[10] Sisters who taught in Toledo's growing suburban schools remember having as many as seventy-two children packed into a classroom, where there was almost no room between the students' desks and the blackboard. Official diocesan statistics from 1959 admitted to an *average* class size of forty-three students per teacher. Almost all pastors reported their schools were strained beyond capacity, and yet only about half of all Catholic children were enrolled in parish schools. Out of necessity, priests stopped vocally disparaging the public schools and instead promoted after-school catechism classes.

For generations, Catholic parents had been told that parochial education was better: It combined faith with knowledge, acknowledged the contributions of Catholics to Western Civilization and American culture, and was taught by selfless and devoted women (and a few men). Most importantly, it helped secure one's immortal soul. When Margaret and her mother had gone to Sacred Heart elementary school, they wore everyday clothes. Now, in postwar America, schoolchildren outfitted in uniforms became an integral part of Catholic identity.

The goal of parish life, especially in the suburbs, was education. As soon as their parish was conceived, Christ the King parishioners started raising money for a school that would also house their church. By 1955 they had the $211,000 needed to construct a building with three classrooms on the second floor and a mix of classrooms and worship space on the first. When time and finances permitted, an actual church would be built and the space originally used for worship would be converted into classrooms. Throughout the country, Catholics were constructing such school-churches made of concrete blocks covered with bricks. The hybrid buildings looked just like the public schools popping up in new neighborhoods. With their simple, rectangle forms and their flat roofs, architects designed school-churches as transitory spaces. As the number of schoolchildren grew, additional floors were added. A pastor could transform any interior space from a sanctuary to an auditorium, to a classroom, and then back again. Other parishes in Toledo—St. Pius, Regina Coeli, and St. Jude—all constructed school-churches during the fifties.

Although there was no difference in the academic goals of parochial and public schools, the full burden of religious education fell on Catholic schools. Parents assumed that teachers instilled the practices and beliefs of Catholicism in their children. The Sisters of Notre Dame who taught at Christ the King not only made sure their students went to Mass every day and Confession once a month, but they also took the children into the church and taught them the parts of the Mass and the symbolism of the vestments. Sister Immaculé, the parish's first princi-pal, made sure that in the fifth grade the children were given missals and taught how to use them. She remembered how important it was that students were well prepared to receive their First Holy Communion and did so in a group, underscoring the importance of Church unity. Or-ganizing the religious lives of schoolchildren rather than concentrating on the spiritual lives of the adults in the congregation was the focal point of Christ the King parish during the years that Margaret and Ken were parishioners.

PUTTING A CHURCH in a building designed to be a school meant that the church's sanctuary space had distinct limits. The simplicity and intimacy that would become a hallmark of Vatican II churches were already evi-dent in many of the churches of the fifties. At Christ the King, each Sun-day the staff had to set up and take down chairs in two classrooms so everyone could be seated. Churchgoers from this era remember that Fa-ther Goes barely gave a sermon during the summer months because the low ceiling made the room excruciatingly hot. Even in the winter, Mass rarely lasted longer than forty minutes.

Always watching his budget, Father Goes's scavenging efforts netted an altar for his new church from one of his former parishes. On either side of this hand-me-down altar were statues of the Virgin Mary and St. Joseph. The sanctuary, however, lacked other signs of being a church that would have been found in the older, downtown churches. There was no stained glass, no large organ, no formal pulpit, no ranks of devotional candles, no pointed arches, and no bell tower. Even when the parish put up a larger building in 1961, they did not build a conventional church; in-stead, they erected an auditorium, put in wooden pews, and then disas-sembled and moved in their old altar. Parishioners were told that when the "real" church was built, the school would take over this auditorium for its gym. In 1983 the auditorium was renovated and a new altar in-stalled, but to this day, a "real church" has yet to be built.

Catholics at Christ the King and the other new churches built after the Second World War did not create a sense of the divine through grand architecture and statuary. Instead, they made the space holy by maintaining the minutely regulated etiquette of traditional Catholicism. Women and girls wore hats in church, whereas men and boys removed theirs. Upon entering, the neatly dressed parishioners dipped their fingers in holy water, made the Sign of the Cross, and genuflected. The light in front of the tabernacle told them that the Eucharist was present on the altar and that they must not talk to each other. Even on Sunday after Mass, Father Goes never greeted his parishioners within the worship space. Social activities took place in the parish hall. Babies who cried during Mass were removed. Margaret recalled an embarrassing moment when her misbehaving toddler had to be dragged out of the church as she shouted, "Daddy, don't spank me!" Christ, as the divine king, was as much present in their church-school as he was in the bishop's cathedral downtown.

Unlike the downtown parishes, with their stately churches in Gothic or Romanesque styles, the school-church did not convey an image of holy permanence. Parishes were in continual flux: Babies were being born, new families were moving in and out, and buildings were being rearranged. The popular Vatican II image of a "pilgrim church" was already evident in many suburban parishes. New parishes built in postwar America signaled to Catholics that the Church was a work in progress, not a finished product. Although Catholic theology and rituals were thought of as unchanging, the reality of living in Christ the King parish underscored the dynamic and evolving character of religious experience. As one parishioner recalled, "We had to ride with the waves."

The frantic pace of Catholic growth at Christ the King necessitated a constant demand for the labor of parishioners. Pastors of new parishes struggled to get the work done without sounding like hectoring nags. Unlike an urban church sandwiched between houses, a suburban parish needed parking lots and lawns. "All the men of the parish who can help are asked to be on hand Saturday at 8:00AM to work the ground and sow seed," the parish bulletin reported in 1955. "Please bring whatever equipment you have—rake, shovel, roller, seeding cart. We'll need them." Ken remembers helping put in the black top for the parking lot, and Father Goes expected help to pour concrete for the parish center floor: "The men who are free to come evenings this week we ask to come then and the following nights until the job is done." The bulletin noted that the garage got finished, but where "were the volunteers to paint the garage yesterday morning? The paint was there but not the help. Let's try again this Saturday." As soon as one job was finished, there were pleas for help for something else. Christ the King parish functioned like a new home in a subdivision: As soon as it was built, it needed paint and a lawn; then it had to be enlarged, remodeled, and updated.

At Christ the King, Father Goes was the boss, but parishioners remember that they were actively engaged in bringing about the very physical existence of the church. A popular story still circulating among parishioners reports that when Father Goes recruited his volunteer masons to finish building a garage, he promised to supply them with all the beer they needed to finish the job. For years afterward he joked that he had naively miscalculated how much they could consume.

Father Goes showed little interest in helping his congregation "find God." He chided his parishioners not to leave Mass early, to receive Communion frequently, and to behave properly when he came to visit the sick, but he made no effort to educate adults as to why they should do these things. Other parishes in Toledo hosted chapters of the Christian Family Movement, which taught couples how to integrate social justice concerns with liturgical awareness—but not Christ the King. More militant Catholic groups, like the Legion of Mary or the Blue Army, who said the rosary to end communism, were also absent from the parish. For many new parishes of the Baby Boom years, the physical needs of a growing congregation promoted lay engagement while it simultaneously distracted both the priest and the people from reflecting on theological or ritual matters.

For a parish to succeed, openness and respect between priest and people was necessary. Suburban congregations demanded a high degree of competence from their priests and from each other. This was the most educated generation of Catholics in the history of the country, and a pastor who treated his parishioners like children soon found that he had no one to blacktop the parking lot.

Furthermore, the needs of the suburban parish required the efforts of both men and women. From advising the priest on financial matters to putting up chairs for Sunday Mass in school classrooms to participating in parish sports teams, men actively took part in parish life. As soon as Christ the King was established, Father Goes picked twelve men to run for the parish council, of which the congregation elected six to help their pastor make decisions. In the parish bulletin, Father Goes explained that these men needed to be practical Catholics who financially supported their church, sent their children to the parish school, and did not belong to a society like the Masons, which was condemned by the Church.

Christ the King also had an active Holy Name Society, a group of men who met once a month, went to Communion as a group, and put on fund-raising activities. In some cities Holy Name Societies put on large public rallies, but mass displays of Catholic piety was on the decline. Suburban men tended to be more interested in socializing with one another than they were in collective prayer or asserting Catholic power. At Christ the King, monthly Holy Name meetings typically included a quick prayer and then a sports movie or a man from the Toledo Municipal League who spoke about "the metropolitan complexities of annexation and incorporation."

Of the five Sunday Masses celebrated at Christ the King, all but one were low Masses with no singing during the Mass itself. The music director at Christ the King tried with little success to assemble a male choir to sing for the 8 a.m. Sunday high Mass. He knew that choirs performed a liturgical office and, therefore, should be comprised solely of men. In 1956 he had six men and "a few more would help." A year later he chided the congregation that only one third of last year's number were turning up for practice. "Surely from about 500 men," he wrote in the parish bulletin, "we have 20 who can give a return to God of their vocal gifts through our church choir." Sister Immaculé recalled with pride her ability to teach a mixed choir of schoolchildren how to chant for their daily Mass, but parish men showed no interest in music. The Liturgical Movement's preference for Gregorian Chant never caught on in the suburbs.

Given that no tuition was charged for their school and that all salaries and building costs were paid out of parish funds, the demand for fund-raising was high. Men raised money by going door-to-door for yearly pledges, but women raised money and bought needed goods by collecting trading stamps, holding neighborhood parties, selling the parish cookbook *Fit for a King*, organizing "feather parties" where turkeys were raffled, putting on seasonal dances, and charging for Holy Name breakfasts. In 1956 the women's fall raffle was double the Easter Sunday collection. In 1958 Margaret became president of the women's Altar Society. Traditionally, these women sewed, repaired, and cleaned vestments and altar cloths and also decorated the altar with flowers. Ready-made vestments, the popularity of dry cleaners and local florists, as well as the simplicity of Christ the King's altar meant that their sanctuary responsibilities were minimal. Like the Holy Name Society, the women spent most of their time enjoying each other's company. While the men watched sports movies at their meetings, the women heard a representative from the Singer Sewing Machine company. Margaret thought that these meetings were useful and practical, presenting good advice to women about their roles as wives and mothers.

Parish life had always had its social components, but Margaret's generation was particularly fond of doing things with others rather than by themselves. Her cohort has been called the civic generation. They bowled in teams. The men joined the Elks and the Shriners and the women their auxiliaries. Workers joined unions. Voters went to political party meetings and ran for local offices. Groups of couples played bridge at each other's houses, sticking their kids in the basement to play. They attended church dances and fashion shows. One reason that the generation who lived through the Depression and World War II gravitated to organized religion was because they enjoyed expressing themselves communally.

However, such continual preoccupation with socializing and group activities had its critics. "What is open to me? The women's Guild program, lawn parties, fashion shows, bazaars, suppers," complained a woman from a New Hampshire parish. "I am looking for God and I haven't found him in any of the fashion shows."[11]

BY THE SUMMER OF 1958, Margaret was settled into her house, her neighborhood, and her church. The couple had adopted a son. Caring for a two- and a four-year-old took its toll, but she still found time to help Ken organize the parish lawn social, raising $200 by selling donated ice cream and cake, "in spite of the bad weather," according to the parish bulletin. Toledo was close enough to Erie that she could easily visit her parents and brother. At thirty-two, she figured her life had finally settled down.

Ken thought differently. A position had opened up in Washington, D.C. to work for the federal parole board. A part of the Bureau of Prisons, the parole board oversaw the release of men and women from federal prisons. Working for the federal government would be a new challenge, and so Ken took the job when it was offered to him. Reluctantly, Margaret helped put their house up for sale and prepare for the move. The couple bought a home in a new subdivision just built in Alexandria, Virginia. On her living room wall Margaret hung up her house blessing signed by Father Goes, dedicating the family to the Sacred Heart.

That October, not long after the family left Toledo, Pope Pius XII died at his summer house on the outskirts of Rome. He had been pope since 1939, and his career had been controversial both theologically and politically. In the almost twenty years since the last papal death, funeral, and electoral concave, Americans had developed a taste for Catholicism. From the clerical wisdom expressed in *Going My Way* to the meditations of Thomas Merton to the scathing attacks of Paul Blanshard, Catholicism *sold*.

The death and funeral of Pope Pius XII began a barrage of media coverage that brought the minutiae of Vatican traditions into American households. The papal funeral was televised, and news magazines detailed how the body was placed in a triple coffin (oak, lead, and cypress) and buried along with a red bag containing a sample of every Vatican coin minted during his reign, a parchment copy of the final funeral eulogy, and the pieces of his broken Fisherman's Ring. What other exotica, the media seemed to be asking, would accompany the election of a new pope?

chapter three

GATHERING IN
LOS ANGELES AND ROME

With the death of Pope Pius XII, the parish-oriented, local Catholic world in which Margaret lived gained a new international dimension. The funeral of Pius XII and the eventual installation of Pope John XXIII were covered in loving detail by the American press. The foreign aspects of Catholicism—once considered negative characteristics—were rehabilitated. As the news media became increasingly visual, the sensual and ceremonial nature of Catholicism held new intrigue. The drama and visual spectacle of Roman Catholicism made for good television and for full-color photo spreads in *Life* and *Look* magazines. Americans wanted glimpses of what was going on around the world, and the exotic nature of Catholic ceremonialism fit their tastes precisely.

After the elaborate funeral of Pope Pius XII, fifty-one cardinals from around the world gathered in Rome to pick his successor. Locked together in a room in the Vatican, they were not to come out until they elected a new pope. White robes and crimson slippers in three different sizes were readied for the new pontiff. As the cardinals voted, their ballots were burned in a special stove whose smoke could be seen from St. Peter's Square. When no consensus had been achieved, wet straw was added to the burning ballots to produce black smoke. When the ballots were burned without the straw, the smoke would then burn white, signaling to the outside world that a new pope had been chosen. A prospective pope needed to receive one vote more than a two-thirds majority to merit white smoke.

On the third voting day of the conclave, Angelo Roncalli, a cardinal from Venice, was elected. At seventy-seven years old, the media at first speculated that the new Pope John XXIII would be a caretaker pope who might attempt basic reforms of the Vatican bureaucracy. The new pope, however, soon made it evident that he was not cut from the same cloth as his predecessor.

The son of a northern Italian sharecropper, John XXIII possessed a wry sense of humor and an unmistakable concern for the average Catholic. "In Italy," he quipped after his election, "there are three ways of losing one's money: women, gambling, and farming. My father chose the most boring way of the three. He became a farmer."[1] In his first address as pope, he explained that his hope was simply to be a good shepherd to his flock. Breaking with traditions that kept the pope isolated in Vatican City, John XXIII visited prisoners in Roman jails and the poor of the country's hospitals.

The new pope's humble origins belied his astute awareness of the political and social challenges of the twentieth century. A former Vatican diplomat, Pope John XXIII was well traveled and multilingual. He recognized the importance of the press, meeting with them shortly after his election and quickly gaining their affection. A plump man with an informal manner and confident personality, John XXIII quickly became a favorite of the international media. Reporters helped him spread his message: that he would devote his pontificate to people struggling in the modern world.

Barely three months after his election, Pope John XXIII surprised both his councilors and the world at large by announcing his desire to assemble an ecumenical council. His brief mention of this to a gathering of cardinals left them in stunned silence. There had not been such a gathering of Catholic bishops and heads of religious orders for almost one hundred years. Pope John XXIII had given no earlier hints he was considering such a monumental undertaking. None of his cardinals had been consulted about the wisdom of *aggiornamento*—the "updating" of the Church and her laws. The world's press scrambled to find out the history of ecumenical councils: What would be the scope and purpose of such a meeting?

Unlike the First Vatican Council, which had clarified the meaning of "papal infallibility" and was closely associated with the condemnation of modern trends in theology, the Second Vatican Council was to focus on helping people live their faith. Pope John XXIII believed this Council should address concrete, practical, and pastoral problems. For him, a Council of religious leaders was needed to generate a positive but searching look at the whole life of the Church. Such a renewal of Catholicism would also serve as a gesture of outreach toward other Christian and religious communities.

A YEAR AFTER JOHN XXIII'S unexpected announcement, another John captured the attention of American Catholics. John F. Kennedy, a senator from Massachusetts, held a press conference on the second day of 1960. Noting his service as a naval officer and his fourteen years in Congress, he announced his candidacy for "the most powerful office in the free world."[2] Young, wealthy, and Catholic, Kennedy was not a typical candidate. His supporters struggled to persuade fellow Democrats to give Kennedy the party's nomination instead of the more established politician, Hubert Humphrey.

Kennedy's run for president stirred up lingering anti-Catholic sentiments in the country. Mainstream Protestant magazines, ministers who ran big-city churches, and well-educated journalists all voiced concerns that, as president, Kennedy could be controlled by the Vatican and the Catholic clergy. In their opinion, Catholicism, like communism, was by its very nature undemocratic. Some of their skepticism was allayed after Kennedy told ministers in Houston that he believed in the absolute separation of church and state, that no Catholic prelate would tell him how to act as president, and that parochial schools should not be granted public funds. Still, fear of a Catholic in the White House lingered. Kennedy's slim margin of victory over the Republican candidate, Richard Nixon, was at least partially the result of concerns over religion.

Although both Margaret's and Ken's families had been active in local Republican politics, the couple voted for John Kennedy. More than a specific political platform, the youthful Kennedy represented the ascendancy of their generation. Kennedy and his family demonstrated that loyalty to Catholicism could effortlessly accompany intelligent patriotism, urbane sophistication, and coolly detached cosmopolitanism. The election of the new president signaled that old suspicions about Catholics were dead.

Margaret was ecstatic when Ken told her that he had snared tickets to the Kennedy inauguration. The day before the event, however, a massive snowstorm hit the East Coast. Government offices closed early, and it took Ken's car pool two hours to drive the short distance across the Potomac River to Alexandria. The storm continued into the morning of January 20. Not even snowplows were venturing out. The fates had conspired against the couple, and so they joined millions of other Americans in front of their television sets.

Listening to the new president address the nation, their disappointment with the weather faded as they were caught up in his message: "Let the word go forth from this time and place," he declared, "that the torch has been passed to a new generation of Americans—born in this century, tempered by war, disciplined by a hard and bitter peace, proud of our ancient heritage—and unwilling to witness or permit the slow undoing of those human rights to which this Nation has always been committed, and to which we are committed today at home and around the world."

Kennedy observed that the world had been split into two powerful groups of nations, each with the ability to enact humanity's final war. Fearing this potential outcome, he called for civility, the mutual exploration of common problems, and a new world of law where "the strong are just, and the weak secure, and the peace preserved." Kennedy addressed Americans as individuals and called them to join in this historic effort: "And so, my fellow Americans: ask not what your country can do for you—ask what you can do for your country."[3]

Ken and Margaret took Kennedy's request very seriously. Soon after his inauguration, Kennedy appointed his brother, Robert, as attorney general. Early in 1961 Robert Kennedy approved the funding of three experimental "pre-release guidance centers." Located in New York, Chicago, and Los Angeles, these centers would house young federal prisoners during the last months of their incarceration, where staff at the centers would teach inmates how to cope with life outside of prison. They would help them find jobs, set up savings accounts, and show them legitimate forms of leisure. Rather than thinking only in terms of isolating and punishing, the Bureau of Prisons of the Kennedy administration created a pilot program focused on rehabilitation. Although he had worked for the parole board for only a few years, the opportunity to participate in such an innovative form of corrections could not be ignored. Ken applied for the new job.

THAT SUMMER THE FAMILY was packing again, this time to move across the country to California, where Ken would head the pre-release guidance center in Los Angeles. Margaret was beginning to accept that her family life would forever be mobile. They could not rely on mother for babysitting or mother-in-law for helping out with Thanksgiving dinner. Margaret's brother, Charles, was busy with his own family, and with four kids, he had managed to get to Washington, D.C., for only one springtime visit. Margaret had learned that moving—first for her husband to go to college and then for him to secure more interesting jobs—meant that she had to develop friendships quickly. Her husband and children, rather than an extended network of relatives, became the focus of her attention.

By Christmas of 1961 the family was settled in a rental house in Monterey Park. Ken had located a site for the pre-release guidance center in a former Baptist seminary in East Los Angeles, and he and his staff began their work with federal inmates. Eight miles from Los Angeles, Monterey Park had begun as the former Spanish land-grant estate of Rancho San Antonio, but prior to 1910 only a handful of people worked its walnut trees and grain fields. Developers eventually tried to sell plots of land for homes, but even with the Pacific Electric car line bringing men into the city to work, only 5,000 people lived in the area by 1920. The collapse of the real estate bubble in 1929 stymied that growth. Only after World War II and the rapid population expansion of Southern California did Monterey Park flourish. Families from around the country used their GI Bills to move into the new homes springing up around Los Angeles. By 1951 Monterey Park had a population of 21,000, and ten years later the population had doubled. In 1960 the city's racial composition was 3 percent Asian, 12 percent Hispanic, and 85 percent white.

While Ken settled into his new job, Margaret entered the life of her community through two Catholic churches. The family's house was in the parish of St. Thomas Aquinas, a quick walk up the hill. Newly built in 1960, it did not yet have a school. St. Stephen's was a well-established parish two miles away. The parish had already built three churches since its founding in 1921, and it had just torn down its old school and built a new one. Six lay teachers and seven Sisters of the Holy Names of Jesus and Mary taught almost six hundred students in two classes of eight grades. The parish was justifiably proud of its school—built in the modern style with outdoor corridors and plenty of light.

Margaret and Ken agreed that the education of their children—understood to be an intellectual, cultural, moral, and spiritual endeavor—was to be their highest goal. Although women across the country were entering the workforce in ever-greater numbers, Margaret joined the 70 percent of married white women who were stay-at-home moms.[4] Margaret could have easily gotten a job in the booming postwar California economy, enabling the couple to save for a down payment for a house, but she did not. For this couple, working outside of the home was something a mother did only if she had to. Margaret believed that mothers needed to make sure their children were doing their homework and eating healthy meals. She knew the sisters needed help on the playground and the parish needed fund-raisers. Ken continued to tell Margaret she did not need to work, and she agreed. Margaret helped in the church office and drove the nuns to get school supplies.

THE SAME CHRISTMAS of 1961, Pope John XXIII formally announced that the Second Vatican Council would open in the fall of 1962. Three years of preparation had clarified the purpose and scope of the meetings. In the text in which he described the point of the Council, the pope explained his belief that the world was at a critical period of its history and the Church must engage with it. Modern society had achieved great progress in science and technology, but it also convinced itself that God is superfluous to that story. There was not a corresponding advance in morality to that of material progress, so the modern world must be brought into closer contact with the message of Christ. The upcoming Council, the pope declared, would demonstrate that the Church is alive—always young, always radiantly reflecting the rhythms of the times—and yet always the same. This would be the challenge of the Council: to change, as all living bodies change, but at the same time to remain consistent with its own truth.

Pope John XXIII indicated that the Council deliberations would not seek to remedy specific deficits in the Church. Indeed, in his announcement he gave no indication that there was any problem with the current state of Catholicism. Unlike the earlier popes who had called ecumenical councils to address specific deficiencies in the Church and the world, this Council was intended to be positive. Always the optimist, John described the Church of the day as "vibrant with vitality." The pope charged the future Council Fathers not to change the faith but to fortify it. When the Council was finished, the resulting documents would serve to promote greater efficiency, instill deeper holiness, and spread the Church's revealed truth.

Other ecumenical Councils were exclusively Catholic affairs, but Pope John XXIII believed that this twenty-first council should be relevant to Protestants and even to non-Christians in the larger world. Acknowledging previous Catholic efforts to strengthen Christian unity, he predicted that the forthcoming Council would continue this trend by clarifying Catholic beliefs and thus smoothing the way to a return to Christian unity. It would also offer men of goodwill an opportunity to turn their thoughts toward peace, a serenity that came from acknowledging spiritual and supernatural realities.

ON OCTOBER 8, 1962, Cardinal James Francis McIntyre boarded a flight at the Los Angeles International Airport bound for Rome. Accompanying him were his secretary, Father John A. Rawden, and Father Lawrence J. Gibson, the archdiocesan director of vocations. His auxiliary bishop and Council Father, Timothy Manning, had left the day before. There were at least fifty clergymen on the flight, and thirty of those were bishops. To demonstrate that Pan Am understood the historic nature of their trip, the airline had printed the flight instructional brochure entirely in Latin and included the Catholic table grace. After landing, McIntyre joined two other cardinals (Richard Cushing from Boston and Joseph Ritter from St. Louis) to live for the next few months at the North American College, where generations of American men had received theological training in Rome.

McIntyre held a privileged position in the American Catholic hierarchy as one of only five cardinals. He had led the Archdiocese of Los Angeles since 1948, and within five years of his arrival he became the first cardinal of a western city. His jurisdiction spanned from the coastal town of Santa Barbara to just north of San Diego. If all those living in that area were counted, it would have been the largest diocese in the nation. In 1962 the Catholic population of the archdiocese was 1,421,478.

McIntyre had overseen the immense growth of Southern California's Catholic population. Eighty-seven new parishes had been established by 1962 and hundreds of others had completed renovations. He managed to revoke California's taxing of private schools and to fend off efforts to reinstate the tax. Each year more and more children were taught in parish elementary and high schools. The period between 1952 and 1962 saw a 115 percent increase in enrollment, a rate almost double that of the public schools. Trained as a manager and accountant on Wall Street prior to entering the priesthood, McIntyre oversaw New York City's archdiocesan finances before the move to Los Angeles. McIntyre adroitly and meticulously managed church monies, making sure that all church construction was approved by his office. Strong, traditional, and opinionated, McIntyre was an American Catholic success story.

Cardinal McIntyre was one of 2,908 men eligible by Canon Law to attend the Second Vatican Council. Most of the Council Fathers were like McIntyre—bishops who administered Catholic sacramental and social life in distinct geographical areas. Other Fathers were the heads of religious orders like the Jesuits or the Dominicans. Still other Council Fathers were leaders of Catholic communities—patriarchs and bishops—from countries in the Middle East and Asia who followed the rituals and customs of "Eastern rite" Catholicism. These "Oriental Fathers" submitted to the authority of the pope in Rome, but their congregations followed ritual, theological, and disciplinary traditions distinct from those of the "Latin" West.

Two thousand five hundred and forty Council Fathers processed into the nave of St. Peter's Basilica for the Council's opening on October 11, 1962. Those of the lowest rank entered first. At the end of the procession, the pope was carried aloft on his *sedia gestatoria*, a portable throne. Once inside the Council Hall (known as the *aula*), the Fathers sat in order of their seniority on two tiers of bleacher-like seats, ten rows high. Each bishop had his own small writing desk. Above them were eight galleries constructed between the pillars of the Basilica for theological advisors, who were official representatives of bishops who were unable to attend, and other authorized observers. In true Roman fashion, coffee bars were built in two side chapels so that the Fathers could take a break from the proceedings and enjoy an espresso.

The largest contingent of Council Fathers came from Italy. Although Italian Catholics comprised only 9 percent of the total Catholic population, 430 Italian clerics took their seats in the aula—about 17 percent of the Council Fathers. Over the centuries, in addition to monopolizing the Vatican institutional bureaucracy, many tiny dioceses were created in southern Italy—each with its own bishop. The Italian force at the Council was formidable. Even though many Italian citizens did not attend Mass or involve themselves in lay organizations, their taxes supported a vast array of church buildings and paid clerical salaries. The Italian language was close to the ecclesiastical Latin used in church rituals and documents. Of all those who arrived at St. Peter's, the Italian Council Fathers were the most comfortable with the style of religious discussion that took place in the aula.

SOME OF THE ITALIAN BISHOPS were also members of the *Curia*, the governing arm of the Church. These men possessed the legislative, juridical, and administrative powers to enforce the teachings of the pope. Though not all members of the papal bureaucracy were Italian, the vast majority was.

As the power of the pope increased over the centuries, so did the power of the Curia. When Pope Pius XII became ill in the years before his death, he withdrew from Vatican affairs. The curial bishops took over the day-to-day government of the Church, thereby expanding their influence. Consequently, these Italian bishops (most of whom were cardinals), who had no pastoral responsibilities and who took pride in their cultural isolation, wielded considerable authority. They held, for instance, the chairmanships of all the preparatory commissions who produced the drafts of the texts to be discussed by the Council Fathers.

From the beginning, the American media was fascinated by the Curia. For audiences used to a comparatively open democratic political process, the Curia represented the secretive and exotic parts of Catholicism. News reports from the Vatican introduced into the homes of average Catholics an aspect of Church leadership that had previously been the concern of bishops and theologians only.

The Curia valued protocol and custom and rejected direct challenges or public humiliation. Trained in the "Roman School," they felt most comfortable making sense of faith by using the scholastic theology developed by Thomas Aquinas in the thirteenth century. Even more importantly, they understood the technical language of Catholicism that was rooted in nineteenth-century interpretations of Aquinas.

At the time of the Council, the curial perspective on humanity was dark. In his opening address to the Council, the pope was probably referring to the Curia when he mentioned the "prophets of doom" who were always "forecasting disaster."[5] Most members of the Curia believed that human beings are bent toward evil because of the existence of Original Sin inherited through Adam's disobedience. Even after Baptism erases this stain, a serious effort had to be made by both individuals and societies to keep Christians on the right path. Because the Curia had played a critical part in defining what Catholicism looked like, that they wondered why the Church needed changing at all is not surprising.

AFTER THE ITALIANS, the next largest contingent (241 Council Fathers) came from the United States. By most definitions, the American Council Fathers were theological and social conservatives. Some, like Paul Hallinan of Atlanta and John Dearden of Detroit, became more liberal over the course of the Council, but others, like the Californian Cardinal McIntyre, were skeptical of change.

During the first two annual sessions, the American bishops rarely spoke in the aula. They came to Rome with little interest in theology or experience with innovations in Catholic worship. Most American bishops were practical men who were used to spending their days balancing budgets, meeting with civic leaders, and trying to keep their churches staffed and their schools full. Neither the diplomatic intrigues of the Vatican Curia or the subtleties of scholastic theology held much interest for them; their worries were material rather than spiritual. Although the American heads of religious orders may have visited communities outside of the United States, most of the bishops did not concern themselves with the variations in liturgical languages, rituals, and theology of a global Catholicism. Nor, given their overwhelmingly practical bent, did they spend time reflecting on the implications of that variation for the Church.

American bishops differed from other Council Fathers in that they directed growing and increasingly middle-class Catholic communities. The children of immigrants no longer marginalized by poverty and prejudice continued to support their parishes, send their children to parochial schools, and integrate their faith into their everyday lives. Men were entering the priesthood and women the convent in record numbers. Well-placed Catholics in the movie industry meant that popular representations of the faith were positive. Unlike in Latin America, where Protestant missionaries aggressively sought converts, civic ecumenism reigned in the United States. Whereas European bishops hoped to stop sharp declines in church attendance and vocations, American bishops wondered what all the fuss was about.

If, however, the American bishops had come to the Council armed with data from social scientists, they would have had a bit more sympathy for their European and Latin American counterparts. Embedded within the very successes of American Catholicism were a series of problems not unlike those in other industrialized Catholic countries. Although church attendance was still strong, it was declining from an all-time high in 1958. The large numbers of Catholics in parish schools and attending Mass put pressures on nuns and priests, and vocations were not keeping up with rising demand. Lay Catholics who often had theological training from college and high school were less patient with clerical incompetence and paternalism. Many wanted their parishes to be more than social centers. Their educational achievements made them less sanguine when they discovered that the sisters teaching their children had barely graduated from high school. Catholic censorship of books and movies looked distinctly old fashioned as Protestants and Jews moved to embrace modern literature, arts, and entertainment. The United States had not experienced "dechristianization" or persecution by communist regimes as had Western Europe, but the Council did occur at a particularly critical time for America's Catholics, regardless of how ignorant the American representatives may have been of that fact.

THE NEXT MOST POPULOUS national group, after the Council Fathers from the United States, was the 204 Fathers from Brazil. The First Vatican Council had been dominated by Europeans, but the Second Vatican Council was shaped by bishops from Latin America, Africa, Asia, and the

Middle East. Africa, for instance, sent 250 Council Fathers, although only sixty were black bishops or cardinals. Council Fathers like the Brazilians came from countries where poverty and social injustice were endemic. Some Council Fathers came prepared to take strong stands against what they understood as the economic and political exploitation of the weak by the strong. Other Fathers, often from the same country or language group, believed that such a focus on earthly matters distracted Catholics from the spiritual core of their faith.

These Third World Council Fathers were often concerned about the mismatch between their native cultures and the culture of Catholicism. Were the rules and practices of the Church based on biblical and theological principles or simply on the social customs of Europeans? The visual diversity of a multi-ethnic and multinational clergy dressed in a stunning array of robes posed against the baroque architecture of Rome made for exciting magazine spreads. At the same time, this assortment of clergymen raised the question of whether or not a universal—a truly catholic—Church could move beyond surface issues and unify itself in order to address real global problems.

THE COUNCIL FATHERS who were most excited about the possibility of theological and liturgical reform came primarily from the countries that bordered the Rhine River: Germany, Austria, Switzerland, France, the Netherlands, and Belgium. This European faction came to the Council poised to present their case for *aggiornamento*. Unlike American bishops, many of these men had taught on university faculties or had embraced new developments in theology. They had overseen liturgical reforms in their diocese that were already successfully engaging lay Catholics in the sacraments. In comparison to the national contingents of bishops, the number of reformers was small; only sixty-eight Council Fathers, for instance, came from Germany.

Progressive Council Fathers from Europe increased their influence on the Council by bringing with them well-trained, articulate, and committed *periti*. Periti, or experts, were priest-specialists in Canon Law, Scripture, Church-state relations, theology, or liturgy. Most taught in seminaries or in university theology departments. These advisors worked as consultants on those Council committees that prepared the draft documents, especially after the Council had begun and the initial drafts proved to be unpopular. Periti also helped the Council Fathers understand what was being said in the general meetings.

Over the course of the four years of the Council, over four hundred men served as periti. Some of the most famous—Karl Rahner, Henri de Lubac, Yves Congar, Marie-Dominque Chenu, and John Courtney Murray—were senior theologians who had experienced censorship of their ideas by the Vatican. Edward Schillebeeckx attended as a theological advisor to Dutch bishops but was never granted official status as a peritus. Other periti, like Gregory Baum and Hans Küng, were younger men who would become famous proponents of the changes introduced at the Council. Still another peritus, Joseph Ratzinger, would later become Pope Benedict XVI. Unlike the First Vatican Council of 1870, Vatican II was strongly influenced by the perspective of professional theologians. During the sixties and early seventies, their writings would be read by American Catholics trying to make sense of the ideas behind the Council documents.

In an unprecedented move toward openness, Pope John XXIII, together with Cardinal Augustin Bea (the newly appointed director of the Office for Christian Unity), invited thirty-two "separated brethren" to attend the general meetings at St. Peter's. "Separated brethren" was the term used in the Council to refer to Protestant and Orthodox Christians. These non-Catholic observers were seated high in the central nave, at a rostrum on the same level as the cardinals. Because they were not expected to know Latin (the language of the Council proceedings), they were given simultaneous translation. Once a week they met with Vatican officials, at which point they expressed their opinions on the ideas discussed by the Council Fathers. The number of non-Catholic observers increased for each of the four Council sessions, signaling a permanent end to Catholic isolation from the larger Christian community.

MAJOR NEWSPAPERS, magazines, and news services from around the world sent journalists to cover the events of the Council because they found that their non-Catholic readers were also interested in what was happening in Rome. The strict secrecy of the First Vatican Council had led to a proliferation of rumors and misinformation that the nineteenth-century press amplified. A hundred years later, to announce one's engagement with the modern world and then to exclude the press was not possible. When *Time* magazine named Pope John XXIII its "Man of the Year" for 1962, it was the third time his image had appeared on its cover. This pope understood the importance of public opinion cultivated through the media. The press office set up inside a converted movie theater and stories filed by reporters served as vital interpreters of the discussions of the Council.

American reporters underscored their participation in the Council by insisting that this was a revolutionary moment in history. The world, they reported, should pay attention because change was in the air. Everything Catholic was up for grabs: clerical celibacy, fish on Fridays, priestly dress, the Latin Mass, and doctrines like Original Sin and the real presence of Christ in the Eucharist. From their perspective, they had been given an unprecedented glimpse of the inner workings of a spooky, exclusively male club. The press had covered the election and early days of a Catholic president; now they would lay open the workings of his Church.

Not surprisingly, the press often covered the Council as if it was taking place in Washington, D.C. rather than in Rome. Reporters did not understand the difficult theological language or an Italian culture that valued ceremony and tradition. Many interpreted the Council using models drawn from political reporting. They saw the pope as an "of the people and by the people" president and the various Council Fathers as either pro-reform liberals or anti-reform conservatives. During the Council's first year, restrictions were placed on what could be said to the press, so reporters were left to off-the-record stories, background panels, rumors, and their own imagination to document what was happening at the Council. By the second session a more open relationship was established, but the slow character of religious change all conspired to make reporting from Rome difficult.

To help English-speaking reporters understand the issues discussed at meetings (meetings they were never allowed to attend), the U.S. bishops set up a series of daily press panels. Every afternoon in the basement of the Rome USO, religious experts and Council Fathers tried to provide historical and theological contextualization for the papers read from the floor of St. Peter's. The more articulate and impassioned Fathers could go into depth on their positions, and the press could report on them without breaking secrecy or spending a fortune courting theologians at Roman restaurants. The National Catholic Welfare Conference News Service provided summaries of these panels to over six hundred diocesan weekly newspapers. Even the mysterious and immensely popular author Xavier Rynne (whose real name was Father Francis X. Murphy), who chronicled the Council for the *New Yorker* magazine, used the materials generated by the press panels to arouse the interests of the general reader.

None of the reporters who covered the opening of the Council noted the irony of a crowd of over two thousand men dressed in lace and silk solemnly striding into St. Peter's on the feast day of the Maternity of the Virgin Mary without being accompanied by a single woman. All of the Council Fathers, the non-Catholic observers, the periti and most of the press who attended Vatican II were men. There were no women included on the preparatory commissions—not even those that dealt with women's religious orders. When the Catholic wives of the members of the press corps tried to receive Communion during the daily Masses that preceded the Council's general sessions, they were turned away. Only after the press corps protested did Church authorities allow the Swiss Guard to permit the women to approach the altar. The paper of noted economist Barbara Ward, who had been asked by the lay observers to report to the Council on world poverty, was read by a male associate because a woman's voice was not to be heard in the solemn assembly.

This total absence of women was remedied only at the end of the third session when a few Catholic women were invited to join Catholic men as *auditores* (which means "listeners"). By the fourth session, twenty-three women—thirteen lay women and ten religious women—attended the Council. Of the ten sisters, one was an American. Of the lay women, only one was married at the time. The women were excluded from the two coffee bars that were set up in the side altars of St. Peter's, thus restricting their conversations with the Council Fathers and the periti. After some grumbling, a separate coffee bar was built for the female auditors, where men were permitted to visit. Because the men's coffee areas were called Bar Jonah and Bar Abbas, the women nicknamed theirs Bar Nun.

THE LOS ANGELES archdiocesan newspaper *The Tidings* covered with great enthusiasm the opening of the Second Vatican Council. Cardinal McIntyre sent a letter to all of his parish priests, encouraging them to have their parishioners say a specific prayer for the success of the Council. At Holy Rosary elementary school in Sun Valley, first- and second-grade boys celebrated the gathering in Rome by dressing up as Council Fathers in "grave solemnity." A particularly plump third grader sat in the middle of his classmates as Pope John. Student nurses from St. Vincent's College in Los Angeles formed a living rosary one evening on their college lawn to pray for the success of the Council. Each student represented a bead by holding a flashlight, and when the night descended, they formed a glowing star in the darkness.[6]

Margaret read about the Second Vatican Council in *Newsweek* and *Time* magazine. She watched Council Fathers being interviewed now and then on television, but there were more pressing things going on in her world. On October 22, 1962, President Kennedy interrupted the evening television programming to announce that there was unmistakable evidence of an offensive nuclear missile site being built by the Soviet Union on the island of Cuba. For two weeks Margaret, along with millions of other Americans, worried that nuclear war was imminent. Then, a year later, as the second session of the Council began, President John F. Kennedy was assassinated. As little John-John Kennedy saluted the casket while the funeral cortege passed by, Margaret watched her husband cry.

For Margaret, the events of the sixties continually rivaled the news of the Second Vatican Council. Civil Rights protests in the South burst into violence as marchers were attacked by police dogs and water cannons. Four little black girls were killed when a white racist bombed their church. In the summer of 1965, as Cardinal McIntyre finalized plans to return to Rome for the final session of the Council, a Los Angeles neighborhood burned. A white police officer had arrested a young black man who he believed was driving drunk. The arrest was a flashpoint for anger against the police and for the economic and social segregation that plagued Los Angeles. Six days of rioting left thirty-four people dead and almost a thousand buildings burned, looted, or damaged. Margaret, who was recovering in a downtown hospital after a breast biopsy, watched the smoke from Watts out of her window. She told Ken to make sure the children were kept inside because she heard that rioters were roaming the freeways with guns.

The Second Vatican Council was formally closed on December 8, 1965, but Margaret has no recollection of the celebrations that marked its ending. Her mother, who had been ill with breast cancer, died the week before that Christmas. There was no time to read magazines or listen to television reports about what was going on in the world. While Ken stayed home with the children, she flew across the country for the funeral. Two months later the couple flew to Erie for the funeral of Margaret's father. With the deaths of her parents so close together, the world seemed to be closing in on her. For her, there was prayer, but she had little interest in what had happened at St. Peter's in the Vatican. The debates and the documents that the Council Fathers produced initially had little relevance to Margaret and millions of other Catholics. In the Vatican, Catholicism was being reimagined. The compromises that they were generating would call Catholics like Margaret to participate in their faith in new and unexpected ways.

chapter four

THE COUNCIL AND ITS DECISIONS

In his opening address, Pope John XXIII charged the men who gathered in the *aula* of St. Peter's Basilica with a nearly impossible task. They were to renew the spiritual core of Catholicism while safeguarding its essential truths. The documents they were to write must display a new enthusiasm and joy for the message of Christ. Though acknowledging the limits of modernity, a positive engagement with contemporary society would enable Church doctrines to be more widely known and better understood. The future must be faced without fear. Perhaps the most challenging requirement the Pope expressed that day was that the Council provide a "balm of mercy" rather than an "arm of severity" in correcting error. The Council was to demonstrate to the whole world that the Church was gentle, patient, and full of tenderness in its spiritual guidance.

In response to those charges, the Second Vatican Council produced sixteen documents over a period of four years. Although those documents provided serious reflections on the nature of the clergy and religion, their greatest innovation lay in what they said to the average churchgoer. Many Catholics were already experiencing changes in their parish life. The newly composed documents provided a theoretical explanation for why church renovations looked a certain way or why people were asked to engage in improving the social conditions of their communities. Participation by lay men and women in the spiritual dimensions of their faith was clearly articulated as the goal of church life.

The documents of Vatican II offered a new framework through which Catholics could develop further theological and ritual reflections.

The lofty goals set out by Pope John XXIII were to be accomplished by men more comfortable articulating and enforcing rules in their diocese and religious orders than in fortifying Christian holiness. The assembled leaders spoke vastly different languages, worked in a variety of global cultures, and had diverse theological orientations. Each Council Father had his own sense of the strengths and weaknesses of the Catholic tradition. Consequently, crafting a finished document would be an involved and intense process.

Arriving at a finished document entailed a complicated procedure of reflection, writing, debate, compromise, and revision. Both before and during the Council, committees called "commissions" composed drafts (known as "schemas") on specific topics. These commissions were headed by powerful cardinals who shaped these early drafts. Cardinal McIntyre, for instance, was a member of the initial preparatory commission as well as the commission on bishops. During each of the fall sessions, individual Council Fathers stood up in the aula and read, in Latin, statements concerning each schema. The commissions then had the task of altering the schema in light of the discussions. Eventually they would vote to accept or reject a specific amended chapter of the evolving document.

Though this was meant to be democratic, it made for a tedious process. Ideas moved back and forth between the commissions and the discussion on the floor of St. Peter's. Council Fathers delivered lengthy speeches defending their positions. In informal discussions over coffee at Bar Jonah and Bar Abbas, *periti* and Council Fathers worked out their thoughts and considered compromises. Council Fathers also met in larger language groups or national bodies to hammer out their positions, which were then taken to the commissions or made into interventions. At the end of the first session, one American bishop complained about the lengthy process: "I don't see what we've accomplished. They talk about it, but I don't see it. I get more work done before breakfast than we did here all session. I'll come back but I don't like the idea. I've been getting so bored that I go for a walk every morning about 11 o'clock."[1] Eventually a final vote would be taken on a document. The pope "promulgated" it by formally making it known to the public. This was how change was accomplished.

As it turned out, the reformers had a distinct advantage in this complicated procedure. Council Fathers and periti who wanted to make substantive changes in Catholicism quickly discovered that the pragmatic skills they had learned as bishops, university professors, and cosmopolitan modern citizens came in handy when shaping the opinions of the less committed. As proponents of engaging with modern culture, reformers were open to the media and made efforts to translate their ideas into concepts that the press could understand. In turn, reporters spent more time interviewing reformers than they did interviewing those satisfied with the status quo. To the consternation of many Italian bishops who valued the formality of their serious endeavors, periti even passed out handouts promoting their ideas.

In contrast, conservative Fathers, who sought to maintain Catholicism as it had been in the past, made little effort to persuade the uncommitted Fathers, the international media, or even other conservatives of their positions. As leaders in their communities who almost exclusively commanded rather than asked, they were not used to giving brief, to-the-point reflections on the topic at hand. Within the Council sessions, they were not skilled in speaking concisely or learning how to compromise. This meant that they tried the patience of even those open to their cause. When the most powerful cardinal in the Curia, Alfredo Ottaviani, exceeded the time limit for speaking and ignored a warning bell, his microphone was switched off and other Council Fathers clapped with approval.

Within the first weeks of the Council, there was an atmosphere of a "palace revolt." [2] As the initiator of *aggiornamento*, Pope John XXIII made certain that those who preferred to maintain the status quo would not stymie renewal. In addition, the Council Fathers were not simply rubber-stamping the schemas drafted by the preparatory commissions; rather, reformers who wanted the Church to feel more comfortable with a dynamic of change and openness gained the upper hand. More and more Council Fathers came to value dialogue, compromise, historical contingency, and the demystification of absolutes. The shift away from confrontation and reproach supplied an unprecedented energy and drama to the first session of the Council. By the end of the first session, it became obvious that those who had traditionally controlled Catholicism no longer had a monopoly of power.

Session One: How to Worship?

Of the various preparatory committees, the one least dominated by the conservative Curia was the group discussing Catholic rituals. Liturgical reform had occurred in northern Europe, and as a result, specialists on the Mass, sacraments, and other Catholic practices tended to be liberal and non-Italian. Even the commission's head, Archbishop Annibale Bugnini, was a rare curial reformer who had worked on liturgical changes during Pius XII's pontificate. His committee had given focused attention to shaping the schema on divine worship because they were interested in doing more than merely acceding to the status quo. Consequently, when the schema on the liturgy was the first to be discussed, it was a triumph for the reformers at the Council.

In the aula, the Council Fathers did not actually discuss, but rather they gave and listened to speeches called "interventions." Interventions were in Latin, as were all Catholic rituals and formal Church documents. Many of the Council Fathers could not understand spoken Latin, and those who did often stumbled over the poor diction of their colleagues. "Scarcely anyone can understand Cardinal Spellman," reported several Council Fathers, stating that his "Latin is universally agreed to be unintelligible."[3] Cardinal Richard Cushing from Boston left early from the first session, telling everyone who would listen that he couldn't understand a word of the Council proceedings. Even those proficient in Latin faced the problem of how to translate modern terms like "race" or "nuclear arms" into an ancient language that had stopped evolving. There were no official translations of the oral or written interventions. Even Council Fathers who understood spoken Latin relied heavily on the press to report what was happening in the sessions.

At the second session the following fall, Cardinal Cushing offered to pay for simultaneous translation. The proposal was accepted, but nothing came of it. Instead, a summary of the day's speeches was given in English to the Americans. Only by the fourth session were English-speaking Fathers permitted to huddle around two priests who translated what was being said from the Latin. The Los Angeles diocesan newspaper *The*

Tidings was silent on Cardinal McIntyre's facility with Latin, but it reported that his associate Bishop Timothy Manning was having "no difficulty in understanding the Council sessions." For Manning, Latin was "the natural vehicle of faith."[4]

Did Latin provide a universal language for a global church that stimulated a deep spirituality? Or was it simply a legacy of the European past that stood in the way of comprehending fully the promises of Christ? Others may not have relished Cardinal Spellman's Latin, but he believed it gave Catholics a special identity. As such, the discussions regarding the role of Latin in the Church took on a new relevance within the aula of St. Peter's. Council Fathers had to decide how meaningful—or how useful—this language was as a sacred tongue. Some experienced the practical drawbacks of the language, but the debate centered on whether it was a "natural vehicle of faith."

Although American Council Fathers may have had the most difficulty understanding what was being said, the Fathers from Asia and Africa were the ones who strongly argued for replacing Latin with the vernacular languages their people actually spoke and understood. Council Fathers from the Middle East pointed out that this was not a council of the "Roman" Catholic Church, whose liturgical and institutional language was Latin, but rather an ecumenical (meaning universal) council, where all groups in communion with Rome were participating.

Language was not the only issue that had diverged; the rituals themselves were different throughout the Church. Over the years and across the continents, various rites for celebrating the Eucharist had been incorporated—rites that used languages other than Latin. Shortly after the Council opened, a Byzantine Rite Mass was sung in its traditional languages of Greek and Arabic. The discussions on the place of language in the liturgy mirrored the very problems of a world Catholicism that contained a Latin-based, Europe-oriented Catholicism as well as a culturally diverse, global Catholicism.

The main priest who celebrated the Byzantine Rite Mass was the Melkite Patriarch, Maximos IV Saigh. Making a point of breaking the "Latin only" rule, he gave his intervention in French rather than Latin. Living and praying in the multiethnic Middle East, he stressed the linguistic diversity of Catholicism. Saigh pointed out that, for his community, Latin was actually a "modern" language because it was newer than their own liturgical language of Greek. Jesus, he reminded the Fathers, spoke the language of his contemporaries and offered the first Eucharistic sacrifice in the language his followers understood, Aramaic. Why not, he suggested, let groups of bishops at episcopal conferences, decide which language should be used in their geographical area? Language, like faith itself, was meant "for men and not for angels."[5]

Council Fathers from communist countries also backed the use of the vernacular. Bishop Otto Spülbeck from East Germany explained that in his country, the state controlled every means of communication. To have the liturgy in Latin meant that the Church lost a significant opportunity to educate the people in their faith. With even the gospel read in Latin, how could the liberating message of Christ be heard? Furthermore, Council Fathers from Vietnam said they were often accused of being tools of colonialism because their Church's language was the language of foreigners.

Council Fathers from Western Europe also supported linguistic reform. Experiments with the wider use of the vernacular in liturgy in Germany and France had been successful. Reformers hoped to make them permanent. They argued that Latin was not appealing to the young, the poor, or workers in an increasingly secular Europe. If the vernacular took its place, it would serve as a conciliatory gesture toward Protestants, who had long argued that people needed to hear the words of Christ in their own language. Preserving the essence of the sacramental life of the Church in Latin meant that the people were missing the heart of their faith.

The speeches given in support of the vernacular as a liturgical language revealed a changing balance of power in the Council. Church leaders from the Middle East, Asia, and Africa had no interest in prolonging the use of Latin in their congregations. If the Church was serious about missionary work and spreading the message of Christ, it had to acknowledge that those outside of the West have difficulty with Latin. Likewise, many religious gestures that seemed unquestionably Catholic—like giving a ring at a wedding or kneeling to show respect—had no intrinsic meaning in non-Western cultures. Council Fathers argued that the Church should have no culture of its own other than the culture of Christ. To insist on Latin—or rings or kneeling—was merely to wed faith to colonialism. From the first session onward, non-Western Council Fathers demanded the Church recognize that social custom did not equal religious truth.

Many conservative Council Fathers felt that Latin was too closely tied to the sacredness of the Mass and other sacraments to be easily removed. Language was not merely a practical tool of communication; rather, Latin supported the drama and beauty of Catholic ceremony. Although Cardinal McIntyre himself delivered his views to the Council in halting Latin, he did not need an anthropologist to tell him that liturgical languages were powerful. In the United States, Catholic identity was derived from rituals conducted in Latin. McIntyre predicted that if the vernacular were adopted, "it would be an immediate scandal for our people." Attending Mass was essentially a private, internal, spiritual affair because the Mass was structured around "the contemplation of the mystery of Eucharist." For the Los Angeles cardinal, those interventions that stressed the importance of "active participation" in the Mass missed the point and, therefore, were "receiving more consideration than needed."[6]

Pope John XXIII thought differently. Although he did not attend the Council meetings so as not to directly influence its outcome, he did watch them from closed-circuit television. At a public audience that took place at the time of the debate over the vernacular, he explained that the Church was not a collection of precious objects found "in some old museum." Although museums and ancient monuments are good for appreciation, real life is about change. "We live to advance," he observed; "we must move ever further onward along the road which Our Lord has opened up before us. The Christian life is not a collection of ancient customs."[7]

Eventually the vast majority of Council Fathers approved of this sentiment. The Constitution on the Sacred Liturgy (also called by the first two words of the Latin text, *Sacrosanctum Concilium*), with its openness to vernacular languages, was promulgated on December 4, 1963, at the end of the second session.

Sacrosanctum Concilium: Renewing Ritual Life

Although the Constitution on the Sacred Liturgy may be best known for breaking Latin's dominance in church rituals, this change actually comprised only a small part of the Constitution. More important was the conclusion that lay involvement in the spiritual life of the Church was a responsibility and valued principle. To help the average churchgoer understand the meaning of that involvement, a new language was crafted to describe the Church's nature, function, and mission.

The language contained within the document on the liturgy was influenced by the Council's discussion of the role of the Bible in Catholic life, which also took place during the first session. When the first draft of the Constitution on Revelation (or *Dei Verbum*) was presented to the Council Fathers, the majority found it unacceptable. Pope John XXIII ordered it withdrawn and a new commission convened to rework it. The discussion of the place of Scriptures in Catholic life was intense, and the final text of *Dei Verbum* was not promulgated until the start of the fourth session. However, in writing the Constitution on the Sacred Liturgy, many of the ideas that would eventually be found in *Dei Verbum* were sharply articulated.

Unlike Protestants who use Scripture in every aspect of their religious lives, up until the Second Vatican Council, Catholics did not routinely read from the Bible. Children were taught Bible history, but were not encouraged to read directly from the text. Catholics learned biblical stories from listening to the Gospels and epistles read at Mass. The Mass also included passages from the Old and New Testaments, but because the liturgy was in Latin, parishioners did not see the connection between the Bible and worship.

Pope Pius XII's 1943 encyclical on Catholic biblical scholarship had encouraged priests to integrate the Scriptures into their sermons, but it never mentioned the person in the pew. *Sacrosanctum Concilium* drew the average Catholic to the Bible. It called on ideas and images taken directly from the Scriptures to define the liturgy. By using biblical language to explain the importance of community rituals, the document exemplified what would be enjoined in *Dei Verbum*: Catholics were to cultivate a "warm and living love for Scripture." Catholics should be familiar with the Bible, so clergy needed to make sure it was accessible. The Bible—and not theological speculation—should serve as the source for homilies, prayers, and liturgical songs. Because the New Testament told the story of Christ's saving acts, all rituals should be linked to biblical texts.

The Constitution on the Sacred Liturgy stressed that Christ was the center of Christianity and so his enduring presence in the Eucharist should be reinforced. Through the Mass, Catholics participated in the sacrificial death and resurrection of Christ. Holy Communion (the body and blood of Christ) needed to be made the focal point of Catholic spiritual life. Bishops could allow the distribution of the Eucharist in both the forms of bread and of wine. As this was the heart of Christianity, the Constitution explained that all other pious devotions or sacraments were to be connected to the Mass. Baptism, ordinations, marriages, funerals—all these rituals required an accompanying Mass.

The other sacraments were also to be renewed. Council Fathers concluded that the sacrament of the Last Rites (also known as Extreme Unction) had become too closely associated with death. Consequently, the Constitution renamed the sacrament "the anointing of the sick," offering it to all those threatened by the physical and emotional disorientation of illness. Likewise, Catholic funerals were not to dwell on the inevitability and sorrow of death but rather on the Christian promise of the Resurrection. A funeral should instead evoke Easter, and Catholics should utilize whatever colors their communities use to symbolize hope and glory.

The majority of Council Fathers accepted the diversity of Catholic life across the globe as a positive characteristic, so the Constitution acknowledged the importance of local devotional customs. Popular devotions were "warmly commended," but they must also be connected to the sacred liturgy and the story of Jesus as represented in the liturgical seasons. As long as local devotions do not promote superstition or error, they may be preserved.

The Constitution did not criticize the cult of the saints. Continuing a long-standing Catholic tradition, it recognized that in "venerating the memory of the saints, we hope for some part and fellowship with them." However, because the Mass symbolically reenacted the death and Resurrection of Christ, it far surpassed any of the devotions to Mary or the saints.

Assuming that images of Christ, Mary, and the saints will continue to be placed in churches, the Constitution explained that the veneration of images by the faithful "is to be firmly maintained." What was of concern was not the act of veneration but rather the proliferation of images. In order to avoid causing confusion for Catholics, the number of images was to be moderate and their placement within the church to reflect "right order."

The saints and their representations, like the question of the vernacular, were not of pressing concern in the document. What was stressed
instead was the communal nature of Catholic worship. The Mass was
defined as a "sacrament of unity" not a private function. Catholics should
attend Mass as a "holy people united and organized under their bishops"
and not as "strangers or silent spectators." Repeatedly the document emphasized that the participation of the faithful was to be active, thoughtful, devout, intelligent, full, and without strain. By reason of their
Baptism, Catholics have the right and the duty to participate in the
sacraments. Reverential silence should be observed at the proper times,
but the faithful should also take part in acclamations, responses,
psalmody, and antiphons. True worship engages the body through actions, gestures, and postures.

Sacrosanctum Concilium legitimized a diversity of worship styles. Although Gregorian Chant was still accorded "pride of place" in the liturgy
and the organ "held in high esteem" in the Latin Church, other types of
music for worship could be introduced. The Constitution was sensitive
to the needs of Catholics living in Asia and Africa who had their own musical aesthetics. As long as congregations upheld the sacred character of
the Church and the edification of the faithful was kept in mind, other in-
struments could be used in divine worship. Throughout the document, a
balance was attempted between the eternal and sacred character of the
liturgy and the needs of local communities to craft rituals in ways that
facilitated the full participation of the faithful.

The many Council Fathers from countries outside of Europe and
North America had an intuitive understanding of the importance of regional cultures that differed from Western customs. What Council Fathers lacked, however, was a more sophisticated understanding of the
sociological and psychological functions of rituals. As theologians, they
were interested in renewing rituals so that they reflected the truth of a
Christian ideal. That ritual had an emotional element and an identity-
producing function apart from its ability to reflect belief was not considered relevant. Council Fathers steeped in an authoritarian spirit never
considered the possibility that the world's Catholics might strongly resist
change. The Council Fathers lacked understanding of the complex function of rituals, and this was particularly evident in the Constitution's
preference for "noble simplicity."

The rites of the Church were to be distinguished by being "short, clear, and unencumbered by useless repetitions." Over the years, genuflecting, kissing the altar, and making the sign of the cross had increased to the point that they distracted the priest and the congregation from the actual words of the Mass. Liturgical reformers argued that the Mass needed to be simplified so as to communicate its meaning and symbolic power more directly. Consequently, the Constitution asked religious historians to uncover what important elements of the sacraments had vanished over the centuries. This process would help restore the norms of worship experienced by the early Christians.

The periti who drafted documents on the liturgy were particularly influenced by the theological movement of *ressourcement* (meaning "return to the sources"). A group of French and German scholars encouraged Catholics to look to the early Church for clues to authentic Christian life. Theologians of ressourcement understood the Bible and the writers of the first four centuries—rather than the authors of the nineteenth century—to be the foundation on which renewal should be built. The early texts of Christianity contained the clearest picture of a nourishing spirituality because they were produced closer to the time of Jesus. The theologians of ressourcement did not want merely to duplicate the rituals and beliefs of the early Church; instead, they sought a more engaged relationship with the past in order to enliven and stimulate modern Christian life. New ideas and a fresh understanding of the present would emerge from studying the beginnings of Christianity.

One of the key ideas to emerge from the study of early Christianity was the importance of systematically explaining the meaning of Christ's message to the gathered community. The liturgy needed to teach the faithful. Consequently, the Constitution indicated that priests were to include a sermon at each Sunday Mass that drew from Scripture and proclaimed "God's wonderful works in the history of salvation" and the "mystery of Christ." This ministry of preaching was to be fulfilled with exactness and fidelity, zeal, and patience. The faithful were to be instructed with a sensitivity that took into account their age, lifestyle, and religious cultures.

If the faithful were to be more engaged in the liturgy and the celebrants more thoughtful in teaching about the mystery of Christ, then there would have to be a change in the way the clergy were taught. No longer would it be sufficient for priests merely to study theology and church history. Seminarians needed to learn how to touch the emotions of their future parishioners. The Constitution specifically mentioned that renewing Catholic ritual life entailed training priests in liturgy, music, and the history of sacred arts. Having a proper liturgical formation would enable the clergy to create a setting in which the full and active participation of the people could be secured.

Reformers who hoped for a definitive statement by the Council that Latin was to be fully retired were disappointed. The Constitution on the Sacred Liturgy declared that the existing laws on language remained enforced, and that "Latin is to be preserved in the Latin rites." The faithful should be taught to sing or say texts pertaining to them in Latin. In the spirit of compromise that pervaded all of the Council documents, the text also stated that the "mother tongue" may be of "great advantage to the people," and so the limits on its use could be extended. Readings, directives, some prayers, and chants could be in the vernacular. Most importantly, the Constitution directed groups of bishops belonging to one country (called "territorial ecclesiastical authorities") to decide to what extent the vernacular was to replace Latin. The pope would have to approve and confirm their decisions, but linguistic authority would lie with a nation's bishops. The Council opened up the *possibility* of linguistic change but did not make it mandatory.

By permitting national groups of bishops to decide on something as important as liturgical language, the Council significantly changed the way the Church operated. National episcopal conferences, in addition to individual bishops, would now determine how Catholicism would be practiced within a particular country. The Constitution required episcopal conferences to set up worship commissions composed of specialists in order to revise liturgical books, approve adaptations, and oversee translations. The increase in the power of episcopal conferences, with their teams of experts, meant a decrease in power of both individual bishops and of the Vatican Curia. Thus, another layer of authority had been introduced into Catholicism.

The Constitution on the Sacred Liturgy, as with the other fifteen documents of Vatican II, attempted to synthesize a series of opposing elements. There was to be Latin but also the vernacular. Rituals were to be simple and understandable, but they were to reflect the eternal liturgy of heaven. Catholics could venerate the saints but not too many of them. Popular devotions were fine but not if they had no connection to the story of Christ. Local customs showed the genius of humanity but superstitions were condemned. Holding together such opposing ideas would be the challenge the Church would face after the Council ended.

By the end of the first session, many Council Fathers had become convinced that they could enact changes to the universal Church. Vatican II would not simply rubber-stamp the schemas prepared by the Curia-headed preparatory commissions; there could be enthusiastic disagreements, backroom politicking, misleading press reports, and uneasy compromises without the unity of the Church crumbling. Although intellectually the Fathers knew that they belonged to a universal religion, meeting each other face to face made the multicultural nature of Catholicism real. Bishops found others who shared their problems and concerns. By joining with those who spoke their same language or shared their same theological orientation, Council Fathers discovered that they could be active participants in shaping the Church. Reformers discovered that movement toward renewal was possible. For them, it was the power of the Holy Spirit—not the success of political maneuverings—at work. For the Curia and other conservatives, the liberal momentum was frightening.

What was less clear as the Fathers left for their home countries after the first session in December of 1962 was exactly what grand concepts like "full and active participation" meant. Did it mean that parishioners should be encouraged to use the missals they already owned, or did it mean a far more basic realignment of the relationship between priest and people?

How these questions would be answered became less clear after the death of Pope John XXIII during the summer between the first and second session. In the September before the Council opened, the pope had been diagnosed with stomach cancer, but he kept his illness secret. Although his successor, Pope Paul VI, could have suspended the Council, he was also committed to continuing the renewal processes. With a degree in Canon Law, the former bishop of Milan was more exacting and organized than his predecessor. Pope Paul VI continued the Council, but he did not have the charisma that excited Catholics about the possibility of reform nor the enthusiasm for aggiornamento to ensure that conservatives in the Curia were always contained.

Session Two: What Is the Church?

In October 1963 the cover of *Newsweek* magazine featured a photograph of five U.S. cardinals who were attending the second session of the Second Vatican Council. Cardinal McIntyre was among the elderly white men dressed in scarlet robes posed to exude regal authority. Emblazoned across the bottom of the magazine cover was a headline that read, "Catholicism in America." It was precisely this representation—a group of elderly men in church garb—that would be challenged by some Council Fathers when they returned to Rome.

What exactly is the Catholic Church? The photo editor of *Newsweek* chose to display the prevailing image of Catholicism up to that point: It was a hierarchical organization in which the most important religious actors were high-level clergymen. In this image, the Church was made up of professional religious experts. Unordained churchgoers (the "laity") did not appear in the picture because they were peripheral to the real power of their religion. The laity served the Church only to the extent that the clergy allowed it.

During the second session, the Council explored this conception of the Church. In so doing, they returned to questions left over from Vatican I: Who makes up the Church and how do the various parts relate to each other? Vatican I had clarified the powers of the pope, but what about the roles of bishops, priests, and the laity? After the production of the Constitution on the Church (or *Lumen Gentium*), it was no longer accurate to equate "the Church" with "the hierarchy." Catholics sitting in the pews, the 650 million baptized Christians who recognized the authority of the pope, were "the Church."

A first draft of the document on the nature of the Church was initially introduced during the final week of the first session. This initial schema reflected the orientation of the chairman of the commission who drafted it, Alfredo Ottaviani. As the Secretary of the Holy Office, Ottaviani was responsible for safeguarding the faith and morals of Catholics by ensuring that errors and false doctrines were not promoted. Given the Council's unprecedented hunger for change, however,

Ottaviani's conservative schema seemed too timid, too triumphal, too clerical, and too legalistic.

Ottaviani shared with many Catholics the notion that the Church was a perfect, hierarchical, and unchanging society. His episcopal motto was *Semper Idem*: "always the same." For Ottaviani, the best way to understand the Church was to use the precision of essential definitions. Out of a set of ideals, fixed laws and rituals were made. Christ was fundamentally a ruler who established those laws, and the Church saw to it that they were properly interpreted and followed. The clergy, especially the bishops, were the ones who clearly defined the distinct character and mission set forth by Jesus. Consequently, from Ottaviani's perspective, a Constitution on the Church should focus on the men who have exclusively devoted their lives to the Church—priests—and only secondarily deal with the laity.

His colleagues at the Council, however, were more comfortable thinking about the Church as a "mystery." For them, the Church was a paradox that united that which is perfect with that which is not. Like Christ himself, the Church was a union of the divine with the human. Unsatisfied with the first draft, they sent it back to the Theological Commission. A second draft was introduced for discussion in September of 1963, and a final version was approved in November of 1964.

DISCUSSIONS DURING the second session often centered on what kind of image or metaphor should be used to describe the Church. Rather than using the traditional monikers "Church Militant" or "Church Triumphant," reformers preferred the term "People of God." This term stressed the paradoxical nature of the Church: It linked God with human beings. The phrase echoed the New Testament message that Jesus came to serve people, not to ordain a set of special leaders. It also opened up the possibility that the Church, like people, could err. "The people of God is not only a holy people," explained Cardinal Albert Meyer from Chicago, but it is also a "refuge of sinners. The Church is a welcoming Mother. And Christ has already told us, 'For I came not to call the just but sinners.'"[8]

Council Fathers who were not satisfied with the Theological Commission's initial draft called on earlier papal documents to support their desire to foreground the importance of the laity in the Church. Reformers looked to previous encyclicals that discussed the role of individuals in the

Catholic community. For example, in 1945 Pope Pius XII wrote the encyclical, *Mystici Corporis Christi*, which directed attention to the importance of lay men and women in the Church. The Church was the "mystical body of Christ," and every Catholic had a function to perform within that body. *Mystici Corporis Christi* served to stimulate reflection on the role of the laity in the ritual and theological life of the Church. Nonetheless, Pope Pius XII made it quite clear that there was order and hierarchy within that body. The pope encouraged greater lay involvement, but the encyclical was not an invitation to outright church democracy.

With this earlier encyclical in mind, various Council Fathers argued that all people were members of the Mystical Body of Christ. All Catholics had a duty to help establish the reign of Christ in the modern world. The unordained had unique spiritual and practical gifts. Council Fathers spoke up, stating the obvious: Church leaders were underutilizing the laity. Why were all 200 pereti priests? For a vocal number of Council Fathers, the answer to the question was equally obvious: The clergy had devoted their lives to spreading the faith and were trained in theology.

Cardinal Giuseppe Siri from Genoa, Italy, wanted the final document to stress the obedience of the laity to the clergy. Although it is true that lay people could have useful gifts from the Holy Spirit, he worried about the danger of deception that would lead to too much independence. Whoever had special expertise always needed to make sure they were subject to the teaching authority of the Church. If not, a "church within the Church" might emerge. Bishop Arturo Tabera of Albacete, Spain, an opponent to empowering the laity, worried that the new revisions to the schema put "Christian life in the world and the religious life on exactly the same level."[9] Carefully crafted structures of obedience would crumble if they were not properly maintained.

The discussion about who constituted the Church became particularly heated during a debate that did not explicitly deal with either the clergy or the laity. Though all Catholics held the Virgin Mary in high regard, the Council probed the question of where she fit into the wider conception of the Church. Some Council Fathers argued that Mary was someone so different from other Christians that made up the Church that she merited her own document. Others felt that, like other righteous believers, she should be discussed within the Constitution on the Church. This difference of opinion prompted a discussion that asked questions such as: Should a separate text elaborate the unique characteristics that enabled Mary to mediate between humanity and Christ as a "mediatrix of all graces"? Or should those characteristics be downplayed? What did it mean to call Mary the Mother of the Church?

Mary minimalists sought to contain the influence of Mary among Catholics. They were aware of a rise in devotion to the Virgin during the fifties. In 1950 Pope Pius XII had declared as an infallible dogma her bodily Assumption, and 1954 was named a Marian Year. In the minimalists' eyes, this trend was unfortunate because it accorded the Virgin Mary so much attention that it placed her outside the normal body of the Church. Minimalists also believed that devotion to the Virgin was particularly annoying to Protestants, who bristled at any person or thing that came between the individual and Christ. Council Fathers who sought to ease the split between Protestants and Catholics wanted Mary to find a place within the Constitution on the Church. Reformers who supported ecumenism did not want Council documents to present Mary as anything more than the biblical mother of Jesus.

Opponents of the minimalists disagreed. Mary "maximalists," like Cardinal Francis Spellman from New York City, argued that all of the titles attached to Mary by past popes—such as coredemptrix, reparatrix, Queen of Heaven—should have their place in a separate document, as Mary was more than just another lay member of the Church. Furthermore, Spellman argued that the attitude of Protestants toward Mary was irrelevant because the task of an Ecumenical Council was to "teach the members of the Church, rather than those outside it."[10] To include Mary within the Constitution on the Church was to overlook significantly her importance in world Catholicism.

ANOTHER CONTROVERSIAL TOPIC that generated fiery interventions was the question of the permanent diaconate. The diaconate referred to the position held by deacons, a term that comes from the Greek word for servant. In early Christian history there were many different roles for individuals to play in their religious community. Deacons collected and distributed alms for widows, the sick, and the poor. They maintained order inside churches, read the gospel, and performed other rituals. Over time, however, a more dramatic split between the clergy and the laity occurred. The office of deacon, rather than being a permanent job, became a steppingstone to becoming a priest. Consequently, a man was a deacon for a limited period of time before being ordained. Like priests, deacons needed to be unmarried men.

Council Fathers, particularly those from missionary countries in Asia, Africa, and Latin America, argued for the permanent diaconate to be restored in order to broaden religious opportunities for laymen. Between 1955 and 1965 thirty African countries had gained independence from colonial powers and joined other postcolonial nations trying to eradicate the trappings of colonialism. Native-born priests and sisters were rare, and missionaries were suspect. The lack of ordained clergy in those regions severely limited bishops' ability to maintain Catholic communities and win converts.

By restoring a permanent diaconate, supporters hoped to spread the tasks once assigned only to priests to responsible married men. Ordained deacons would be able to do everything a priest did except hear confessions, anoint the sick, and consecrate the Eucharist. Married deacons already existed among Catholics of the Middle East, who followed Eastern-rite Catholicism. Proponents were not arguing for revolutionary changes; they did not suggest that priests be permitted to marry or that women become ordained priests. Female deacons were not even mentioned. A celibate, male priesthood was never questioned at the Second Vatican Council.

Council Fathers who did not want to reestablish this office tried to table the discussion entirely. Cardinal Spellman reminded the Council Fathers that whether a deacon was permitted to marry or not was a disciplinary issue and so did not merit discussion in a document on the nature of the Church. Natural or divine law did not mandate celibacy for the clergy; it was a rule of conduct established by the Church. Although he did not mention this in his intervention, theologians later explained to reporters that as a Church discipline and not a moral law, priestly celibacy could be changed.

Other Council Fathers took a practical approach. They argued that instituting a class of permanent deacons would actually make the clerical situation even worse. Wouldn't men choose to become deacons and marry rather than become celibate priests? Cardinal Antonio Bacci from the Curia warned that young people would take the easy way out and that soon the Church would be inundated with calls for married priests. Critics believed that blurring the lines between laity and clergy would be detrimental to the future of the priesthood.

Lumen Gentium: A Pilgrim People of God

When the final Constitution on the Church (*Lumen Gentium*) was approved in November of 1964, it generally reflected the concerns of the reformers. By using biblical imagery rather than theological language, the text engaged the average Christian rather than only those trained in scholastic thought. The Constitution opted for poetic language: The Church was a land to be cultivated, sheep to be led, a dwelling place of God among people. Christ loved the Church as his bride. By using the Bible as its primary source, the Constitution worked to dissolve the boundary between Catholics and other Christians.

Poetic biblical language also helped define the Church as a mystery, "a reality imbued with the hidden presence of God," as the newly elected Pope Paul VI explained when he opened the second session. The Constitution stressed that the Church was not simply the product of its structure, its hierarchy, and its set of laws; rather, within the community of those who believed in Christ was a supernatural spark that allowed the organization to transcend simple sociological categories. Animated by a divine reality inserted into history, human thought or language could never fully capture the essence of the Church. Therefore, to exclusively evoke models of perfection and strength (such as "Church Militant") was at the same time to overlook the human dimension of the Church. Because the Church was the paradoxical union of the human and the divine, it was simultaneously perfect and flawed, holy and sinful. The Church, the Constitution insisted, was "a loving mother of all."

The Constitution reiterated the Catholic conviction that Christ communicated not simply through individuals but also through communities. Human beings, by their God-given nature, were social creatures who communicated with God in their own ways. A Church, a People of God, was necessary both for salvation and for the betterment of humanity. The People of God was a community who came together to love and care for each other. At the same time it was a visible religious organization with structures of order, authority, and obedience. Again, the Council Fathers sought to synthesize contrasting characteristics. The Church was a site both of love as well as of hierarchy; it was a family and an organization.

All of the People of God were called to holiness—not merely the professionally religious. The Council Fathers underscored the importance of the laity by providing a lengthy discussion of their roles in the Constitution on the Church as well as in the Decree on the Apostolate of the Laity (*Apostolicam Actuositatem*), promulgated on November 18, 1965. These texts described how, through Baptism, all Christians are given a type of "priesthood." Lay men and women exercised their priesthood by receiving the sacraments, by prayer and thanksgiving, and through the witness of a holy life. Through acts of self denial and active charity in their workplaces and homes, men and women served as living examples of the gospel of Christ. In addition to providing charity to those in need, the laity must ensure that the benefits of economic progress were available to all. The laity was to spread the gospel by engaging in conversations with both believers and nonbelievers. To do this, they should be trained properly in theology, Catholic doctrine, and Scripture. God did give the laity special gifts, but those who preside over the church must judge the genuineness of those gifts and make sure they are used properly.

None of the roles accorded to the laity described in the Vatican II documents broke new theological ground, but what had changed was the *attention* paid to the average churchgoer and the enthusiasm in which the texts called for their full participation. However, the Constitution was silent about whether or not the laity was to exercise authority in the Church, especially regarding religious matters. Instead, it indicated that pastors should work with the laity and be open to their expertise and opinions.

Although the Constitution encouraged the laity to assume their proper "apostolic activity," this did not alter the need for a "ministerial priesthood." The laity was fundamentally equal with the clergy, but priests still held sacred powers unavailable to those not ordained. Thus, the clergy were to mold and rule the people, bishops were to work with each other, and the pope was still the head of the People of God. The Council approved additional documents on the pastoral roles of bishops, the ministry and life of priests, and priestly formation. Seminaries were asked to reform their curricula to make priestly training more relevant to parish life and to deepen student understanding of philosophy, theology, and the Bible.

The majority of Council Fathers decided that restoring the permanent diaconate would not blur priestly and lay roles. The worries of bishops in developing countries accorded with the fears of European bishops, who were themselves experiencing decline in priestly vocations. Reestablishing the permanent diaconate was a practical response to a serious problem.

As a result, the Constitution stated that regional groups of bishops might ordain mature—even married—men as deacons. These men were given the same responsibilities as those deacons scheduled for ordination to the priesthood. The deacons' "ministries of service" included administering Baptism, distributing Communion, blessing marriages, presiding over public worship and prayer, and officiating at funerals and burials. With papal approval, older deacons were allowed to have wives, but for younger men, "the law of celibacy must remain intact."

The laws of celibacy were also mentioned in regard to the "religious"— those sisters and brothers who voluntarily dedicated themselves to God and lived under vows of poverty, chastity, and obedience. Although these men and women were not ordained, they were consecrated and their desire to live under vows was a special gift. The Constitution on the Church explained that the vows that the religious took permitted them greater freedom from earthly cares and obstacles that drew individuals away from the "fervor of charity" and the "perfection of divine worship." As with the various decrees on the priesthood produced by the Council, the Decree on the Adaptation and Renewal of Religious Life also called for the adjustment of orders to contemporary life. The Decree asked religious communities to deepen their spirituality and rethink their mission based on their order's history and the needs of the modern Church and humanity.

Perhaps the most significant innovation of the Constitution was to introduce the notion of a "Pilgrim Church." Historically, pilgrims sought to be in close proximity to the divine, so they traveled to holy sites across Europe and the Middle East. Pilgrims were not exclusively members of the clerical elite—like those men who graced the cover of *Newsweek*— but also included average men and women, saints and sinners alike.

Journeying with other fellow pilgrims to Jerusalem or Rome or Santiago de Compostella or Lourdes, pilgrims faced perils along their routes. Their voyage was not unlike the greater voyage that every Christian undertook during his or her life. Although these travels could be exciting, pilgrims were not tourists. Pilgrims were expected not to forget that their final goal was to be in the presence of God.

In its emphasis on the pilgrim, the Constitution employed two contrasting images of the Church. On the one hand, the Constitution described the perfect goal of the pilgrim: Christians make their way toward heaven, often represented as the Heavenly City of Jerusalem. Pilgrims have a distinct objective in mind, and this goal was desirable, real, and fixed. The Constitution explained that it was the "special urgency" of the modern era that required the Church to bring "all men to full union with Christ." At the end of the travel—at the end of time—a new heaven and a new earth would be established. Then Christ would eternally rule his perfected people. Even before that time, the Constitution clarified, those who have "gone to sleep in the peace of Christ" and were in heaven could intercede for those still on earth and strengthen the pilgrim in his or her travels.

On the other hand, as a Pilgrim Church, the institution was traveling toward perfection, but it was not yet perfected. Christ brought the promise of heaven and the eventual establishment of his kingdom on earth. In Christian history, pilgrims could not avoid being at times robbed, tricked, or distracted from their goals. According to the Constitution, then, as deeper investigations into faith produced new insights, the Church needed to adjust and renew itself. Just as a wayward pilgrim made amends for misbehaving on the path to the Sacred City, the Church needed to be aware that at times it had left the pilgrimage route.

To what extent the Church "incessantly pursues the path of penance and renewal" was tested in later Council discussions of non-Christian religions. For example, the Pilgrim Church had certainly lost its way in its treatment of the Jews. Too many times in its history, Catholic interaction with Jews and Judaism was clouded by unrelenting hostility. In 1215 decisions made at an ecumenical council required Jews and Muslims to wear special dress in order to alert Christians not to mix with them. Jews were forbidden from going out in public during Holy Week. No Jew ("a blasphemer of Christ") was allowed to hold public office because he would have power over a Christian. As late as the nineteenth century in Italy, Jewish children who had been secretly baptized could be taken from their families by Vatican authorities. Although some Catholics heroically sheltered Jews during the Nazi era, many ignored the persecution or even actively supported the Holocaust. To what extent would the Council Fathers recognize such acts as sins and repent?

The Declaration on the Relation of the Church to Non-Christian Religions (*Nostra Aetate*), promulgated on October 28, 1965, was groundbreaking in recognizing the common patrimony that Jews and Christians share. It forcefully stated that Christ freely underwent torture and death because of the sins of *all* people so that all could attain salvation. Jews should not be "repudiated or cursed by God." However, the final document also dropped a line from an earlier schema that specifically condemned the notion that the Jews killed God (*deicidii rea*). It also contained no specific reference to how Catholics, as individuals or as Church officials, persecuted the Jews. Rather, the Declaration deplored anti-Semitism in general, "directed against the Jews at any time and from any source." It would be left to later theologians and historians to articulate the specific sins of Catholics toward Jews and to find ways of rethinking New Testament statements on the Jews.

The last section of the Constitution on the Church dealt with the role of the Virgin Mary. The minimalists who wanted Mary's role downplayed won the argument, but the vote was exceedingly close. There were only forty votes that separated the minimalists and the maximalists—the closest of all Council votes.

As in other cases where there were strongly contrasting views, the Council Fathers tried to bring together opposing theologies of Mary. On the one hand, only Christ and not Mary was the one mediator between God and humanity. Mary belonged "to the offspring of Adam," so, like all humans, she was in need of salvation. Thus, devotion to Mary was not an end in itself. Through meditating and contemplating her, the faithful were led into a deeper understanding of the mystery of Christ's incarnation. Mary cared for humanity and modeled the virginal purity of the Church, but she had no saving power herself.

On the other hand, Mary was preeminent and singular in the Church. She was more than just a mother: She was the Mother of God and Mother of the Redeemer. For this role, she was eternally predestined, which was how she could be prophetically foreshadowed in the Old Testament. The Constitution made a point of mentioning previous papal assertions about the character of Mary: She was free from the guilt of Original Sin, her body did not decay at her death but rather was wholly raised into heaven, and she was exalted by Christ, her son, as queen of all. Consequently, her liturgical cult should be fostered and treasured. Veneration of her image was to be religiously observed. Only excesses, such as too little devotion or too much devotion, should be avoided. The faithful should express "filial love toward our mother" but without "fruitless and passing" emotion or "vain credulity."

In addition, Mary maximalists also had a powerful supporter who tempered the trend to downplay the Virgin's influence: Pope Paul VI. Unhappy with how the vote turned out, the pope gave Mary the official title of "Mother of the Church" at the close of the third session. Just as Pope John XXIII had intervened during the first days of the Council to make sure it did not move off the path to reform, Paul VI made a gesture to reassure traditionalists.

The Constitution on the Church introduced powerful metaphors into Catholic vocabulary that were modeled on biblical images. What was unclear, however, was how the rich array of metaphors would inform and inspire Catholic imaginations. If the Church is truly the People of God, what new roles would clergy and laity assume for themselves? How would authority be distributed between them? If the Church was a Pilgrim Church, what was the correct route to the Heavenly Jerusalem and who would decide which path to choose? Whether or not this new language could act as a foundation from which to criticize older understandings and structures of the Church remained uncertain.

Session Three:
How Should the Church Relate to the State?

The Council Fathers who came from the United States did not distinguish themselves in the aula until the fall of 1964, during the discussion the Declaration on Religious Freedom (*Dignitatis Humanae*). Although the American Fathers had often sided with conservative bishops and the Curia on issues such as the permanent diaconate or the importance of the Virgin Mary, they were strongly on the side of the reformers when it came to promoting religious liberty. During the third session, a session that frequently became bogged down, their voices were distinct and uncompromising.

The positions on religious freedom were evenly split. Those Council Fathers who came from multireligious countries like the United States, Germany, the Netherlands, and France tended to believe that when a variety of religious communities lived harmoniously together, Catholicism would flourish. Those from predominately Catholic countries like Spain and Italy insisted that keeping the faith strong meant keeping other religions out of the public limelight. Thus, whereas reformers wanted to keep the state and religion separate, conservatives looked to the state to reinforce Catholicism.

Political history shaped Council discussions on church-state relations. In Italy, for a hundred years the Vatican had been in competition with the secular and often anticlerical Italian state. Only in 1929 did the Vatican sign an agreement with Benito Mussolini that finally recognized the legitimacy of the Italian government. This concordat—which is an agreement regarding religious matters between the Church and national government—also established Catholicism as the country's religion, secured papal control over Vatican City, prohibited divorce, and required Catholic instruction in all public schools.

Other such agreements were forged in Europe. Concordats with many other regional and national governments (including one with Nazi Germany in 1933) gave the Catholic Church special privileges. In 1953 Ferdinand Franco's concordat with the Vatican declared Catholicism to be the only religion of the Spanish nation and prohibited public exercise of any other types of worship. It also stated that Protestants could not establish private schools for their children or teach in public schools; they also could not be officers in the armed forces, operate their own hospitals, broadcast over the radio, or maintain their own bookstores. The strict curtailment of the activities of non-Catholics followed from the assumption that if individuals were following a false religion, they had no right to promote their erroneous faith. The state, with the support of the Church, must act as a correcting parent for the immature masses by seeing that only the true religion was promoted.

Many Latin American bishops also desired unity between the political and the religious spheres. Following the First World War, Protestant missionaries (especially from the United States) had increased their activities in South and Central America—long a primarily Catholic sphere. North American Protestants argued that capitalist economic interests could never be secure in nations where Catholic culture propped up medieval forms of antidemocratic governments. Progress necessitated that Catholics be converted. During the debates on religious freedom, Council Fathers from Latin America argued that the only way to stem the pressure of Protestant missionaries and their foreign supporters was to blend the national government with Catholic leadership.

Looming in the background of the discussions about freedom of religion was the Catholic Church's history of persecuting heretics. Although the various inquisitorial tribunals that the Church established did not actually execute the convicted—it left such nasty activities up to the civil authorities—it had condoned torture, promoted intolerance, and legitimized oppression. The philosophy that energized such behavior was that principles always took precedence over the bodies of individual men and women. Theological, moral, philosophical abstractions were of a higher worth and thus overruled specific, historical situations. To allow false doctrines to exist and spread was to harm the one true Church.

Catholics in the United States had a very different experience. They witnessed in their day-to-day lives what happened when "false doctrines" were permitted to exist alongside the true Church. Even conservative bishops in America recognized that Catholicism was thriving among Protestants and secularists. Increasingly, Catholic intellectuals in America were wondering how long they would have to put up with their Church's political philosophy that made sense in medieval Europe but did not reflect the reality of life in the United States.

Jesuit theologian John Courtney Murray contributed the most perceptive reflections on how to integrate Catholic traditions and American freedoms. Beginning in the early 1940s, Murray outlined how liberalism in Europe came to be anticlerical but in the United States it did not. He stressed that by guaranteeing the freedom of all religions, the American government guaranteed the liberty of the Catholic Church. Unlike most political theorists, Murray did not see the government as a purely natural and distinctly secular entity. "Through the medium of democratic institutions," he wrote, "the people themselves bring the demands of their religious conscience to bear upon the acts and legislation of the government."[11] God worked through people. Although in itself error had no rights, *people* who thought or acted in error had rights. God gave us our human dignity, argued Murray. Even believing in false doctrines did not merit the relinquishing of God-given rights. A coerced faith was valueless.

As uncontroversial as those ideas now seem, they stimulated Vatican censorship. In the summer of 1954, the pro-secretary of the Holy Office initiated a formal procedure against Murray. As the upholder of orthodox Catholic doctrine, the Holy Office charged that Murray's ideas were erroneous and that he must not publish any more on the topic. The pro-secretary who initiated the silencing, Alfredo Ottaviani, would continue to reject Murray's ideas on church-state relations throughout the sixties. Murray was "uninvited" from participating in the planning commissions of the Council, but due to the insistence of Cardinal Spellman, Murray was eventually permitted to come to Rome as a peritus. Beginning in 1963 he took up the chairmanship of the committee that was preparing the draft document on religious freedom.

Ottaviani strongly disagreed with Murray and the other reformers. For Ottaviani, religious pluralism had nothing to recommend itself. "Man in error is deserving of charity and kindness," the Italian declared, "but it is not clear if he is entitled to honor."[12] The Catholic Church was the only one true Church, and it was God's will that that Church should prevail. For conservatives like Ottaviani, advocating freedom of religion came perilously close to the sin of indeferentism, which upheld the notion that all religions were basically the same. From Ottaviani's perspective, tolerance of other religions was an unfortunate practical necessity, not a value to be defined by doctrine. Unjustifiable liberty permitted to false religions harmed the one true religion. Under normal conditions, then, the state should closely collaborate with the Church to produce a just society.

Ottaviani spoke for many Council Fathers who felt that the schema on religious freedom focused too much on the rights of individuals and not enough on God and community. Individual conscience could be followed only if it was objectively correct, otherwise it must submit to the proper authority. Council Fathers who came from countries with concordats, such as Italy and Spain, argued that freedom of religion would weaken Catholic nations. They worried that ideas like those promoted by John Courtney Murray would diminish the prestige and authority of the Church by severing it from the political sphere.

Supporting the traditional perspective on many other topics, the American Council Fathers had little patience with the medieval orientation of Ottaviani and his supporters. Cardinal Cushing reminded the Fathers that throughout Catholic history the Church demanded liberty for herself, which was her right. "Today," he concluded, "she demands a similar liberty for all men without exception." Cardinal Ritter of St. Louis argued that religious liberty was only a case of human liberty, which was a natural right—something we all should have by the mere fact of our humanity.

Stephen A. Leven, the auxiliary bishop of San Antonio, pulled no punches in his intervention. "Not a few Fathers have spoken of separated Christians [Protestants] as if they were children to be talked down to in a catechism class," he observed. But such speakers, he declared, "have perhaps never encountered one separated Christian in the flesh. Such approaches to the problem have unduly exaggerated the possible danger of ecumenism." At a later press panel, his irritation continued to be evident: "All my life I have worked among Protestants, it is unbearable to hear Protestants talked about as if they were a strange entity."[13] The American Council Fathers were quick to point out that Italy was where people voted for the Communist Party and did not go to church, but in America, Catholics—living among Protestants, Jews, and nonbelievers—actively supported their Church.

Ottaviani, however, did not represent all Italians. In the spring just before his death, Pope John XXIII had issued his encyclical *Pacem in Terris* (1963), which sharply broke with the tradition Ottaviani represented. For the first time in Catholic history, a pope stated that democratic governments were the most in accord with the dignity and freedom of humanity. The encyclical rejected the attempts by the Curia to present monarchy as the best model for church-state relations. Instead of looking backward to an idealized medieval past, Pope John XXIII noted the positive accomplishments of the modern world: the emancipation of women, the growing prosperity of workers, and the end of colonial rule.

Dignitatis Humanae: The American Decree

After two years of debate and five versions of the schema on Church-state relations, on December 7, 1965, a sixth was approved and eventually promulgated. The Declaration on Religious Freedom (*Dignitatis Hu-*

manae) came to be known as the "American Decree" because its formal acceptance by the Church ended the doctrinal differences between Catholic teaching and American political theory. Religious pluralism was presented as a fact and religious freedom became enshrined as a principle.

The Declaration on Religious Freedom stated that God ordered, directed, and governed the entire universe and human community. One of his gifts to all of us was the right to human dignity. Human dignity was not something that needed to be earned or that was accorded only to those who follow the "correct" path; rather, human dignity was an eternal, objective, and universal divine law. Thus, the Declaration was addressed not only to Catholics and "separated brethren" but also to all people—those who believed and those who did not.

Closely attached to human dignity was the right to personal and civil liberty. People have the right to act on their own judgment and to follow their own conscience. Following one's conscience not only made for better governments, but it was also through the conscience that men and women came to know God. Thus, in order to hear the inner voice of God, people needed to be immune from coercion in civil society. Responsible freedom (which, to the Church, meant freedom within "due limits") must be the basis of society.

The Declaration called on all people to love and to search for truth. The pursuit of truth was accomplished through education, dialogue, and constructive communication. In matters religious, no one should be forced to act in a manner that violates his or her beliefs. Humans are communal beings. We express ourselves through group activities, so the organized act of individual conscience—religion—needed to be accepted. Non-Catholic religious communities were to be able to hold public worship services, start schools and charitable institutions, and maintain their own organizations. Catholics had to recognize the rights of members of other religions not because they behaved well in the civic sphere but because of their very humanity. The Catholic Church had to be a "free church"; it could not compel people to belong to it.

If the Church had to forsake coercive power, then civil governments had to do the same. Council Fathers who lived in communist countries were particularly adamant that governments had no right to meddle in religion. The state must not try to train or appoint clergymen, build churches, or use church monies for its own affairs. No one was to tell parents where to send their children to school. There should be equality of all before the law, and the courts must be blind regarding an individual's religion. Only in cases in which public order was threatened by abuses of religious freedom should governments intervene in the business of religion.

As in the Constitution on the Church, the Declaration on Religious Freedom acknowledged that the Church had acted in the past in ways "which were less in accord with the spirit of the gospel and even opposed to it." Although the Declaration did not give any specific, historical examples, it did restate the principle that must guide all Church activities: Jesus was not a political Messiah who ruled by force, but rather he came to serve and to give his life for all humanity.

The value of humility was particularly evident in how Catholics were to relate to those of other faith communities and to the separated brethren. The Declaration on Religious Freedom as well as the Decree on Ecumenism (*Unitatis Redintegratio*) did not forsake the goal of Christian unity; instead, these documents insisted that the pursuit of that goal had to be conducted in dialogue and not in isolation. The Decree on Ecumenism called on Catholics to have a change of heart and to ask for grace "to be genuinely self-denying, humble, gentle in service of others, and to have an attitude of brotherly generosity toward them." Christian unity was practiced not through self-confidently asserting the superiority of Catholicism but rather by living according to the gospel. Indeed, the Decree on Ecumenism asked in "humble prayer" for forgiveness from God and the separated brethren for "sins against unity."

All those who believe in Christ and who were properly baptized have the right to be regarded as Christians and "brothers" to all Catholics. Like Catholics, the separated brethren worship God, have the Bible, and led lives filled with faith, hope, and charity. However, the Decree on Ecumenism stipulated that only the Catholic Church was still "endowed with all divinely revealed truth and with all means of grace." "It is through Christ's Catholic Church alone," the Decree summarized, "which is the all-embracing means of salvation, that the fullness of the means of salvation can be obtained." The Decree went no further in clarifying the nature of salvation for those Christians who do not fully participate (as Catholics do) in the "blessings of the New Covenant." The goal of the text was to bring Catholics and Protestants together, so the Decree on Ecumenism did not dwell on the implications of Christian difference.

To facilitate Christian unity, the Declaration on Religious Freedom explained, Catholics would be permitted to join in prayer services during ecumenical gatherings. Such communal worship underscored the ties that connected Catholics and Protestants together. To better understand the outlook of the separated brethren, the Decree on Ecumenism encouraged Catholics to study their distinctive doctrines, history, and liturgical life. Studying Protestantism would deepen Catholic understanding of Christianity in general as well as clarify the distinct beliefs of Catholics. The goal was to incite all Christians to a more sophisticated realization of their faith and an unambiguous expression of the riches given by Christ. Not only were Catholics no longer permitted to persecute other believers or to isolate themselves from Protestants, the Decree on Ecumenism stipulated that only through civil dialogue with non-Catholics would Catholics come to understand their *own* faith.

The Second Vatican Council rejected the traditional Catholic goal of gaining moral influence through accommodation with national governments. The majority of Council Fathers believed that whatever power the Church might lose in uncoupling religion from politics, it gained in moral righteousness. In addition, the Declaration on Religious Freedom and the Decree on Ecumenism stressed that Catholics can benefit spiritually from improving relations with the separated brethren. The texts placed the onus on Catholics to value Christian unity by adjusting their attitudes rather than assuming that non-Catholics must change.

The openness to other religions was a major innovation of the Second Vatican Council and one that was welcomed by the non-Catholic world. This restraining of the "Church Triumphant," however, raised another set of questions that would shape Catholic discussions after the Council. These questions centered on the acceptability of dissent within the Church. The Declaration on Religious Freedom clearly stated that non-Catholics have the right to follow the dictates of their conscience, but would the Church be accepting of diverse theological speculation by its own thinkers? With the Church relinquishing its influence in the public sphere, what would be appropriate moral leadership—inside and outside the Catholic community—in the future?

Session Four: How to Live in the Modern World?

Pope Paul VI made it clear that the session in the fall of 1965 would be the Council's last. This decision stimulated a rush to finish discussion on the many schemas the Fathers had yet to finalize. One minute Council Fathers were listening to opinions on what constituted marriage, and the next minute they were voting on the pastoral duties of bishops. Final voting came almost every day—on religious life, on Christian education, on the lay apostolate, on non-Christian relations.

The most important votes were taken on the various chapters of what would become *Guadium et Spes*. As the only draft document that originated from the Council Fathers themselves and not from one of the preparatory commissions, "schema 13" became the Pastoral Constitution on the Church in the Modern World. The longest and most repetitious of the documents produced by the Second Vatican Council, it sought to provide guidance on how Christianity could help people understand and solve contemporary social problems.

By the time *Guadium et Spes* was promulgated in December of 1965 at the close of the Council, there were twenty-nine Catholic lay men, thirteen Catholic lay women, and ten nuns in attendance in the aula. The Council Fathers had become more comfortable consulting lay experts on matters that ranged from sex roles to economics. Still, the summer before the last session, Pope Paul VI decreed that one of the most pressing concerns for the laity—birth control—was not to be discussed at all during the Council. In order to give sufficient thought to the problem, a papal commission was being established that would present its findings on the regulation of birth to the pope at a later date.

Schema 13 focused on other wide-ranging social problems that faced modern men and women: war, racism, poverty, and inequality. These problems were not to be left to governments to solve but must be faced head-on by all Christians. Bishop Joseph Blomjous from Tanzania summarized the schema's concerns when he asserted that the Church was not only designed to "save men for heaven" but also "to humanize man's social life, to inspire a sense of personal responsibility in all men, and to foster a social order that sins less flagrantly against divine justice."[14] For those Council Fathers like Blomjous who lived daily with the negative legacies of colonialism, an inward focus on personal sin was a cowardly rejection of Christ's call to love all humanity. The human-designed systems that encouraged hunger, disease, torture, and injustice were the sins that needed to be addressed.

European Council Fathers who intimately knew the terrors of warfare sought strong language that promoted disarmament and peace. The twentieth century had survived two world wars, and it now faced the possibility of global annihilation by nuclear weapons. A document that addressed the whole world, and not just Catholics, needed to clearly lay out Jesus's hatred of war and violence. Peace had to be a chief concern of the modern Church.

The American Council Fathers were quite sensitive to the schema's negative attitude toward war. Archbishop Philip M. Hannan of New Orleans worried that the condemnation of nuclear stockpiling, with its concomitant balance of terror, could be construed as an indirect rejection of the U.S. involvement in Vietnam. Archbishop Hannan specifically did not like the phrase that stated that "any use of nuclear arms is absolutely illicit" or the notion that the mere holding of nuclear weapons increased the possibility of war. "A greater part of the world has been saved from Red aggression by our possession of nuclear weapons," he explained to a newspaper reporter.[15] Cardinal Spellman wanted to make sure that the document did not rule out governments drafting men into the military.

Although a number of American Council Fathers hoped to temper the schema's condemnation of war, all supported adding a rejection of racism to the text. Speaking on behalf of all the American bishops, Cardinal Patrick A. O'Boyle of Washington, D.C. asked for the "forthright and unequivocal condemnation of racism in all its forms."[16] He echoed the sentiments of Bishop Tracy of Baton Rouge, Louisiana, who explained during an earlier session that a reference to racial equality would bring to light the problem of people around the world who suffer discrimination not because of any transgression on their part but only because they belong to a certain race. Racism was an uncontroversial evil at the Council; even the conservative curial Fathers did not hesitate to condemn it.

For a large number of the Council Fathers, the greatest evil facing the modern world was neither war nor racism, but rather communism. Strong condemnations of communism came from around the globe. With this in mind, American Council Fathers wondered why nuclear arms were being condemned if they served to contain communist expansion. They supported their country's anticommunist political involvements around the world. Bishops who had been persecuted in Eastern Europe wanted the final text to reflect the brutality of governments that threatened Church leaders and were hostile to any expression of organized religion. Missionaries had been expelled from China and Southeast Asia, and Catholics who remained had been tortured and even killed. Four hundred and fifty Council Fathers signed a written intervention asking for a condemnation of atheism and Marxist communism.

Still, there was some disagreement on this issue. Strong arguments were made to continue Pope John XXIII's wish for the Council to make positive statements about modern life rather than condemnatory ones. French bishops, for example, sought to deal with communism in a more dispassionate and open manner. They wanted the document to acknowledge the complicated nature of why people might actually choose to become communists. Could it be that Europeans voted communist because they felt that communist parties had a more sophisticated understanding of modern social ills? Had the Catholic Church actually contributed to the rise of communism by not seriously fighting for social justice? Following this line of thought, a bishop from the Canary Islands argued that the problem lay not with communists. He wanted to "vigorously denounce" liberal *capitalism* because the unbridled pursuit of wealth actually caused atheism. For this bishop, communism was the economic system most closely aligned to the sentiment that "the goods of the earth should be destined for all."[17] This argument found no supporters.

Schema 13 emerged from this debate an unwieldy document. With this schema, the Church hoped to provide guidance for all parts of human existence, from eliminating the production of nuclear weapons to regulating family size. Church, political, and private matters all came under the purview of the Council Fathers. Although they might have all agreed on the evils of racism, traditionalists and reformers had different understandings on how men and women should join together to build Christian families.

Reformers wanted a more positive approach to marriage and sexuality that encouraged mutual love rather than dwelling on the mechanics of procreation. For them, marriage and the family was a cause for celebrating human and divine love and commitment. To dwell on control and regulation, reformers argued, detracted from the joy God intended for his human family. Delineating the primary or secondary aims of marriage and other such theological niceties failed to help modern Christians understand the dignity of domestic life.

Traditionalists preferred to praise the traditional large Catholic family and the sublime nature of marriage. Cardinal Ottaviani reported that he was the eleventh of twelve children from a poor family, and his parents always trusted in the goodness of divine providence. However, even a reformer like Cardinal Léon Joseph Suenens from Belgium did not hesitate to voice his worries about the impact of modern culture on family life. Suenens echoed conservative fears when he attributed the decline in strong marriages to "the wave of immorality flooding our streets, movie screens, and literature."[18]

However, the most controversial intervention on marriage did not come from Council reformers like Cardinal Suenens: Two weeks after the final session opened, an Egyptian Council Father raised the issue of divorce. Archbishop Elie Zoghbi, a patriarch of the Melkite rite, asked his colleagues to consider the possibility of granting divorce in cases of adultery. In the Catholic Church, a marriage could never be annulled (which means to dissolve the union) due to sin. Even if one partner remained faithful and the other was a philanderer, an annulment could not be granted. In such a situation, the faithful spouse could not remarry even if his or her partner deserted the family.

Archbishop Zoghbi asked that a "merciful eye" be cast on those individuals who had been abandoned by their spouses and thus forced to live the life of a single person.[19] He noted that among Protestants and Greek Orthodox Christians, the injured party could be granted permission to remarry. Or, in another case, why should an innocent person have to endure a marriage with a spouse who was permanently insane? Not all people could be so heroic as to follow current Church law and remain celibate.

The Egyptian Council Father's intervention was so revolutionary that the aula filled with an attentive silence as he spoke. Council Fathers did not dash out for a cup of coffee, as they had been doing regularly during the long speeches. Later in the week, experts on the U.S. bishops' press panel provided the context for Zoghbi's intervention. Church historians described how, up until the eleventh century in eastern Christendom, when Orthodox and Eastern Rite Catholic Churches were united, remarriage was permitted in cases of adultery and death. Other cases of remarriage existed in the Western Christian history, such as when women were carried off by warring tribes. In recent years, American theologians noted, the Vatican was granting more annulments in cases involving mental illness or marriage with non-Catholics. Nevertheless, since the Council of Trent, divorce had been enthusiastically prohibited.

The press interpreted Zoghbi's intervention to mean that the Church's stand on divorce was not an intractable, eternal doctrine. If the Church could, at times, permit people to use their own languages in the Mass, could not Catholics, at times, be permitted to divorce?

Cardinal Charles Journet from Switzerland offered a resounding "no" to that question. The Church's teaching on the indissolubility of marriage was the teaching of Christ himself, as he clearly stated in Mark 10:9: "What God has joined together, let no man put asunder." Journet quoted additional biblical verses and corrected Zoghbi's understanding of Church history. Unhappy situations in life such as infidelity or insanity are only unhappy when seen "from a purely human point of view without reference to the Gospel or to divine help."[20] Other Council Fathers, including Zoghbi's own colleague from Egypt, joined in to reject any discussion of the dissolubility of marriage. The matter was put to rest.

DURING THE COUNCIL'S discussions on marriage, Pope Paul VI effectively removed the topic of married priests from the discussion table. On October 11, 1965, he announced that not only would the Latin-rite Church continue the ancient law of celibacy, but he also sought to "reinforce its observance." "Public debate," he informed the Council Fathers, "is not opportune on this subject."[21] The pope's decision caused little stir in the Council.

With the controversial questions of clerical celibacy, divorce, and birth control removed from discussion, the Council turned its attention to women. Sixteen Council Fathers submitted interventions on the role of women in the Church, with most merely duplicating the sentiments laid out in earlier Church documents. The most progressive of those statements, however, was never read aloud in the aula. The intervention of Archbishop Paul J. Hallinan of Atlanta did not come with the support of the American Council Fathers. Hallinan's written opinion was filed with the general secretariat, but the Council Fathers did not see fit to discuss his ideas.

Hallinan wrote that because women comprised half the people of God, they should be given equal consideration in the schema on the Church in the modern world. Although the Church acknowledged great women saints and honored "Mary Our Lady," it had been slow in denouncing "the degradation of women in slavery, and in claiming for them the right of suffrage and economic equality."[22] In many places in the world, women's education, working conditions, and wages were inferior to men's and women chaffed under unfair marriage and property laws. To stand for justice, the Church needed to be a front-runner in freeing women from their place as second-class citizens both in the secular society and within its own institution.

The Church, then, needed to make specific gestures to bring real women into Catholic sacramental life. Simply honoring the Virgin Mary or praising womanhood and "woman" in the abstract was not sufficient. At Mass, women should be permitted to act as lectors and acolytes, which are altar servers. After proper religious study, women should be able to be ordained as deacons. Women should be trained as theologians and encouraged to run apostolic organizations. Those women who were nuns or sisters should always be represented and consulted in matters concerning their interests. Women should even be on the commissions that would be set up to revise Canon Law.

In many ways, Hallinan's ideas were as controversial as Zoghbi's on divorce. Because they were not read out in the aula, they did not come up for general discussion. There was no far-ranging debate on the role of women in the Church because few Council Fathers considered their status to be a pastoral problem that needed to be addressed. The Archbishop's bold thoughts were not supported by the other American Council Fathers or by progressive periti. Monsignor George Higgins, a member of the U.S. Bishops panel, was correct in observing that since the forties the struggle for racial justice had occupied the attention of the American Church, but the rights of women had not. "Women must work harder to make their cause known and felt," he concluded, "before a change could come about in the Church practice."[23]

Gaudium et Spes: The Church in the Modern World

On December 7, 1965, the day before Pope Paul VI declared the Second Vatican Council officially over, he promulgated the Constitution on the Church in the Modern World (*Gaudium et Spes*). The Constitution portrayed contemporary society as filled with inequalities: There was wealth and power but there was also hunger and poverty. Individuals were capable of both the most noble and the foulest deeds. There was profound technological progress but also the possibility of "war which would reduce everything to ashes."

The goal of the Church was not to create a perfect society isolated from the troubles caused by sinners and unbelievers but rather to show how the benefits of the modern world should and can be extended to everyone. Engagement with the world, rather than withdrawal from it, was demanded of the Church. And so the Constitution addressed its message not only to believers but also to the whole of humanity.

The Constitution understood human nature as torn between the positive parts of the individual that reflect the original goodness of God's creation and the negative aspects that pull the soul toward darkness. Men and women were created by God in a state of holiness, but "at the urging of personified Evil," they abused the freedom God gave them. People set themselves up against God and tried to find fulfillment apart from God. They sought to serve each other rather than serving God. All human life, then, whether expressed by individuals or in communities, was a "dramatic struggle between good and evil, between light and darkness." Sin was the cause of the social imbalances in the world.

Humanity would lose this battle if it was not for the fact that Christ came to free and strengthen people against the "bondage of sin." Christ offered individuals both inward renewal and his efforts at "casting out the prince of this world." Through Christ, people were released from their bondage to "the devil and sin" and opened to their God-given destiny. At the end of life, Christ offered humanity the ability to vanquish bodily death and to live "a divine life beyond corruption." Then, at some unknown time would come "the consummation of the earth and of humanity" and the establishment of a new earth where justice would reign.

Although the text is addressed to all people, it does not waiver in seeing the world in Christian terms. The Constitution presented as relevant to the modern world the Christian story of creation, fall, and redemption. There was sin, a personified evil called the devil, and a divine savior who aided humanity in the battle against darkness and misery. Without God, human beings were out of balance and could never fully attend to the problems that beset the world. The Constitution called for engagement with the modern world, but it never lost sight of standing on a Christian foundation.

Because every person had "a godlike seed" sown in him or her, the Church offered to all of humanity its aid in cultivating basic goodness. True, people had the tendency to do wrong, but because God created them, they were inherently good. The task of the Church was to foster that goodness. As with all the other Council documents, the Constitution on the Church in the Modern World looked to the Bible with its story of Jesus to discover exactly how the Church should encourage the good. Like Christ, the Church must give witness to the truth. Just as Christ entered the world in order to rescue "and not to sit in judgment," the goal of the Church must be "to serve and not to be served."

Consequently, the Church must not have any earthly ambitions that distracted it from acting as Christ acted. Like yeast in bread, the Church must work as a leavening agent to make the whole of society rise. For the world, the Church must serve as a kind of soul. Its purpose was not to have a mission in the political, economic, or social order but rather to safeguard the gospel of Christ. Each in their own unique way, Church members were called by Christ to serve humanity.

The Constitution described how God's plan for humanity unfolded through history. Because God spoke to people in the language they understood, studying the contemporary world and "its expectations, its longings, and its often dramatic characteristics" was important. Within the modern world were signs of God's greatness and the "flowering of his mysterious design." God's plan, then, was not in tension with modernity; rather, the Constitution argued, unchanging realities that have their foundation in Christ were embedded within the culture of each generation. There was no one time period or geographical culture that had a monopoly on godly expression.

Given that God acted within the world and not against it, people learned his mysterious designs by studying not only society but nature as well. The Constitution admitted that science and technology could foster a detached orientation toward matter that encouraged the denial of God's involvement in life, but this need not be the case. Conducted in the correct spirit, science and technology could greatly improve the conditions of humanity. Science as well as philosophy, history, mathematics, and the arts served to elevate humanity to a "more sublime understanding of truth, goodness, and beauty."

Individuals must, therefore, be encouraged to grow in their ability "to wonder, to understand, to contemplate." Modern methods of science that demanded "strict fidelity toward truth" correctly assumed positive value in modern society. Culture, as with science, was to be freely formed without pressure from the Church. Creators of culture and practitioners of science, however, should not engage in study simply as an end in itself. Intellectual understanding leads people to make personal judgments and thus "to develop a religious, moral, and social sense." Just as God was behind the order of history, contemplation led people to have more refined behavior and commitment to the common good.

Although the Constitution stressed the importance of autonomy in the sciences and the humanities, conditions existed that can limit freedom. People possessed the independence to voice and publicize their ideas through the arts, theology, or technology but "within the limits of morality and the general welfare." What exactly comprised the limits of morality was not outlined. The Constitution reflected the desires of reformers to eliminate the role of the Church as a censurer of the arts and sciences, but the text also retained the wishes of the conservatives by stating there were limits to creative autonomy.

The major abuse of the freedom that God has given humanity was atheism. Atheism notoriously asserted that individuals were ends in themselves; that they were the sole creators of their own lives. Modern technological progress fooled people into thinking that they—and not God—were in control. The Church repudiated such notions as "poisonous doctrines" and pointed out that true liberation, including economic and social emancipation, could not come from focusing exclusively on earthly affairs.

At the same time, however, the Constitution pointed out that atheism was not simply the problem of atheists. Believers themselves "can have more than a little to do with the birth of atheism." Atheism arose from a variety of causes. If Christians neglected their own religious training or taught incorrect doctrines, then they actually concealed the true face of God and religion. Atheists did error because they neglected the voice of their conscience (which is how God speaks), but ignorant believers also bore some responsibility for the spread of atheism.

The Constitution on the Church in the Modern World never directly connected atheism with communism nor did it specifically condemn Marxist communism. Those Fathers who hoped for a sharp denunciation of oppressive political regimes in Eastern Europe or Asia were disappointed. Instead, the Constitution supported all economic structures that upheld human dignity and worked for the good of society as a whole. With this neutral stance, the problem became not communism nor capitalism *per se*. God intended the goods of the world for all people, not for a small elite. The purpose of productivity must not be an excessive desire for profit and domination; rather, productivity must be geared to providing for the common good of the world's people.

The Council Fathers affirmed in the Constitution that people have the right to work, form labor unions, and strike for fair wages. They have the right to private property and land reform if need be. All nations must help each other develop, so investments should be directed toward providing people with employment and sufficient income. Developing nations, however, must not simply look for outside help but must also cultivate their own resources. The Constitution approved of a diversity of economic models that ranged from communitarian patterns of ownership to industrial capitalism, but all must be set within "the limits of morality."

Political systems also may be varied as long as each promoted an "inner sense of justice, benevolence, and service for the common good." Citizens should develop patriotism toward their nations but without being narrow-minded. Everyone needed to look out for the welfare of the whole of humanity. Public authorities who oppressed their citizens should be obeyed to the extent that the common good was upheld, but when governments threatened their citizens, those citizens may "defend their own rights." Genocide was condemned as criminal, and indiscriminate war against entire cities or regions was defined as "a crime against God" that merited "unequivocal and unhesitating condemnation."

The Americans who sought a defense of nuclear armaments were disappointed. Although *Gaudium et Spes* maintained the spirit of the

Council by presenting positive goals to strive for rather than specific ideas to condemn, it did take a strong stand against certain kinds of war. If countries undertook military action "for the just defense of a people" that was one thing, but "for the subjugation of other nations" was another. The Constitution ignored the American Council Fathers' attempt to put a positive spin on the arms race. It concluded that the arms race was "not a safe way to preserve a steady peace." Rather than eliminate the threat of war, a balance of terror actually made the possibility of war stronger. Peace came from trust, not fear.

In addition, the cost of the arms race unjustly injures the poor. War thrived on injustice, economic inequalities, and from the slowness of social reform. Thus, all people should strive to uphold human rights, eliminate the quest for power, and work to contain the basic emotions of jealousy, distrust, pride, and egoism. In its one bow to the concerns of the American Council Fathers, the Constitution admitted that members of armed forces could be "agents of security and freedom." Soldiers also could contribute to the establishment of peace.

The Constitution on the Church in the Modern World took a strong stand for economic justice and world peace, but it did not elaborate on the evils of racism and sexism. Archbishop Hallinan's push to recognize women in the Church and society was entirely ignored. Discrimination based on sex was placed in a list along with race, class, social conditions, language, and religion. It was one of many forms of prejudice that must be overcome. Without elaboration or reference to women within the Church, the Constitution simply stated that the fact that women in parts of the world could not choose their own husbands, acquire an education, or have cultural benefits equal to those of men was "still regretted."

The family, not the status of women, was what the Constitution sought to better understand and support. Throughout the world certain "disfigurements" threatened family life: polygamy, divorce, free love, the use of "illicit practices against human generation," and the "worship of pleasure." Because the married state was integral in fostering communities of love, marriage could not be placed on a lower level of spiritual worth from that of celibacy. Sexual intimacies within marriage were "noble and chaste" and, when expressed "in accord with genuine human dignity, must be honored with great reverence." Although the Constitution discreetly used the term "conjugal love," it was clear that the Council

Fathers sought to eliminate a common Catholic assumption that sex, even in marriage, was dirty. Marital love, including its physical dimension, was ennobling.

Reproduction, even if it was not placed at the top of a hierarchy of marital values, was still the aim of conjugal love. God created men and women such that they would mate and create offspring that would enlarge his world. In the creation of families, men and women cooperated with God in his creative efforts. The proper task of married couples was to educate their families.

The Constitution made one tentative step toward recognizing that unlimited reproduction might not be in the best interest of families and the world. It asked couples to take into account their own welfare and that of their communities in deciding how they might "fulfill their task." It was acceptable for couples to consider the material and spiritual resources available to them in raising children. This was a cautious move toward recognizing that a couple might sincerely believe that their God-enlightened conscience was asking them to limit their family size.

Parents could legitimately *think* about not having any more children, but they could not undertake methods "found blameworthy by the teaching authority of the Church" to control family size. Because from the "moment of its conception" life must be "guarded with the greatest of care," abortion and infanticide were described as "unspeakable crimes." Consequently, although Council Fathers from developing countries presented interventions about the pressures of global overpopulation, the Constitution praised couples who raise large families.

THE REPORTERS who covered the Second Vatican Council went to Rome thinking that the Catholics were going to make revolutionary changes in beliefs, rituals, and institutional structures. By the end of the Council, however, pointing to clear-cut changes was difficult. The core tenets of Christianity remained: The priesthood was still an all-male celibate institution, debates over birth control were postponed, and divorce was still prohibited. Many journalists were left wondering: What changes, then, *did* occur?

Although reporters may have been disappointed that renewal was not dramatic and traditional Catholics may have been convinced that nothing significant *could* change in a Church that claimed possession of the full truth, something did happen at Vatican II. Both the Catholic and non-Catholic world observed that not all bishops and theologians agreed on the structures and images of their faith. The Council revealed divisions within Catholicism, but those divisions did not render the organization ineffectual. Debates and disagreements actually led to meaningful compromises. The collaboration and dialogue of the Second Vatican Council modeled an institutional style that challenged an earlier attitude of "pray, pay, and obey" for the laity. By the end of the Council, including laymen and -women as observers and minimal discussion partners suggested that the Church had a capacity to observe and revise its own process of stating the truth.

The sheer number of bishops, theologians, official and unofficial observers, and media representatives who gathered in Rome spoke to the continued relevance of Catholicism in modern society. Because the Council made the unprecedented gesture of inviting and listening to non-Catholics, religious communities from around the world paid attention to the Council debates and documents. The Council addressed the world not in a commanding manner but rather in a way that encouraged interaction and involvement. What the world heard was that Catholics believed that Christians had more in common with each other than they thought. Friendship and reciprocity rather than competition and suspicion would be the values promoted at the highest levels of the Church. Even the attendance of twenty-three women as auditors signaled the beginning of including women in the official realms of Catholicism.

The Second Vatican Council broke the European monopoly over defining Catholic practices. Council Fathers from Asia, Africa, Latin America, and the Middle East not only took part in the proceedings in large numbers, but they also made substantial interventions that shaped the final documents. Their concerns about global poverty and social injustice as well as their criticism of Western cultural dominance pushed the Church toward recognizing its global responsibility. In addition to raising awareness of economic and social problems, Third World bishops secured the legitimacy of local customs in worship. Art, music, church design, and vestments could all reflect indigenous cultural styles. This emphasis placed on the global nature of Catholicism decentered the exclusive role of the West in defining Catholic identity.

Although non-Western bishops added a new international dimension, the Council was also central in revitalizing the relevance of European theology in the lives of average Catholics. The Council stimulated and fed theological creativity. In sharp contrast with the First Vatican Council, the Second Vatican Council was indebted to academic theologians for producing its documents. These theologians, many of whom were proponents of the "new theology" that had been condemned in previous decades, understood the ideas behind the sixteen promulgated documents. They would go on to author books elaborating on those ideas and then travel across the globe explaining the significance of the Council. The works of Karl Rahner, Hans Küng, Edward Schillebeeckx, and Yves Congar would be translated into English and serve as the standard interpretations of the theology of Vatican II. American bishops, not all of whom were enthusiastic about the Council documents, would have to contend with European theologians for interpreting the impact of Vatican II.

Theologians became religious celebrities after the Council because lay Catholics were brought more directly into the intellectual and ritual life of the Church. The Council documents consistently call for the laity to be actively involved in their faith and for the clergy to pay attention to their ideas. The Second Vatican Council succeeded in fulfilling Pope John XXIII's desire to create pastorally oriented documents. American Catholics had always been essential in financially supporting their parishes, but now they were expected to be involved in their church's ritual life.

The Council documents not only required the increased ritual involvement of Catholics; the "People of God" also needed to understand the social and economic forces that shaped cultures and societies. The sharp economic divisions that limited the lives of many on the planet needed to be addressed and remedied. Modernizing the liturgy without altering one's understanding of social justice was to underestimate the power of Christ's mission on earth. Though not always clear in detailing the abuses of prejudice, war, and economic exploitation, the Council documents articulated a straightforward connection between spiritual and social reform.

Social reform was tightly linked to Jesus's actions in the Scriptures. By preferring biblical language to the legalistic language of nineteenth-century establishment theology, the Council turned Catholics toward the world of the New Testament. The foundation of the Church was the message of Christ as found in the Scriptures, and this must serve as the basis for renewing ritual and directing belief. Catholics, who had not been avid Bible readers, were asked to bring the Scriptures into every part of their religious lives.

The style of the Council documents also indicated a change in the way Catholicism would be taught. The precise, legalistic language of documents from earlier Councils was replaced by a more symbolic, poetic idiom. Terms like "People of God" and "Pilgrim Church" served to present an ideal rather than a definition. Such rich images were designed to open up thought and reflection rather than close down discussion and regulate. As rhetorical texts, the Council documents were meant to inspire readers rather than lay out codes of conduct. Through both the content and style of its language, the Council concluded that modern people would not respond well to statements of condemnation: The Church needed to be inviting and encouraging rather than judging.

Although the Council documents called on Catholics to have a social conscience, they also sought to emphasize the importance of the inner spiritual life. Outward conformity to Church law was not stressed as much as the inner pursuit of holiness. Christ speaks to people's hearts, so it does no good to threaten or force them into behaving in a certain way. What the Church needed to do was to cultivate a love of God, Christ, and the message contained in the Scriptures. A deep Christian spirituality could be obtained only through love and desire, not through fear. In the modern world, the Council concluded, only a free and willing acceptance of the gospel would lead to the creation of an authentic Christian community and to serving others as Jesus did.

The high ideals articulated in the documents of the Second Vatican Council would now have to be put into practice by the bishops of the United States. Cardinal McIntyre returned to Los Angeles realizing that a monumental task lay ahead. Although he disagreed with elements of the discussion, as a loyal Church leader he knew he would have to follow the dictates coming from the Vatican. Throughout the country, the extent and pace of change would be dependent on the enthusiasm that bishops, priests, nuns, and average churchgoers brought to this call for a renewed Catholicism.

chapter five

UNEVEN ACCEPTANCE

Hard as it may be to believe, the Catholic Church is not the tightly run organization it has been made out to be. There is a common misconception that decisions, made with confidence, are implemented quickly and efficiently throughout the world. People believe that, like the military, once an order is given from on high everyone below falls into line. One moment rituals are in Latin and the next they are in English. One moment churches are filled with the statues of saints and the next they are empty. This school of thought claims it was as if someone had come into your house and stolen all your furniture.[1]

In reality, implementing the Council decrees was uneven, disjointed, and disorganized. This was in keeping with Catholic practices throughout the ages, in which, in the Church, change came slowly—if at all.

Although the Catholic Church is the oldest international bureaucracy, at the same time, it is profoundly local. New orders from Rome gradually filtered through countless theological, social, and cultural layers. American bishops in particular were accustomed to running their dioceses with little influence from Rome. Pastors had long structured their parishes to fit the ethnic traditions and social class of their parishioners. The religious orders of nuns and priests who maintained colleges and high schools had their own perspectives on reform. True change took time.

Catholics of the sixties and seventies faced a monumental task in actually executing the documents handed down by the Council Fathers. Telling people that their faith needed to be updated was one thing, but putting together a policy that would alter the thoughts and behaviors of real Catholics was quite another.

Part of the problem was a lack of planning and education. In the United States there was no coordinated national strategy of theological education to explain what the Council Fathers' documents meant. Bishops had the sole authority to regulate rituals (within the limits left open by pontifical documents), so it was up to them to educate their priests and congregations. Because the Council documents were deliberately designed to be evocative rather than precise, sorting out their meanings was no easy task. In addition, many in the Vatican bureaucracy whose task it was to implement the Council decisions were not enthusiastic about reform in the first place. As a result, change was slow in coming.

Region by region, parish by parish, reforms occurred at very different rates. If Margaret and her family had stayed in Ohio at Christ the King parish, their experience after the Second Vatican Council would have differed sharply from what they experienced in a suburb of Los Angeles. Midwestern Catholics were much more open to liturgical change than were Catholics in southern California. The stable heartland of the country—not the sunny West Coast—moved consistently toward bringing English into the Mass, involving laymen and -women in church leadership positions, updating sacred music and art, and liberalizing the customs of religious orders.[2] Lay Catholics in Kansas City, for instance, had established the first nationwide newspaper, the *National Catholic Reporter*. Not under the control of any bishop as diocesan newspapers were, the *National Catholic Reporter* eagerly detailed the story of Catholic reform.

The Midwestern progressive spirit can partly be explained by the longstanding support of German American Catholics for meaningful ritual and theology. Changes in the structure of the Mass, church architecture, and even gender roles took early root in the Midwest. German American parishes in the Midwest were longstanding innovators in the "Dialog Mass," where the congregation gave responses in Latin. Religious orders like the Benedictines, who had roots in Germany, brought reforms into the parishes and colleges they served. In 1962 modernist architect Marcel Breuer designed the abbey church for the Benedictine monks of Collegeville, Minnesota, setting new standards for church designs. Two years later, Benedictine Father John Bloms from Ada, Oklahoma, became among the first in America to use girls as altar servers. That same year the Ursuline motherhouse in Paola, Kansas, approved a pilot study of two sisters who would wear suits rather than habits. Long before the Council closed at the end of 1965, parishes in places like Missouri and Oklahoma had already begun to change.

The evolving story of reform differed across the country, but the avenues of implementation were consistent. Putting into practice the reforms of the Second Vatican Council depended on several Catholic organizational bodies: Pope Paul VI sent out letters and documents clarifying the call for renewal. The Vatican established commissions and committees that oversaw the process of updating. Those various commissions then approved decisions made by bishops, religious orders, and other Catholic organizations around the world.

The Council's Constitution on the Sacred Liturgy (1962) gave national groups of bishops (also known as "episcopal conferences") the power to determine how much and when the vernacular would be used. In the spring of 1964, the U.S. National Conference of Bishops issued two decrees that permitted the partial use of English in parts of the Mass and the other sacraments beginning on the first Sunday of Advent, November 29, the beginning of the Catholic liturgical year. At first, English was permitted to replace Latin only in the teaching sections of the Mass and the places where the faithful expressed their prayer and devotion. Eventually, however, the entire Mass was reworked, and a translation into the vernacular was provided in 1970, with a final approval in 1974. The U.S. National Conference of Bishops also organized translations and approved liturgical books.

Until the early seventies, local bishops determined the pace of religious change in their dioceses. Each bishop set up a liturgical commission to inform priests in his jurisdiction on developments regarding Catholic rituals. Some bishops encouraged reform by allowing experimentation by priests, nuns, and laypeople. These bishops permitted a certain level of freedom in their dioceses. Other bishops feared the results of unregulated change. They directed their attention toward ferreting out what they believed was spurious theology and rituals. Liturgical commissions languished.

SOME PARISHES also dragged their feet in enacting the reforms. Margaret and her family never heard the Mass in English before leaving California in 1967. Sister Rose, who taught elementary school during the years immediately after the Second Vatican Council, remembered that at St. Stephen's parish in Monterey Park, "things moved a lot slower than in other places."

Not only ritual but architecture was at issue as well. In September 1964 the Vatican had approved the construction of freestanding altars where priests could stand facing the people during Mass. Five years later nothing had been renovated at St. Stephen's. The Sisters of the Holy Names of Jesus and Mary, who staffed the parish school, continued to wear their traditional habits until the fall of 1969. No statues were taken from the church. No wall decorations were painted over. No altar rails were removed. The thief had entered, but the furniture still remained untouched.

While the sixties flared across town in the burning riots of Watts and up north in the student protests at Berkeley, "the Catholic sixties" did not arrive at St. Stephen's parish until 1972. That was the year Monsignor Charles O'Carroll retired after thirty-two years as pastor.

Monsignor O'Carroll had never been in favor of change. In 1966, when the Council Fathers returned to their dioceses to enact the documents they had approved, Monsignor O'Carroll was sixty-nine years old. Born in 1897 into an Irish family in Edinburgh, Scotland, he was ordained in 1922 specifically for the Archdiocese of Los Angeles. Unlike the Archdioceses of Boston or Chicago, Los Angeles never produced enough priests to staff its own growing parishes and schools. A direct conduit was therefore established between the well-known Irish seminary of Maynooth and the priest-hungry parishes of Los Angeles. Immigrant Charles O'Carroll became pastor of St. Stephen's in 1940. Eight years later James Francis McIntyre came from New York City to become his bishop, and in 1953 McIntyre would become the first cardinal west of the Rockies.

Although he headed St. Stephen's parish throughout the turbulent sixties, like many priests of his generation, Monsignor O'Carroll upheld the Catholic values of an earlier era. Parish life must facilitate institutional growth, which would in turn enable spiritual development. O'Carroll and his cohort believed that the efficient running of a large church and school was the highest earthly goal a priest could achieve. McIntyre enthusiastically cultivated the perspective that Catholic education held the key to both religious and social stability.

The immigrant priest did not disappoint. Monsignor O'Carroll oversaw the construction of a church and two schools in his Monterey Park parish. In 1928 a Spanish mission-style design replaced a small wooden church that had been built in 1918. Before long, however, even the new church wasn't big enough. Young families were rapidly moving into California after the war.

By the fifties, O'Carroll realized he needed an even larger church. Rather than merely expand the existing sanctuary, O'Carroll launched a building drive. He hired a local Alhambra architect, J. Earl Trudeau, to design a modern church of reinforced concrete to replace the old one. With twice the seating capacity, the new church accommodated over 850 parishioners. The main altar's dramatic focal point was a large wooden crucifix suspended in front of a marble backdrop. The Eucharist was kept in a gold tabernacle that sat atop a solid block of marble. A "crying room" with soundproof glass for women and their noisy babies was placed to the left of the altar. The new sanctuary had a magnificent marble pulpit that lifted the priest above his congregation so all could better hear his sermons. O'Carroll approved designs that included two simply carved statues, one of the Virgin Mary and the other of the Sacred Heart housed in equally simple side altars.

Trudeau's plans for a contemporary church echoed the artistic taste and theological orientation that preceded Vatican II. The concrete and marble building radiated a feeling of size and strength. The clear windows brought plenty of light into the worship space. There were no architectural ornaments (like neogothic spires) to link the church to an earlier era. St. Stephen's reflected the modernist preference for the plain and efficient. Following the current trends in Catholic artistic reform, the few statues in the church had a simple, almost primitive feel to them.

Monsignor O'Carroll hired well-known Catholic artist John Henryke de Rosen to decorate the walls of his church. De Rosen took six months to paint the Stations of the Cross in a band around the side walls of St. Stephen's. The painted figures were over five feet tall and included Roman soldiers on rearing horses and silhouettes of women draped in classical robes. De Rosen painted his murals in the "hieratic style," which is solemn and majestic. Hieratic art had a ritual stiffness to it that emphasized the characteristics of abstraction, stasis, and severity. Large and bold, the murals contributed to the church's impressive atmosphere and size.

Ritual life also emphasized the solemn and majestic. The spacious church was designed with no interior columns to obscure the view of the altar. With only two simple side altars, nothing distracted the congregation from their devotion to Christ in the Eucharist. Mothers with babies sat in isolation from their families in the crying room, but it was located at the front of the church, where they looked directly out the soundproof glass onto the altar. The parish sponsored no novenas nor other devotions to the saints, but Monsignor O'Carroll said the Stations of the Cross at Lent and the school children put a wreath of flowers on the statue of Mary in May. The church and its rituals were formal, focused on the Eucharist, detached from the daily lives of the parishioners, and under the control of the parish's priests.

Although Monsignor O'Carroll could have said the Mass in English as early as November of 1964, he chose not to. O'Carroll did not say his Masses in English because the Archdiocese of Los Angeles did not require him to do so. The National Conference of Bishops did not *mandate* a change in language; they merely *allowed* English at prescribed times. A letter from the Los Angeles Archdiocesan Liturgical Commission to the city's priests underscored that point. The letter stressed that "It is well to remember that the use of English is permissive. It is not required or directed. . . . The entire Mass may be said as at present in Latin without making a substitution of the vernacular."[3] The pastor of the church was to decide how many Masses at his parish would be in the vernacular—if any would be said in English at all.

As each year passed, the Vatican and the U.S. National Conference of Bishops permitted increasingly more of the Mass to be said in English.

There was still no official English translation, however, and Rome still published statements supporting the continued use of Latin. Until the late sixties, priests who said parts of the Mass in English simply used translations of the Latin Mass. Then, on April 3, 1969, Pope Paul VI promulgated the *Novus Ordo Missae*, which translates to the New Rite of the Mass. More than a translation, the *Novus Ordo* Mass simplified and shortened the Mass. It permitted certain variations in gestures and specified places where priests could choose from several alternate texts.

In November 1969 the priests of Los Angeles received a letter about these modifications. The instructions gave the textual changes in Latin, although most of the nations' priests were already saying the Mass in English. The letter indicated that the newly modified Masses could still be celebrated entirely in Latin. It would not be until November 28, 1971, that the *Novus Ordo* Mass, read not in Latin but in the vernacular, became obligatory for all parishes in the United States. Shortly after that date, Monsignor O'Carroll retired.

M ANY PASTORS across the country did not rush to implement Church renewal because they were satisfied with how their parishes were running. By the time Margaret and her family arrived in California in 1962, Monsignor O'Carroll had paid off the mortgage on his church, and with the five Sunday Masses, St. Stephen's parish served over 3,000 parishioners each week. The nuns and laywomen ran a full school. Long-time parishioners remember that people in the parish got along. They also remember that Monsignor O'Carroll had an officious personality, a gravelly voice, and preferred the company of his dog over that of his parishioners. As formal as the church he built, he refused to shake the hands of the parish's women.

Parishioners responded in kind. Margaret never invited him over to dinner as she had Father Goes from Christ the King. Ken never joked with him. But this didn't bother the Monsignor. With his church and school built, he had no reason to curry favor with his parishioners. Any pressures they attempted to exert in order to implement change were ignored. "The pastor was the law," summed up Sister Mary Felicitas, a teacher at St. Stephen's.

This made for a palpable absence in some parishioners' religious experience. Margaret went to Mass and helped out at the school, but something was missing. The parish did not offer any consistent opportunity for deepening her relationship with God. The vast space of the church lacked intimacy. With her children older now and in school, Margaret wanted to cultivate her closeness to Christ and his mother—something that seemed impossible at St. Stephen's.

To find what she was seeking, she had to look outside the parish. When a neighbor suggested she join their rosary prayer group, she saw a special opportunity to have a more intimate and intense experience of divine love. The neighbor, Loli Ceniseroz, had two sisters who had joined the convent. She herself felt drawn to deepen her spiritual life as they had. So Loli invited a few other women to meet once a week to say the rosary. After they got their husbands and children off to work and school, the women met in each others' homes. Their group was multi-ethnic, reflecting their church and neighborhood.

The members took the meetings very seriously. Sue Covello remembers making sure her house was as clean as possible, "even in places I knew no one would go." After their neighbors arrived, the women asked the Virgin Mary to listen to their worries. Loli gave the women a small pamphlet, "The Rosary Crusade," which described the five Joyful, Sorrowful, and Glorious Mysteries that punctuated the life of the Virgin. They began the rosary by reciting together the Apostle's Creed, the basic statement of Christian belief. After one Our Father and three Hail Marys, the first Mystery was read by the day's hostess: "The Angel Gabriel announces to the Virgin Mary that God wishes her to become the Mother of His Son. Mary obeys with humility and joy." A Resolution followed: "I will be humble and courteous toward all. With this picture in mind, say the first decade of the Rosary." The hostess then began the first part of the Hail Mary with the others responding with the second. They said ten Hail Marys for each Our Father and Glory Be to the Father. After each decade of ten beads, another Mystery and Resolution were announced. The women fingered the beads of the rosary and recited the words over again.

After the prayers were finished, the hostess brought out coffee and sweets that she baked especially for the group. The women unfolded TV trays and set their cups and plates in front of them. For the next half hour they chatted about what was going on in each other's lives. They told stories about their children and reported on the course of illnesses. In little over an hour after arriving, they would be hugging each other goodbye and scheduling who would host the following week. The rosary circle was a place where Margaret and her women friends drew closer to each other and to God on their own terms and in their own words.

Although the rosary circle itself was not organized through the parish, saying the rosary was ubiquitous in Catholic life prior to Vatican II. All of the women would have received rosaries as children and learned the accompanying prayers. Teachers told them to carry rosary beads with them at all times. It was appropriate to pray the rosary at church meetings, funerals, at Mass, and before going to sleep. It reassured the sick when recited at their bedside and made those who felt in danger feel protected. Just touching the beads was a comfort to many Catholics. Saying the rosary even had political dimensions. Communism would be conquered and sinners converted if Catholics consistently said the Marian prayer.

Within parishes of the era of Vatican II, priests and people each had their own perspectives on how to cultivate holiness. In the case of Monsignor O'Carroll, liturgical reform held little interest. He made no effort to alter the ways that parishioners worshipped. Catholics like Margaret, who sought a deeper expression of spirituality, looked outside the parish. In the case of Margaret and her friends, she found that the traditional practice of the reciting the rosary met that need. Although that practice had no direct connection to the reforms of Vatican II, it did illustrate two of its themes: worship in the vernacular and the integration of spiritual and everyday concerns.

IN ADDITION TO PRIESTS and people, a third group of Catholics strongly influenced parish life in the sixties. Teaching sisters were responsible both for the academic and the religious lives of their students. They taught prayers, Bible history, and the catechism, and they prepared children to receive the sacraments. Nuns modeled the religious life and insisted on a high standard of morality. In the early sixties, even children who didn't attend parochial school received the bulk of their Catholic faith from the sisters who organized and taught Saturday morning Confraternity of Christian Doctrine (CCD) classes. Although the number of lay women teachers was increasing, teaching sisters still supervised Catholic religious education.

Between 1958 and 1962, over 23,000 young women entered religious orders *each year*. This was the largest cohort of religious women in the nation's history, and by 1966 the total number of sisters would peak at over 180,000. The impact of religious women on the character of American Catholicism was never higher than during the Council years. The timing for new ideas to percolate through communities of women committed to religion could not have been better.

The Sisters of the Holy Names of Jesus and Mary who ran St. Stephen's school juggled an intense professional commitment to their students with a religious lifestyle that attempted to preserve a monastic notion of spiritual perfection. Although parish priests could visit their families, drive cars that they owned, and take the occasional vacation, teaching sisters led a communal life that required them to focus exclusively on prayer, study, and work. Rising at 5:15 every morning, the sisters said prayers, heard Mass, and had breakfast all before beginning their teaching day. Dressed in a heavy woolen serge habit and wearing a stiff white headpiece that looked somewhat like a carriage horse's blinders, they taught fifty students in each classroom. Mothers volunteered to stay with the children during the noon hour so the sisters could return to the convent for a quick and silent lunch.

School was out at 3:15, but the education continued. Sisters stayed late to tutor, help with sports and the choir, or give music lessons. They then walked home to clean, cook, and pray. Supper was at 5:30, and after the meal sisters took an hour of recreation. The Grand Silence began at nine o'clock. There was to be no talking until the next morning. Before lights-out at 9:30, they did their schoolwork: preparing classes, marking papers, and filling out report cards. Sisters remember stuffing towels in the cracks of their doors to make sure Sister Superior would not notice the light that indicated they were working longer. Others collapsed in bed, exhausted after the long day.

This routine held steady throughout the school year. When school ended in June, the Holy Names Sisters cleaned out their classrooms and packed their extra habit and their few personal belongings into a trunk. This was shipped to a different convent where they would spend the summer. As with all religious orders, many of the sisters had entered the convent immediately after high school and began teaching without even an undergraduate degree. During the summer the order paid for them to attend college, either at a school the order ran or at another institution.

The college course work did not provide much of a break for the sisters. Some recall being assigned to specific college classes with little attention paid to either what they preferred to study or if they had the required preparatory courses. Still expected to be in bed by 9:30, the pressure to perform well in their courses while maintaining convent rules was intense.

Throughout the summer the Holy Names Sisters looked forward to August arriving, when they would sit in a room with their hands tucked in the sleeves of their habits and carefully listen to where they would be sent to teach in September. In 1964 the Los Angeles archdiocese paid the orders that taught in their elementary schools $125 a month per sister.

Teaching sisters were generally more aware of the Second Vatican Council's reforms than parish priests. Because the majority of Holy Names Sisters spent their summers on college campuses, in their classes they were exposed to the debates going on in Rome. During summer school, sisters from around the country met informally and exchanged news about what was happening at home and abroad.

Throughout the early sixties, Karl Rahner, Hans Küng, Gregory Baum, George Tavard, and Godfrey Diekmann toured college campuses. These theologians elucidated the insights of Vatican II, stressing the optimism and confidence that the Council produced. They lectured on the new importance of the Scriptures in Catholic thought and the renewed interest in integrating the natural with the supernatural. When pro-reform theologian Hans Küng visited Boston College, three thousand Catholics crowded into a hall to hear his lecture. If local bishops refused to let such controversial theologians speak, sisters and other Catholics traveled to hear them at nonreligious venues.

Even those sisters who had no experience with campus life were expected to spend time in religious retreats where they came in contact with new ideas. The Holy Names Sisters, for instance, cultivated a special relationship with the Jesuits. In their retreats the priests shared new ideas about prayer and communal life. With television frequently prohibited in the nation's convents and only the rare movie allowed, reading theology was a permitted pleasure.

Considerable frustration resulted from the fact that Catholic sisters in Los Angeles had more exposure to the teachings of Pope John XXIII and the debates of Vatican II than parish priests. Many wanted to see reforms in the parishes where they taught, but they had no power to enact changes. "Those padres weren't doing a darn thing," reminisced Sister Mary Felicitas, who went on to recall that "There was always tension." Priests were busy managing complicated parishes and resented being told (albeit subtly) that they were theologically behind the times. "With some pastors, that really did bug them," Sister Felicitas concluded, "and we paid for it." She imagined priests thinking, "Oh, you people, you think you know everything."

But for Sister Felicitas and many nuns of the time, the ideas being discussed were exciting and uplifting. "We wanted to know why. What prompted these changes? What was the reason for them?" Many sisters throughout the United States came into contact with new ideas generated by the Council, but most were not in a position to respond positively to them.

THERE WERE EXCEPTIONS. Within the vast Archdiocese of Los Angeles, varying responses to the Vatican Council were unfolding. In 1964 a new vernacular ritual was evolving among the nuns and girls at a college down the freeway from Monterey Park. Experiments were taking place in parishes and colleges run by religious orders that looked to the upheavals of the sixties rather than the security of the fifties for inspiration.

For years the young women of Immaculate Heart College in Los Angeles had participated in a ceremony to honor the Virgin Mary. One day each May, the students put on their black academic robes and caps and, carrying a single calla lily, solemnly marched in pairs to a statue of Mary. There they placed their flowers in vases in front of the Virgin Mother. Hymns were sung, the rosary recited, and the ceremony finished with a Mass. Margaret had also participated in similar "Mary's Day" ceremonies when she was in high school, and the practice was common throughout the country.

In 1964 the responsibility of coordinating Immaculate Heart College's Mary's Day celebration was given over to art professor Sister Mary Corita. In the weeks leading up to May, Sister Corita's students collected images of food. From the Market Basket supermarket across the street they grabbed discarded billboard advertisements, and they also clipped ads from magazines. Out of the advertisements they made collages and then wrapped the windows and walls of the college with their art. Glued on the collages were advertising jingles, abbreviated to highlight their philosophical nature. "Come Alive" read some signs (leaving out "It's the Pepsi generation."). Other signs contained the words of John F. Kennedy, Martin Luther King Jr., Gandhi, and Pope John XXIII. The students erased the ordinary look of the campus.

Dressed in pastel spring dresses with sweaters to ward off the lingering May chill, students carried signs and balloons around campus. They put their posters on sticks and carried them like one would protest placards. Their creations preached, "Come to the feast," "I like God," "Eat Bread and Speak the Truth," and "God Likes Me." Students picked flowers and wove them into their hair. Even the Immaculate Heart Sisters put festive wreaths atop the veils of their habits and accompanied the girls as they walked. The staff of the college brought their babies, and their children contributed artwork to the event. A leader of the Vedanta Society of Southern California (a philosophical organization), Swami Vandanananda, was the college's special guest. After time for conversation and laughing at each other's attire, an honors assembly acknowledged student accomplishments during the past year. Then the women (and a few men) gathered for Mass.

In the college's auditorium a simple table draped with a white cloth became the altar. Behind it were hundreds of cardboard boxes wrapped with pictures of flowers and inspirational words and stacked to resemble the towering reredos, which is the screen or decoration behind an altar of a Gothic church. As the community assembled singing, "He's Got the Whole World in His Hands" and clapping to its rhythm, they walked between the altar and the towers of boxes. Then each person placed an unconsecrated host into a ciborium, which is a large goblet, and many brought cans and plates of food to be set near the altar. Eventually, the community stacked up five hundred loaves of bread and five hundred baskets of fruit. The auditorium filled with the sounds of bells, noisemakers, a live jazz band, Beatles music, and tape recordings of the speeches of notable Americans. Although previous Mary Days ended with a pious play put on by the students, this one ended with a film. The students

gathered to watch *Pather Panchali* (1955), an Indian film directed by
Satyajit Ray.

THE INSPIRATION FOR Mary's Day was a collaboration between Immaculate Heart students and Sister Mary Corita. Born Frances Elizabeth Kent
in 1918, she entered the convent after high school, like many young
Catholic women of the thirties. After a few years teaching grade school-
she received her undergraduate degree in 1941 from Immaculate Heart
College and began teaching art there in 1947. The order then sent her to
study art at the University of Southern California, where she graduated
with a master's in art history in 1951. By the sixties she had gained a national reputation for her innovative printmaking, which mixed words
with abstract designs. Her forty-foot mural depicting the Beatitudes for
the Vatican Pavilion at the New York World's Fair in 1964 solidified her
prominence in Catholic art circles. Sister Corita frequently said that she
most likely would not have discovered her talent and become an artist if
it had not been for the Immaculate Heart Sisters.

The Mary's Days that Sister Corita would organize showed the influences of the art styles that she studied in college and were popular in the
sixties. Her serigraphs, which are a kind of screen printing, echoed the
pop art of Andy Warhol and the socially aware printmaking of Ben
Shahn. After her order funded her travels to Europe and the Middle East,
she looked to folk arts and handicrafts for design inspiration. This led
her to encourage her students to consider the eclectic architectural
achievement of Los Angeles's Watts Towers. Even Sister Corita's unsenti-
mental portrayals of Jesus and Mary show the influence of the Expres-
sionism of French painter, Georges Rouault. Rejecting the abstract
austerity of modernist art, Sister Corita's style was a harbinger of post-
modernism in its preference for the fragmented, diverse, and uncertain.

Mary's Day, however, was more than an exercise in Catholic art. Sister
Corita and many of the Immaculate Heart Sisters were excited about the
possibility of religious reform. Their order was rethinking its mission in
light of the Council, and their college had embraced *Pacem in Terris*,
Pope John XXIII's final encyclical. Sister Corita and her students knew
that Pope John XXIII had called for *aggiornamento*—for updating
Catholicism in order to make it more meaningful for modern Christians.

They were excited about new changes in the liturgy and were awaiting the promulgation of the other Council documents.

Believing that the existing Mary's Day was "a very dismal affair," Sister Corita asked her art students to brainstorm about how to renew the sterile ceremony. "You know how kids can come up with marvelous ideas," she remembered later. "We just took them all in and discussed them and tried to find ones that were possible."[4] Eventually, she involved students, staff, and faculty from other college departments, until there were over five hundred people working on Mary's Day.

Sister Corita and her students decided to organize the day around the theme of "Food for Peace." The college had spent the previous school year studying *Pacem in Terris* (1963), which laid out a set of human rights, including the right to sufficient food, clothing, shelter, medical care, and rest. The abundance of food in some parts of the world only underscored the lack of it in others. Poverty, hunger, and neglect resulted when food was horded, poisoned, or overconsumed. Peace would be possible only when everyone had enough food. Mary was the nurturer of Christ, the Bread of Life. In medieval art, Mary often was portrayed feeding Jesus from her breast. Food was essential for growth and development, for joy and solace. What better theme to link the spiritual with the physical and the theological with the political?

The goal of Mary's Day was to transport the community of Immaculate Heart College from their everyday concerns into a space where they could look more deeply into themselves, their world, and their God. At the beginning of the day, Sister Corita told her faculty to "face the students in the direction of today and to show them how to look at it." To the students, she encouraged them "to live a little dangerously by daring to act before all the answers were in."[5] Sister Corita intended to give the campus a different look and sound on this Mary's Day. The special sights, sounds, and conversations of the morning would provide the community with "the equipment with which to pray."

Although the rosary had been the primary "equipment for prayer" at previous Mary's Days, by 1964 the Mass was the means by which people created their relationship with the sacred. On the first of May, the Vatican had approved the National Conference of Bishops' April decrees on the use of the vernacular. Although priests were to wait for an approved translation, the celebrant on that Mary's Day said Mass almost entirely in English. Prayers that were once said by altar boys in response to the priest were being said in English by those who gathered. The priest said the Mass facing the community.

The Mary's Day Mass was praised by a journalist from the *National Catholic Reporter*, who noted that there "was no fumbling for rosaries or prayer books."[6] Indeed, saying the familiar Marian prayer of the rosary was absent from Mary's Day. The high point of the day was not the crowning with flowers of a statue but rather the reenactment of the Last Supper. Sister Corita explained to a film crew who was recording the event that although the Mass has many meanings, it could be understood as a banquet where all are served. "We become," she reflected, "what we eat."

The festive character of Mary's Day was only one aspect of the celebration. Student Jan Steward remembered that near the altar, "newspaper galleys, with their messages of disaster, hung down the walls, grim reminder that our work, to make changes, was heavy."[7] Magazine photographs of wide-eyed children with the words "World Hunger, 10,000 Deaths Every Day" were set next to pictures of the war in Vietnam. "Who is Really Guilty of the Bombing?" one label read, and followed with, "Each of Us." Sister Corita, in her address to the gathering, reminded the community that the colors and sounds of the celebration also say, "Mother, I am concerned for my brother who is your son. My brother starves, he weeps, he dies. He is myself. Today is a loud call to our mother asking her to teach us what she knows of filling the emptiness, drying the tears and easing the death of our brother. We ask to be taken out of ourselves and surely this is the burden of *Pacem in Terris*."

Serious reflection on social problems was only one part of the day. What set this Mary's Day apart from the rest of the school year was the importance of laughter. "Yes," Sister Corita told the community, "I think Mary laughed out loud. She laughed wholeheartedly without rancor, with great compassion, and with real reverence. If she were here today in her physical nature, she would surely laugh. She would laugh at our wreaths. She would laugh at our pop art. She would laugh compassionately, I think, at the consternation of some of us at this riot of sound and color; at our uncertainty about its suitability for a day of religious celebration."

For Sister Corita, people could connect with supernatural characters like Jesus and Mary through modern popular culture—including that which was silly. Popular culture also held clues to answer the serious questions of the day. Consequently, that a foreign film ended Mary's Day was not surprising. Sister Corita believed that movies provided visual theology for modern people. Movies helped the community to "think about our own time and our own answers to questions, which is a little bit untidier than taking nice answers to other people's and other time's questions."

Although Sister Corita was a charismatic and nationally known artist (her "Love" serigraph was reproduced on a 1985 U.S. postage stamp), Mary's Day was the production of a whole college community, and it was symptomatic of the changes taking place in the wake of the Church's reforms. Throughout the United States, Catholics were designing similar rituals that embodied what they understood to be "the spirit of Vatican II." Reform, relevancy, experimentation, collaboration, youthfulness, intentionality, openness, humor, protest, and the vernacular were the values taken from the Council debates and documents. A spirit was evolving out of the Second Vatican Council that consolidated and legitimized liberal trends in Catholicism.

Pope John XXIII's aggiornamento dovetailed neatly with the sixties' questioning of authority and devaluing of those things that were fixed and unbending. Reformers insisted that only through honestly reflecting on their own culture could a true spiritual renewal occur. Religion, like art, was not timeless. Assuming that things that last longer are better than things that are closely attached to a specific period of time was a false assumption. Just as the modern art of Andy Warhol or Ben Shahn drew from contemporary life, so should religion.

Mary's Day celebrations were intended to make Mary relevant to the youthful Immaculate Heart College community. That many of the activities appealed to modern college coeds accentuated an important shift occurring in Catholic America. Since the thirties, Catholics were opting to go to college at rates higher than non-Catholics. By the end of the sixties, 33 percent of all students in higher education were Catholic.[8] Young Catholics comprised the largest and most visible social group on secular campuses. The spirit of Vatican II was closely aligned to a style of religion that appealed to the young and the educated.

Sister Corita began the process of renewing Mary's Day by asking her students what such a celebration should look like. A student-generated ceremony challenged the educational and religious hierarchy that had previously structured Catholic college life. Just as the Council Fathers who came from Asia or Africa insisted that their cultures could be used as a source of ritual and theology, so college life could become a source for ritual design and religious expression. The meetings in Rome legitimized the notion that truth could be derived through a process of conversation and dialogue not unlike what educational reformers were promoting for the classroom. Collaboration and creativity became key for renewal.

The progressives at the Council insisted that the Church could survive a period of experimentation in order to rediscover its mission in the modern world. Likewise, Sister Corita encouraged students to be fearless in their attempts to make sense out of their spiritual and social lives. Truth would be discovered not by strictly adhering to a set of customs and rules but rather through a process of trial and error. Catholics had to risk the possibility that their reforms would be failures in order to make their faith lively and meaningful. Catholicism by rote memory must be defeated by the spirit of Vatican II, which required people to search for real answers to the question of why they were Christians.

The Council's focus on the People of God led to valuing the vernacular, even if Latin remained. The vernacular was more than just a language—it was a frame of mind, a philosophy. For Sister Corita, the language of the people was the language of commerce and consumerism. Students looked across their street from their campus and saw the Market Basket grocery store, with its garish advertising signs. Sister Corita taught them to look hard at what was advertised in order to see its deeper dimensions. Don't discard or try to escape the language of popular culture, she warned, but instead uncover its hidden powers. The use of the vernacular, both as a specific language and as a cultural attitude, joined together the sacred and profane, the traditional and the modern.

Mary's Day 1964 did not only look to commercial culture as a source for religious renewal. Immaculate Heart College had cultivated a relationship with the Vedanta Society of Southern California, which had promoted the philosophical Hinduism of Ramakrishna and Swami Vivekananda in Los Angeles since 1930. Including this Vedanta Society signaled that India as well as Italy could be a source of spiritual renewal.

The Declaration on the Relation of the Church to Non-Christian Religions (also known as *Nostra Aetate*) promulgated at the close of the Council legitimized and encouraged such interaction with other religious communities. The isolation of the Catholic community—never fully visible in California—was being dismantled.

Even before the end of the Council, Catholic intellectuals were looking to the East for inspiration. Catholic writer and monk Thomas Merton had studied Buddhist thought, and he later corresponded with Japanese Zen scholar D. T. Suzuki. Merton's reflections would be published shortly before his death as *Zen and the Birds of Appetite* (1968). Because Gandhi's writing had influenced the nonviolent philosophy of Martin Luther King Jr., Catholics who sought models for peacemaking also looked to Asian philosophy. Indian films and philosophies provided alternative perspectives for Catholics to consider.

Engagement with modern cultures provoked a change in the style of religious representations. Both the smiling Pope John XXIII (admired for his sense of humor and playfulness) and the liveliness of the Beatles led Catholics into a world of lightness and color. The youthful acceptance of mischievousness translated into an attitude toward ritual that stressed the joyfulness of celebration rather than the profundity of ceremony. The Mass, devotion to the saints, and prayers to the Virgin Mary need not be crushed by solemnity. Worship should be refreshing and renewing, and it could almost be a "happening," one of those quasi-theatrical events of the sixties that left plenty of room for improvisation, chance occurrence, and cultural relevancy.

The introduction of laughter into ritual life served to not only refresh but also protest against Catholic "business as usual." After three years of Mary's Days, Father Daniel Berrigan explained to *Newsweek* magazine why the lighthearted art of Sister Corita was threatening: "She is not frivolous, except to those who see life as a problem. She introduces the intuitive, the unpredictable into religion, and thereby threatens the essentially masculine, terribly efficient, chancery-ridden, law-abiding, file-cabinet church."[9] Spontaneous and malleable, the spirit of Vatican II was characterized by a continual process rather than simply the Council's written documents.

A deadly serious criticism of political and economic structures accompanied the playful pop culture of Mary's Day. References to the Vietnam

War and the arms race in Mary's Day were explicit protests against American foreign policy. Making collages out of magazine photographs of starving children and American war planes directly challenged the Catholic political involvement of the fifties. Repeated condemnations of communism were replaced with criticisms of American capitalism, racism, and militarism. By 1967 Catholic priest Philip Berrigan and three other war protesters would be jailed for dumping blood on draft records. A year later, Berrigan would be joined by his brother Daniel (also a priest) and seven others in burning similar files in Catonsville, Maryland. The group would be arrested for destroying records taken from a building owned by a Catholic fraternal order, the Knights of Columbus, and rented out to the Selective Service.

Catholics used the Declaration on the Church in the Modern World to stimulate movement away from condemnations of communism and toward a broader analysis of economics and politics. As with *Pacem in Terris*, the documents forming in the Vatican encouraged Catholics to resist all dehumanizing social systems, including capitalism. The Virgin Mary was not a mother who embodied middle-class notions of domesticity; instead, she was a mother who intimately knew the world-obliterating pain of torture and hunger.

The Council documents had been designed by bishops and theologians, but their frequent use of the phrase People of God broadened the claim to Church leadership roles. Nuns and artists also had a responsibility to interpret Council documents and to educate the nation's Catholics. Sister Corita, more than any one American theologian, exemplified this spirit of Vatican II. In 1966 a *New Yorker* article called her a "one-woman aggiornamento," and the *Los Angeles Times* named her "woman of the year." *Newsweek* put her face on its cover in 1967 to illustrate their piece on "The Nun: Going Modern." That same year, *Harper's Bazaar* named her one of 100 American women of accomplishment. A Catholic nun, trained not to draw attention to herself, had suddenly become the public face of the spirit of Vatican II in the United States.

IMMACULATE HEART COLLEGE's innovative take on Marian devotions was not simply an extension of ideas discussed at the Council and implemented by a creative artist. The Immaculate Heart Sisters were

caught up in the spirit of Vatican II that paralleled changes in their religious order and in the culture at large. The renewed Mary's Day was also
the result of decades of women's education and the reformist orientation
of an order of nuns. Founded in 1916, Immaculate Heart College opened
ten years after the Immaculate Heart Sisters established a girl's high
school in the hills above Los Angeles. By the fifties the college had a reputation of being liberal: It showed foreign movies, girls could stay out
later at night than at other colleges, and academic accomplishment
(rather than mere marriage) was stressed. Its Hollywood address made it
a favorite of Catholic movie stars, and the college advertised itself as the
place "Where tradition meets tomorrow."

The college was the jewel in the crown of the California Institute of
the Sisters of the Most Holy and Immaculate Heart of the Blessed Virgin
Mary. These "Immaculate Heart Sisters" arrived in California from Spain
in 1871, coming at the request of the bishop of Monterey-Los Angeles. In
1924 they broke away from the Spanish order because the European
motherhouse was overly restricting their lives in the United States. Rome
recognized the new California Institute as an independent order, with a
slightly modified habit and set of rules.

As with the Sisters of the Holy Names of Jesus and Mary, who staffed
St. Stephen's school, the Immaculate Hearts educated Catholic children.
Unlike the Holy Names, however, the Immaculate Hearts worked almost
exclusively in the Los Angeles archdiocese. By 1967 they staffed 125 elementary schools and seventy-two high schools in addition to the college.
They ran more schools in the archdiocese than any other order. Their
college was not only known for educating the children of Catholic movie
stars, but it also served as a training ground for other California nuns
who came for their degrees. In 1962 alone, 360 sisters took graduate
courses at the college.

During the postwar years, the demands of the Catholic community
were so high and the number of women entering the convent so large
that religious orders were scrambling to adapt their monastic systems to
modern needs. American Catholic girls found the convent to be an admired place for pursuing religious and professional interests without the
limiting factors of husband and children. Superiors of convents worried,
though, that women were being sent into the classrooms or hospitals
without proper spiritual and intellectual preparation.

Religious orders of women during the fifties began to send representatives to national conferences to discuss common problems and to establish achievable goals. The Immaculate Heart Sisters were active
members of this "Sister Formation" movement, which had its first conference in 1954. Sister Formation intended to integrate professional education with theological reflection—to bring together the traditional with
the modern. Some American sisters wanted to continue the flow of
women into the convent by adjusting their rules and regulations so as to
respond to a changing American society and culture. Sisters needed both
secular education and spiritual formation.

In addition to the national Sister Formation Conference, every few
years, orders of nuns would meet among themselves to discuss possible
reforms to the rules that organized their communities. In the thirties, for
example, the Sisters of the Holy Names decided that sisters no longer
had to bathe wearing a chemise. In 1945 Immaculate Heart Sisters decided that sisters no longer had to ask the Mother Superior to borrow a
pencil or to use a piece of paper. They were permitted to wear wrist
watches in 1957, though the Holy Names Sisters still had to use pocket
watches. Sisters from neither order, however, were permitted to eat in
restaurants or to speak once the Grand Silence began after evening
recreation. Principals of the elementary schools in which the Immaculate Heart Sisters taught were asked to make an effort to limit their class
size to fifty pupils.

Catholic sisters received a spur to such convent reforms in 1962 after
the publication of *The Nun in the World* by Cardinal Léon Joseph Suenens. Suenens's call for updating was formalized in the fall of 1965, when
the Second Vatican Council approved the Decree on the Adaptation and
Renewal of Religious Life (also known as the *Perfectae Caritas*). Women
religious were called to discover the original purpose for the founding of
their orders. Orders were asked to look hard at the changed conditions of
modern society and to consider how they might better integrate their
mission with contemporary culture. *Perfectae Caritas* also reinforced the
importance of providing appropriate spiritual and professional education to all members of their communities.

The early optimism of the Council encouraged change among the Immaculate Heart Sisters. At their meeting in 1963, they pressed ahead

with reforms by permitting sisters to attend the weddings of their close relatives (but not wedding receptions) and to experiment with allowing sisters to decide when to go to bed. Sisters could now wear pajamas and sandals. Conversely, Holy Names Sisters still could not attend weddings and were not allowed to hold children or have their pictures taken with babies. Most importantly, the Immaculate Heart Sisters agreed that a long-range study of all their order's rules and rituals should take place over the next five years. Suggested revisions "should be guided by the spirit and decision of the Second Vatican Council," by "any revisions of Canon Law," and "by the lived reality of the Institute."[10]

THE PROGRESSIVE FACULTY and students at Immaculate Heart College were not the only Los Angeles Catholics to rework Marian devotions in response to the theological and cultural events of the early sixties. That same May of 1964, the "Mary's Hour" of the Archdiocese of Los Angeles was held in the city's football stadium. Mary's Hour was a devotional extravaganza that involved the cardinal and his bishop, hundreds of priests, and thousands of Catholic lay people. The ceremony originated in 1948 shortly after James Francis McIntyre arrived to head the archdiocese. After a formal procession, a living rosary was formed in the center of the Los Angeles Coliseum by representatives of archdiocesan lay organizations, students of Catholic colleges, boys and girls of high school sodalities, and parochial school children. In 1961 attendance numbered over 80,000. The sports stands echoed with the sounds and sights of Catholic piety, pride, and power.

By 1964 Cardinal McIntyre's decision to support the conservative side in the debates over the liturgy had convinced many Catholics that the aging prelate had outlived his usefulness in Los Angeles. Mary's Hour attendance that year fell to 51,000. Cardinal McIntyre came to symbolize those Catholics who valued not the impulse of renewal but the physical embodiments of Catholicism: the building of schools and churches, the attendance at Mass rallies like Mary's Hour. His lukewarm enthusiasm for reform signaled an unwillingness to help individual Catholics develop a more sophisticated understanding of their faith via the spirit of Vatican II. Sister Jeanne explained that "a letter would be read from the pulpit that a change was coming, and that was all." For her, "The Church failed in teaching the new theology and the reasons behind the changing rituals to the adults in the parish."

As with many of his generation of priests, McIntyre lived in a hierarchical male world structured by levels of obedience. This meant that when changes were made either by the Vatican's liturgical commissions or the national episcopal conference, he passed them on to his priests. Letters were sent out explaining that the time for fasting before receiving Communion had been shortened from three hours to one hour or that priests should say "Corpus Christi" before giving Communion and the person receiving it should respond "Amen."

No effort was made, however, to educate archdiocesan priests as to why such changes were being made. Although an archdiocesan liturgical commission was established, it never required priests to explain to their congregations the theological and social reasons behind the new liturgy. For the cardinal, the unpredictable experimentation that was occurring on multiple levels of society could only lead to chaos. Until McIntyre retired in 1970, archdiocesan priests like Monsignor O'Carroll were required to enforce the letter but not the spirit of Vatican II.

As late as 1966, McIntyre was still telling his priests to base their sermons on Adolphe Tanquerey's classic *Manual of Dogmatic Theology*, which was first published in Latin in 1914. McIntyre reminded them to include the traditional devotions of Benediction and Forty Hours when setting up their yearly schedules, noting that "the recitation of the Rosary should also have a prominent part in these exercises." As some priests renovated their churches and turned to face the people (known as *versus populum*), McIntyre worried about "an over-simplicity in structure and an abandonment of ornamentation, which in turn has created a bareness of appearance that is not consonant with the dignity of the Blessed Sacrament." To remedy this, he sent out instructions on how each altar was to have a tabernacle, crucifix, six large candles, and three linen cloths. A 1967 letter again mentioned that reforms like *versus populum* were not mandatory.[11]

McIntyre's disinterest in theological and ritual change was accompanied by a resistance to understanding the social transformation that the country was experiencing. As the planning for the 1964 Mary's Hour began, California was in the middle of a contentious debate over how to deal with a society structured by racial prejudice. The housing boom in California had been accompanied by a steady increase in segregation by race and ethnicity. Both formal housing covenants and informal residential patterns limited where people could live based on their skin color and country of origin. In June 1963 the California state legislature passed the Rumford Act, a fair housing bill banning discrimination in the sale or rental of housing. A group of California realtors wanted to repeal the act, so they sponsored an amendment to the state constitution banning fair housing measures. "Proposition 14" stated that the California government could not deny a person the right to rent or sell property to any person as he or she desired. A vote on the proposed amendment would occur that November.

Cardinal McIntyre refused to make a statement regarding Proposition 14. His silence contrasted with the views of five of California's bishops (out of fourteen) who officially opposed the proposition. Although McIntyre signed an earlier statement that condemned deliberate and willful segregation, that statement also upheld the importance of preserving freedom of conscience in the free exercise of suffrage. Proposition 14, the cardinal let it be known, was a political issue, not a moral one.

The Catholic Human Relations Council strongly disagreed, and its president criticized the cardinal's silence as a "puzzling and tragic abdication of leadership on the most serious moral issue ever faced by Catholics in California." Stories in the *National Catholic Reporter* described the cardinal removing priests who supported fair housing legislation and yet ignoring those who promoted Proposition 14. That summer, the *New York Times* quoted Los Angeles priests who complained that the cardinal had "no open policy on civil rights."[12]

Cardinal McIntyre may have intended that year's Mary's Hour as a response to accusations that he was a racist: The event was unusually inclusive. The archdiocesan newspaper *The Tidings* carried on its front page a photograph of an African American student who delivered the main address of the day. The cochairman of the event, Albert Raboteau, was a senior at Loyola University. Two fraternal organizations (one all-white and the other all-black) escorted the assembled clergymen. The newspaper described how the "sunlight glistened on the sabers held in salute by Knights of Columbus and Knights of St. Peter Claver as the cardinal carried the Blessed Sacrament in procession." An honor guard composed of

ROTC air cadets and sodality girls surrounded the statue of Mary. "Slowly on the Coliseum green a great mosaic formed," *The Tidings* reported, "a living rosary made up of men, women and children representing the human family in all of its races, stations and occupations."[13]

In an unusual twist on Catholic diversity, this Mary's Hour highlighted the presence of Eastern rite communities in the archdiocese. Although immigrant groups from Lebanon, Syria, Egypt, and Armenia had lived in California from the late nineteenth century, for the first time the organizers of Mary's Hour in 1964 made it a point to give them visible roles in the festivities. Six priests from various Eastern rite churches led the recitation of the rosary while costumed choirs from their six churches provided music. They intoned the Hail Marys in voices with Slavic accents. Then, as "the late afternoon sun backlighted the black headpieces of the Eastern priests," *The Tidings* reported, "it haloed about the white and silver hair of prelates and the senior priests of the archdiocese. It caught the dull gold brocade of the heavy, ancient vestments of the East and provided an instant reflection on the universality of the people of God." After Cardinal McIntyre presented the Eucharist in a golden monstrance to the thousands of assembled Catholics, Mary's Hour ended with a recessional hymn sung by an Armenian choir.[14]

In its own way, the archdiocese's Mary's Hour was also a response to the Council finishing up in Rome. Under McIntyre's leadership, change would never fully come. Formal, liturgical Catholicism—of "the dull gold brocade"—would maintain its place of prominence in Los Angeles. An African American student might be permitted to give the opening address, but his ideas would be left unreported: A young black male need not upstage the silver-haired prelates and priests. The Eucharist would continue to stress Christ's kingly power. Just as the Council Fathers listened to the stirring interventions of Eastern rite bishops, so would Los Angeles Catholics learn that this ancient faith was a hidden part of their own community. In this way would Catholics draw strength from their wide-ranging, international Church.

In the Archdiocese of Los Angeles, the Council's concern for social justice was appropriate, but only if accomplished through longstanding ritual, theological, and authoritative traditions. African Americans like student Albert Raboteau should improve themselves by attending Catholic universities like Loyola. They would then find their place in the

Knights of St. Peter Claver, who were separate from (but equal to) the Knights of Columbus. Mexican Americans in Los Angeles should look to Armenian Americans for how minority populations should behave. Just as Eastern rite traditions were a part of the Catholic world, so too were Mexican American religious customs. Only by coming together as a "living rosary," which displayed order, hierarchy, and devotion, could social cohesiveness be achieved.

McIntyre clearly rejected the reforms of the sixties. In a letter sent to the priests of the archdiocese the summer before Mary's Day, Cardinal McIntyre stressed that the members of every race "are more than our fellow citizens; they are our fellow men, our brothers." The Civil Rights movement, with its marches and confrontations, would eventually fail to secure this brotherhood: "Discrimination will not come to its final end through demonstrations of protest, no matter how orderly and legal these may be," McIntyre explained. "It will not come to its final end through legislation. Discrimination can finally end only when the charity of Christ overflows the walls of justice . . . it is a matter of heart more urgently than a matter of law."[15] From a prelate who himself called on law far more often than he called on the heart to lead the Catholics of Los Angeles, McIntyre's language rightly perplexed reformers.

WHEN MARGARET and her family left California in 1967, they had no practical experience with the reforms laid out in the documents of Vatican II. Neither Cardinal McIntyre nor Monsignor O'Carroll was in any hurry to implement theological or ritual modifications. Margaret was satisfied with St. Stephen's school. She found spiritual and social support in her rosary circle. There she experienced how a group of laywomen praying in a small group could take control over their own spirituality while still utilizing traditional Catholic forms. As with many Catholics across the country, she had been raised to *practice* her faith rather than to ponder it. Nothing was happening in her parish to alter that perspective. The society around her was in upheaval, but her family and her Church remained familiar.

Although the Sisters of the Holy Names understood the significance of the Council debates and many had studied the new theology in summer school, they knew that change could occur in a parish only when an individual pastor embraced reform. The sisters would have to wait until they were transferred out of St. Stephen's to a parish where renewal was occurring. Unlike Margaret, many Holy Names Sisters were intrigued by the theological and philosophical reasoning that motivated changes in the Mass and the other sacraments. Catholic sisters were intimately aware that the current climate of upheaval was not limited to secular society.

Much of the criticism of Vatican II in Los Angeles was directed at the Immaculate Heart Sisters. Within their order, a vocal minority voiced concern about the new rituals designed by reformers like Sister Corita. Older Immaculate Heart Sisters who took part in Mary's Day complained that "we weren't saying the rosary." Sister Corita remembered that it was hard to please them because "anything you would do would cause criticism because at that point everything we did was wrong." As Mary's Days became more well known, alumnae contacted the college's president and threatened to stop their financial support if such antics continued. "It wasn't their college anymore," Sister Corita observed. Irritated Catholics wrote in to their local newspapers condemning the new trends. "To search the garbage, to decorate the ashcan, to try to make meaning of junk, the waste material of man," fumed one such critic in the *Santa Ana Register*, "is to be preoccupied with the bowels of the earth rather than the heaven above."[16]

In 1967 the Immaculate Heart Sisters finished their long-range study of their order's rules and rituals recommended by the 1963 Eighth General Chapter. The results infuriated Cardinal McIntyre and disappointed others within the order. The majority of the sisters approved a document that called for a total theoretical reorientation of the community. Rather than merely changing a few rules, the document sought to create a climate that fostered personal growth through openness, risk taking, self-responsibility, and authentic spirituality. Drawing from current theology, psychology, and the writings of their own sisters, the document explained that the pilgrim nature of the Church meant that the sisters could experiment with their communal life. Because Vatican II acknowledged the unique talents of the People of God, each sister should engage in a form of work that best suited her and that best served the common good.

On a practical level, this meant that sisters were free to resume their baptismal names and choose their own clothing. Individual convents would decide on their community's government and prayer life. Sisters could receive a small stipend to spend on their personal needs. All teaching sisters should discuss whether or not their work in Catholic schools truly served the needs of the larger community. If they chose to continue to teach, their classrooms should have no more that thirty-five students. Annual contracts for pay would be negotiated with the diocese. Sisters who did not have a degree would immediately return to college to obtain their teaching credentials. Principals of schools would be relieved of teaching so they could attend fully to their administrative duties.

The ensuing conflict between the Immaculate Heart Sisters and Cardinal McIntyre over these changes filled the pages of national magazines and newspapers. McIntyre refused to accept their reforms. The majority of sisters, for their part, refused to alter their decisions. Although the full story is complex, the result was that the Immaculate Hearts had to either conform to McIntyre's understanding of religious behavior or leave the archdiocese's schools. The Immaculate Hearts left their teaching posts.

Both the Vatican and a national organization of sisters failed to support the Immaculate Hearts in their conflict with the cardinal. The Immaculate Hearts were also isolated locally. Although Holy Names Sisters now remember the Immaculate Hearts as pioneers who paved the way for their own renewal, in 1967 the struggle was perceived as a cautionary tale rather than an inspiration to action. After the Immaculate Hearts stopped teaching, the Holy Names and the other eighty orders that worked in the archdiocese took up the vacated positions in the schools. It was "for the sake of the children," Sister Veronica explained. The repercussions for an inappropriate understanding of the spirit of Vatican II had become obvious.

In the years immediately following the Council, conflicts over the letter and the spirit of Vatican II filled the Catholic and secular media. The Oklahoma Benedictine who had permitted girls to serve Mass was ordered by his bishop to stop. A Dominican was removed from his teaching post at La Salle College in Philadelphia after he was arrested for protesting segregation. The Vatican's Commission on the Liturgy warned against unapproved experimentation and specifically mentioned that women may not read aloud the epistle at Mass. Even in convents and all-girls schools, the Bible must be read by a man. Seminarians in Boston were expelled for protesting against their teachers. In Rome the Congregation of Religious rejected the proposed habit of the Sisters of Loretto. In Cincinnati the bishop forbade the Glenmary Sisters from going to night school and required them to get approval for the books that were read to them at mealtime.[17]

The nation's acceptance of social reform was also uneven. In November 1964 Lyndon Baines Johnson was reelected president in a landslide. That summer he had signed the Civil Rights Act, and although a Southerner, he came to symbolize governmental support of racial equality. Margaret and many other Californians, however, voted for the conservative Republican candidate, Barry Goldwater. They also passed Proposition 14, which overturned the Rumford Act fair housing bill. Racial tension was at an all-time high and riots erupted in Los Angeles that summer. Californians Richard M. Nixon and Ronald Reagan (who became governor in 1966) launched careers, thereby capitalizing on the tensions by promising to maintain law and order. Meanwhile, in 1967 hippies called for a "Summer of Love" in San Francisco.

Closer to home, women were shocking their parish priests by coming to church without hats. Some priests warned women that they would not be given Communion without their heads covered. Other priests, frustrated by watching girls pin Kleenex and church bulletins to their hair, concluded that head covering was not mentioned in Canon Law. The problem was that the 1917 Code of Canon Law *did* stipulate that women cover their heads and dress modestly, "especially when approaching the altar" (Canon 1262). Should priests, in the spirit of Vatican II, ignore such violations because hat wearing no longer conformed with the modern world? All agreed that Canon Law needed to be brought into harmony with the Council documents, but could such changes be made in the meantime? Canon 1262 also required women to sit separately from men at church, "consistent with ancient discipline," but this requirement was ignored in contemporary parishes. Why not ignore the head covering rule as well?

The women of St. Stephen's parish stopped wearing hats to church without comment from Monsignor O'Carroll. Margaret wore a lacy mantilla that could be folded into a rectangle and stuffed into a small plastic envelope that fit into her purse. Whereas other Catholics had their faith tested by reform proceeding too fast—or not fast enough—Margaret's remained unaffected. Changes in the Church and the community filled the newspapers and magazines but not the pews of her parish or the streets of her neighborhood. Immune from the battles that tore apart the Immaculate Heart Sisters and rendered the Holy Names Sisters cautious, she made her way as a practicing Catholic in extraordinary times.

chapter six

DESIGN FOR CHANGE

I t was December 20, 1969, Margaret's twenty-eighth wedding anniversary. Although an annual dinner date with Ken was planned, it would have to wait. That Saturday evening the whole family was going off to "Sunday" Mass. Going to Sunday Mass on Saturday night was not what was remarkable; shortly after the end of the Second Vatican Council Catholics had been permitted to fulfill their Sunday obligation the evening before. Rather, the family's excitement in the car was because they were going to the first Mass celebrated in their newly built parish church, St. Jude, outside of Denver, Colorado.

Margaret and her family had moved from California two years earlier in the summer of 1967. They traveled slowly across the West, stopped at all the national parks, then settled at the base of the Rocky Mountains. Ken had been promoted to associate warden of the Federal Youth Center, a minimum-security prison in Englewood built in 1956 to house young offenders. The family moved into government housing adjacent to the prison, in an area where cattle and horses grazed, and prairie dogs populated the fields.

Moving to Colorado was a relief to Margaret. She had come to California in 1961 with fantasies of a sunny paradise but left with memories of angry students occupying university buildings in Berkeley, antiwar critics being dragged off to jail in Oakland, and the billowing smoke of buildings burning in Watts in 1965.

For Ken, a new job and a new home seemed to offer renewed security in a disrupted world. The optimism that led him to work enthusiastically for the rehabilitation of federal prisoners had been tempered by six years of interactions with criminals, government bureaucracy, and narrow-minded local citizens. Both Kennedy brothers had been murdered; Lyndon B. Johnson declined to run for a second presidential term; and the election of Richard Nixon in 1968 came with his call for the "Silent Majority"—those Americans who were not demonstrating in the streets against the Vietnam War—to support his foreign policy in Southeast Asia.

Margaret and her family settled in an area far different from what she had experienced in California. Unlike Monterey Park, where her children could bike to parks and the library, Margaret found that she spent much of her time in the car shuttling her teenagers hither and yon. There was no easily discernable town where the family was living. The prison's address was in Englewood, their home address was in Littleton, and the nearest grocery store was in Lakewood. The Federal Youth Center had been built in rural Jefferson County, not far from other land owned by the federal government. As the government bureaucracy expanded after World War II, families followed the jobs into the outskirts of Denver. Farm land soon gave way to housing developments. In 1940 Lakewood's population was a paltry 1,701, but by 1960 it was 19,338.

The summer the family arrived, a new Catholic parish was founded in the growing area. Given both the excitement and responsibility of building a new parish from scratch, Margaret felt like she was back in Toledo. Going to Mass meant driving to Alameda High School, where the congregation balanced themselves on uncomfortable bleachers in the gymnasium. Father William Sievers tried to establish a Catholic community at "St. Alameda," but his time was mostly consumed with building and paying for the new church. Having no neighborhood community, no church, and no parochial school made it difficult for Margaret to get settled.

So it was with great anticipation that Margaret and her family walked into their new church five days before Christmas in 1969. The modern St. Jude's sat atop a barren knoll surrounded by a large parking lot quickly filling up with cars.

At first it was difficult to find the entrance. What looked like the front of the light red brick building turned out to be a bank of windows. The church wasn't exactly round, but then it certainly wasn't rectangular either. Father Bill (who encouraged parishioners to use his first name) had told everyone that the new church was shaped like a thunderbird. But what did that mean? Was it supposed to look like a sports car or some kind of Indian emblem? St. Jude's asymmetry made the gathering parishioners search for where to enter. From the very start, this parish seemed to be saying, "It's different here."

Once inside the building, Margaret immediately understood what Father Bill meant when he said he was building a church "with no pillars." St. Jude's was laid out in a fan shape with four banks of pews divided by a central aisle. To make the 900-seat church more intimate, the architect had broken up the seating area with two interior extensions. These points of faced brick extended two thirds of the way toward the altar. Within the left point was the room where the priest robed for Mass and in the right was a space for brides to prepare for their weddings. By having the dressing rooms' doors exit into the back of the church, priests and brides could formally process from the back of the church to the altar. This also meant that everyone was relatively close to the altar. Even if you sat in the last pew, you were no more than seventy-five feet from the front.

For a congregation accustomed to services in a high school gymnasium, the avocado green carpet and matching pew cushions offered a welcome change. The upholstery muffled the sounds as the families entered into the main part of the church from the vestibule. With large windows that looked into the church, the vestibule served both as a gathering area and a place where parents could watch the Mass if they needed to attend to children. Insert lighting in the ceiling of the church made the space seem bright and open, even though it was now dark outside.

Three shallow steps slightly raised the sanctuary where the priest said Mass. An altar shaped like a wooden table was positioned midway between chairs for the priest and servers and the first row of pews. This new altar resembled the portable table and credence made by a parishioner for "St. Alameda." Directly behind the altar and slightly to the right was an expanse of brown and white drapery mounted on a wooden frame. When the drapes were pulled back, the congregation could see the organ and an area for the choir. To the left of the altar was a white wall on which were attached three red vigil lamps and a rectangular metallic tabernacle. Two candles and a white linen cloth lay on the altar.

On each of the brick points that reached into the seating area were hand-carved statues of St. Joseph and the Blessed Virgin Mary. Made from unpainted linden wood and imported from Oberammergau, Germany, the statues faced the altar just like the rest of the congregation. Another wooden statue of St. Jude, also made in Oberammergau, was placed in the vestibule over the main doors and facing the front windows.

That wintry evening, the hand-carved Stations of the Cross were mounted along the walls between panes of clear glass. Father Bill reassured the parishioners that stained glass windows depicting the Beatitudes in abstract design would eventually be installed. He also explained that the holy water fonts would arrive sometime soon. St. Jude's would not, however, have a large crucifix. Instead, at each Mass a server would bring in a processional crucifix and place it in a stand near the altar.

Margaret was not disappointed that she had traded a romantic dinner with her husband to go to St. Jude's on "opening night." From the time that Father Bill applied his shovel to the Colorado clay at groundbreaking, he had explained that the physical environment of the church contributed to successful worship. She felt the truth of that statement the moment she entered St. Jude's.

The space was warm and hospitable. St. Stephen's in Monterey Park had always felt somewhat intimidating with its expanses of marble, high ceilings, and dramatic murals. Even Christ the King in Toledo seemed a bit cobbled together because Mass was said in schoolrooms and the gymnasium. Now, with its carpeting, curtains, and upholstery, St. Jude's reminded her of her own living room. When she walked in that night, she felt welcomed into God's home.

Other parishioners felt the same way. A clear connection between the church's modernized design and the changes wrought by Vatican II had been established. Parishioner Bill Campbell thought that the new designs dramatized the Council's desire to make all people feel a part of the Church. "It was an exciting time in the Church," he recalled, "God and Jesus came alive for me."

Susan Clarke remembered her excitement when she noticed St. Jude's did not have an altar rail. It brought her back to her 1964 wedding in Iowa. Susan married a non-Catholic, like Margaret had in Erie. Mixed marriages could now take place in the church, but the couple was not permitted near the altar. Susan and Fred would have to marry outside the altar rail. To Susan's surprise, however, when the bridal party entered the church, the altar rail gate was open. The priest who married them allowed the couple to recite their vows near the altar.

The open floor plan of St. Jude's also encouraged parishioners to think of their church as a place of inclusion rather than exclusion. "They took down the rail and let the people in," she recalled. For Susan and her husband, Fred, the ecumenical outreach of the Second Vatican Council had eliminated the physical barrier that kept Protestants out of the sanctuary of the church. St. Jude's was consciously designed to help Catholics have a more direct relationship with God and with each other. The pews were slightly angled so that the people who came for Mass could see each other. The carpeting and drapes introduced a domestic feel that made the room look less like a hall.

Just as a church built in 1889 reflected the decorative and formal character of a Victorian parlor, the church of 1969 duplicated the informal nature of a contemporary living room. Going to church would parallel still other social interactions that took place in relaxed, cordial environments—a welcome change for parishioners of the sixties.

MARGARET AND HER FRIENDS were excited not only by how the church looked but also by what was happening to the Mass itself. After five years of partial translations and experimentations, on April 3, 1969, a revised Mass had been approved by Pope Paul VI in his apostolic constitution, *Missale Romanum*. By 1970, when the new St. Jude's was officially dedicated, the "new order" (also referred to as the *Novus Ordo*) Mass had been adopted by the archdiocese. Now, in addition to facing the people and speaking the Mass in English, Father Bill would say new words and make new gestures.

The language of the new Mass emphasized the communal nature of the ritual. In the pre-Vatican II version, the priest represented the congregation to God. When it came time to state what the assembled people believed, the priest spoke for himself and his congregation when he said in Latin, "I believe in one God, the Father Almighty." In the new Mass, the entire congregation stood and declared, "We believe." They said the words of the Apostle's creed not as discrete individuals but as a community.

The new Mass also took seriously the idea that language shapes our attitudes about God and ourselves. In older English translations, the generic "men" was used to translate the Latin term *homínibus*. Similarly, in the part of the Mass called the "Gloria," the old translation had the congregation say, "Glory to God in the highest, and on earth peace to men of goodwill." The new order of the Mass translated the prayer as "Glory to God in the highest, and peace to his people on earth." With a new translation, the English word "people" more explicitly embraced both men and women.

Responding to the Council Fathers' request that Catholics become familiar with the Scriptures, the new Mass included more readings from the Old and New Testaments. Every three years the cycle of readings repeated itself. Priests were expected to give homilies, which are talks directly connected to the biblical readings of the Mass and the liturgical season. The traditional sermon, which could touch on any matter of Christian faith, was deemphasized. Announcements about upcoming parish events were segregated from the homily and given at the end of the Mass.

Father Bill experimented with dialogue sermons as well, in hopes of encouraging interaction between people at Mass. Instead of preaching, he asked those assembled to turn to the person behind them in the pew and discuss a particular topic. He remembered that one time he gave them the topic of religious education. A good-natured discussion ensued, punctuated by the occasional chuckle. "The idea of people giggling and laughing," Bill Sievers reflected about this new form of conversation, "having fun . . . you don't do that in church, do you? We were supposed to be very quiet, a pious congregation, we Roman Catholics." Laughter and fun had always played a part in parish life, but after the Second Vatican Council it found a place inside the church itself. Catholics were learning that thoughtful religious conversations could also be relaxed and lighthearted.

The new liturgy underscored the importance of the Eucharist as a celebration of Christ's love. The church was a house for community worship that centered on the ritual act of transforming the bread and wine into the body and blood of Jesus. The part of the Mass once called the Offertory was now called the Preparation of the Gifts, where families carried unconsecrated hosts and wine up to the altar to be used in the Eucharistic celebration.

There was also more flexibility in services. Priests could now choose from three different prayers that could be said during the Eucharist. These Eucharistic prayers, although each different in their styles, all stressed praise and thanksgiving. Just prior to Communion, a "Sign of Peace" was added to remind the assembled community that personal and collective harmony could be achieved through Christ.

For Father Bill and many of his fellow proponents of the "new theology," the Mass was regaining its character of being a sacred meal among friends. Although the Last Supper continued to be connected to the sacrifice on the cross, after the Council, its roots in the Jewish Passover were stressed. As in the biblical story of Jesus's final meal with his apostles, the Mass entailed communal eating and drinking. The documents of Vatican II also called on scholars to unearth the practices of the earliest Christians. They found that rituals in Christianity's first centuries, before it became the state religion, were uncomplicated. A writer in *Today's Parish* observed that "it seems not quite natural, human and even civilized to partake of the sacred food by sticking out your tongue . . . just imagine a picture of the Last Supper with the Apostles sticking out their tongues."[1] The Council documents called for "noble simplicity," and sacred nourishment came to replace sacred sacrifice as the model for the Mass.

Reformers also believed that over the years Catholics had overemphasized the divinity of Christ, transforming him into a distant heavenly king. Father Bill hoped to remind the people of St. Jude that Jesus was as fully human as he was divine. With the new Mass, worship came to look less like the rites of a royal court. Much of the priest's bowing and genuflecting had been eliminated.

By the end of the seventies, Catholics across the country stood to take Communion as adult Christians rather than begging on their knees like servants. Priests placed the consecrated hosts in their hands, and they shared wine from a common cup. To encourage people to receive

Communion at each Mass they attended, fasting was reduced to one hour. Lights were turned on in churches so people could see what was going on. Prior to Mass beginning, everyone was asked to turn to their neighbor in the pew and introduce him or herself. Then, at the Sign of Peace, when the congregants were to shake each other's hands, names could be used. Margaret also remembered that after coming up for Communion, she gave her name and then Father Bill said, "Margaret, the Body of Christ." For her friend Helen Marie Hurt, this routine gesture underscored the values being cultivated at St. Jude: Here was a new Communion etiquette that symbolized hospitality and the importance of paying attention to one another.

Margaret eased into this new understanding of the Eucharist because it resonated with changes she had been experiencing since she was a young woman. In Toledo, the old church of St. Agnes had been renovated during the thirties and a statue of the young saint that had once sat atop the tabernacle had been taken down and replaced with a crucifix. While at Christ the King, the fasting time for Communion had been decreased in order to encourage more people to take part in the Eucharistic banquet. In Monterey Park, a solid expanse of marble formed a dramatic backdrop for the altar and crucifix. For Margaret and many Catholics like her, the Council's decision to refocus Catholic attention on the Eucharist was fully understandable.

The Council documents stressed that Christ came as a servant of humankind and not as a powerful king. They called on Catholics to cultivate the positive and holy aspects of their individual lives—those aspects of their humanity that they shared with Christ. The Mass needed to strengthen what people had in common with Jesus rather than reiterate what separated the human from the divine.

For some who attended St. Jude, this new attitude changed the ways that they imagined God. For example, Mur Hiltenbrand found that prayers and homilies reinforced the idea that God was a loving father. The familiarity and openness of the space encouraged feelings of acceptance. God was present in a place that looked like a family home—not a medieval palace or a museum of sacred art. For Nancy Frenette, the new liturgy cemented a positive image of God in her imagination. She remembers that in the years after the Second Vatican Council, "I was losing the fear of God. I was learning there was nothing I could do to make God love me more than he already does. I didn't have to earn points with God."

As much as conservatives like Monsignor O'Carroll and Cardinal McIntyre resisted change, Father Sievers and the bishops of Denver welcomed it. Father Bill in particular felt that the Vatican reforms were long overdue, and he intended his parish to be a place for the People of God. These ideas created the environment that led Nancy Frenette to feel fully God's unconditional love. Margaret's friend Mary Clydesdale observed that Father Bill was the "backbone of this new parish. It was his parish, no doubt about that."

Bill Sievers was a local boy. Although his grandparents came from Ireland, his father had met his mother while she was working in a hotel in the mining town of Leadville, Colorado. Born in 1929, he attended Denver's parochial schools, entering the seminary after high school. Following his 1955 ordination, he served as a fill-in priest for various parishes until he became a full-time hospital chaplain in 1961. His appointment as pastor of St. Jude's in 1967 came after six years of working with the sick, their families, and their friends.

Serving as a hospital chaplain altered the ways that Bill Sievers understood his faith. Unlike the priests of the fifties who typically had no sustained contact with non-Catholics, Sievers warmly interacted with Protestant and Jewish chaplains. Early on in his chaplaincy, he decided that all the sick and their families needed care, not just the self-identified Catholic ones. He introduced himself to everyone and let him or her decide whether or not they wanted what he could offer. "By nature I am an open person," he reflected. The ill and the dying encouraged him to nurture his ecumenical outlook.

For Bill Sievers, the new theology and rituals that came out of the Second Vatican Council made a great deal of sense. He had seen people struggle with their faith under harsh conditions. Although familiar Catholic routines comforted many, for others the trials of being ill or having a family member who was suffering generated deep and penetrating questions. Those concerns were not easily countered with a few priestly gestures.

Sievers welcomed the Council's insistence that the "sacrament of the dying" be transformed into the "sacrament of the sick." He approved of replacing the black vestments of the funeral Mass for white ones symbolizing the Resurrection. But it was the Mass in English that uplifted him the most: "I went wild," he explained; "it was the greatest thing that happened in my life. No more of this Latin mumbo-jumbo stuff."

Unlike in Los Angeles, Denver priests had no option to hang on to the "Latin mumbo-jumbo stuff." In a letter dated October 6, 1964, Archbishop Urban J. Vehr clearly stated that all the priests in his diocese would follow the recently approved changes in the liturgy.

Although not mentioned in the Council documents, that September the *Consilium* (of Sacred Congregation of Rites) had also made major changes in the design and structure of churches. "The main altar should preferably be freestanding," their instruction stated, "to permit walking around it and celebration facing the people. Its location in the place of worship should be truly central so that the attention of the whole congregation naturally focuses there."[2] In Denver all priests were to face their congregations, and instructions were given on how to construct temporary altars to facilitate that interaction. The parts of the Mass permitted in the vernacular were to be said in English. Pastors were told to install sound systems so everyone could hear the Mass, and "commentators" were trained to help direct the congregation. Everyone was to stand to receive Communion, and the unconsecrated bread and wine was to be brought up to the altar by lay church officials and altar boys. Even a set of approved hymns was sent to parishes.

Archbishop Vehr's organized response to reform built upon a longstanding commitment to Catholic education. Unlike Cardinal McIntyre, who had little personal interest in the complexities of theology or liturgy, Vehr possessed an intellectual bent. Born in 1892 to a prosperous German American family in Ohio, he had advanced university degrees and had studied in Rome. Vehr directed the Cincinnati Catholic school system and a diocesan minor seminary before coming to Denver in 1931. At forty, he became the youngest bishop in the country.

Like all other American bishops, Vehr assumed he would spend his time building churches, schools, and other Catholic institutions. However, unlike McIntyre, who came to California in 1948 along with postwar affluence, Vehr arrived during the Depression, as farmers in eastern Colorado watched their topsoil blow away and miners in the mountains waited in soup lines. The new bishop actually closed parishes. In 1930 the archdiocese had 111 parishes; by 1940 the number had declined to 87.

In spite of their economic struggles, Catholics in Colorado liked the friendly and well-spoken bishop. They bought him a black Studebaker that he enjoyed driving throughout his vast diocese. After World War II and Colorado's ensuing economic rise, he made it his goal to enable every Catholic child to go to a Catholic school. By 1960 one out of every five Colorado students attended a parochial school. Vehr watched where public schools were being built and made sure a parish was founded near each one. Although he was committed to Catholic reform, he did not attend the Second Vatican Council. Plagued by heart trouble, Vehr reluctantly sent his auxiliary bishop David Maloney to Rome as his proxy for the Council discussions.

Archbishop Vehr prepared his flock in a variety of ways for the changes brought about by the Council. In the spring of 1964 he decided to have the annual clergy conference focus on the history of salvation in the Old Testament and the newly written Constitution on the Sacred Liturgy. At a separate workshop, three hundred priests learned how to integrate English into the Mass. Previews of the new liturgy were given to educators and women's organizations. Pastors were sent instructions on church designs, listing the appropriate supportive Vatican documents. All Catholic high schools were expected to offer courses in the new liturgy. Newspaper articles about the upcoming changes appeared in the secular newspaper the *Denver Post*, and the archdiocese even produced a television program on the English language Mass. Vehr urged as many people as possible to watch the telecast "and if possible to express your comments to the station in writing following the program."[3]

The archbishop targeted young priests for indoctrination. In Denver, priests who had been ordained for less than five years had to sit an annual examination. They were evaluated on their knowledge of theology, Canon Law, and Scripture. In August of 1964 they were also asked to write a twenty-minute sermon text on the subject of "The new Liturgical Movement, its meaning and import for our Catholic people."[4] Archbishop Urban Vehr was nothing if not thorough.

The man who replaced Vehr when he retired in 1967 was also a Midwesterner who valued education. James V. Casey came from the farming village of Osage, Iowa, where his father had been a machinery dealer, postmaster, and state senator. Born in 1914, he graduated from a public high school and attended a small Catholic college. Rather than going to a local seminary, he was sent to the North American College in Rome, where top Catholic men were trained for the priesthood. Casey served in parishes and then as a chaplain during World War II, but he also went to Catholic University, where he earned a doctorate in Canon Law. Prior to taking over for Vehr, Casey was auxiliary bishop of Lincoln, Nebraska.

The process of teaching clergy and parishioners about the Second Vatican Council continued through the early seventies. In 1973 the archdiocese formed a Liturgical Commission composed of both clergy and laity. They sent out a monthly newsletter that addressed theoretical issues and practical concerns. The Dominicans came in 1971 and 1974 and gave retreats in parishes on biblical approaches to spirituality in light of Vatican II. Their lay retreats were designed to help Catholics personalize their relationship to God, in addition to providing the more usual instruction on the sacraments and commandments. The diocese supported workshops on various topics, and St. Jude's parishioner Bill Campbell remembered how important the program "Christians in Search" was for his own spiritual development.

Vehr and Casey both had the educational preparation and the desire to articulate a wider vision of the Church than did McIntyre in California. For them, facilitating the basic themes contained in the Council documents served to strengthen Catholic life rather than threaten it. Throughout the sixties and early seventies, the Archdiocese of Denver put mechanisms in place to encourage the smooth transition into new ways of being Catholic. Parishes across the country slowly came in line with the Council's reforms, with some dioceses more active than others in encouraging and supporting the proponents of renewal.

W HEN ARCHBISHOP CASEY came for the dedication of St. Jude's, Father Sievers allowed the teen choir to provide the music. Although some parishioners thought this a bit unusual, the celebration called for the best of what was new in the community. The church did have an organ and an adult choir, but Father Bill was particularly proud of the Masses where singers played guitars and the congregation sang along. Standing behind the altar and facing the people, with their A-line dresses rising high above their knees and their sideburns jutting downward, the teens felt fully comfortable leading the congregation.

Like many Catholic churches of the Vatican II era, St. Jude was experimenting with new musical styles. At guitar Masses, musicians might lead the congregation in original songs written by Catholic pop composers like Joe Wise or Sister Miriam Therese Winter. They could just as well sing a Beatles favorite like "Here Comes the Sun" or "Hey Jude." Cat Stevens' "Morning Has Broken" was popular at St. Jude's, and almost no one knew it was a modern version of an old Protestant hymn.

Looking back on those days, parishioners remember the music fondly. Singer Mur Hiltenbrand recalled that "Music was always fun. We would do the readings for that Sunday and then choose music that was associated with the readings. We were given a great deal of latitude back then." By the midseventies, however, the archdiocese was warning parishes about the perils of copyright infringement, but until then musicians at St. Jude freely chose their music from a variety of sources.

The introduction of guitars into Catholic churches sprang from the same impulse that had brought the vernacular. Social custom no longer equaled religious truth. If the Church was to make sense to those living in the modern world, it had to be sensitive to ever-shifting cultural styles and patterns. Consequently, with the acceptance of the vernacular into the heart of Catholic ritual life, Americans looked to see what local traditions they might adopt.

In the early sixties, a folk music revival hit the United States. The Kingston Trio's rendition of "Tom Dooley" became immensely popular, earning the singers a gold record and a Grammy. They and other groups went on to record songs written by Pete Seeger and Woody Guthrie, musicians who had been blacklisted during the fifties. The Kingston Trio popularized Seeger's "Where Have All the Flowers Gone," and Peter, Paul and Mary transformed his "If I Had a Hammer" into a hit. The Byrds' rendition of Seeger's "Turn Turn Turn" reached the top of the charts in 1965. Bob Dylan wrote the lyrical "Blowin' in the Wind" as well as the more edgy "The Times They Are A Changin'." Joan Baez and Judy Collins captivated audiences both in concert halls and in protest rallies with their soaring soprano voices. All of this music would soon enter America's Catholic churches.

A Belgian nun, however, is the one who finally connected the guitar to Catholic popular culture. In 1964 Ed Sullivan, a prominent television host, flew to Europe and filmed a performance of a young Dominican nun, Sister Luc Gabriel. Sister Luc had entered the convent as Jeanine Deckers, and as most nuns did, she brought her favorite hobby along with her. Sister Luc delighted her fellow sisters with original tunes that she played on her guitar about God and the founder of her religious order, St. Dominic. In order to raise money for their monastery, the nuns recorded Sister Luc's singing and sold albums to visitors.

In 1963, through a series of fortunate events, the Philips recording company began to market around the world the music of Sister Luc (her stage name was Soeur Sourire, or "Sister Smile"). Her single "Dominique" became a smash sensation in the United States, bumping Elvis Presley off the top of the pop music charts. The upbeat song hit the radio shortly after Kennedy's assassination. It seemed to provide Americans comfort in a time of national sorrow. Ed Sullivan intended to put this new musical sensation on his show, just as he had the shaggy-haired group from England who called themselves The Beatles. Over half of the television viewers of the midsixties—somewhere around 50 million people— watched the Ed Sullivan Show. They fell in love with Soeur Sourire. A cloistered nun in a flowing white habit, singing in French about a saint who battled heretics, surprisingly wedded the guitar permanently to Vatican II Catholicism.

THE FOLK SONG REVIVAL of the sixties meshed well with Catholic needs for a new music that linked people's everyday lives to spiritual concepts. Children, teens, and young adults were taking guitar lessons and copying what they heard on the radio. Sixties folk music was designed to be sung, so it depended on basic chordal progressions and straightforward lyrics. With just a guitar, Catholic composers could write songs that linked friendship, peace, and nature with Christian notions of the Resurrection, the lordship of Christ, and the miracle of the Eucharist. Parishes like St. Jude's could then take those songs and, without expensive equipment or much musical talent, integrate them into the Mass. "I welcomed the ability to take the music I heard on the radio and to sing it in church," Mur recollected about her time singing at St. Jude's. "What I thought was, 'God is everywhere. He's not just in church on Sunday.'"

The folk music that came into Catholic churches after the Council was the vernacular of middle-class youth. Of course there was the occasional polka Masses in the upper Midwest or the Mexican mariachi Masses in the Southwest and West, but this music made little sense to postimmigrant Catholics living in the suburbs. Catholic adults were particularly concerned with keeping their young people involved in the Church. In 1960 there were 16.2 million Americans between the ages of eighteen and twenty-four. By 1970 the number had risen to 24.4 million. Of those, over a third attended college, up from 22 percent in 1960. The growth rate of teens was four times the growth rate of the country as a whole.[5] Cultural focus was on this young generation, and many Catholic parents were happy to sing "Morning Has Broken" if it meant their teens would go to Mass.

Not all elements of youth culture were welcome, however. The harsh electronic sound of Janis Joplin or Jimi Hendrix found no home at St. Jude's or most Catholic churches of the sixties and early seventies. Only the parts of the counterculture that upheld the beauty of nature, the importance of human relations, and the quest for authenticity could be brought to church. Sex, drugs, and rock 'n' roll—which Margaret and her generation found nihilistic and disruptive—could not. Furthermore, protests and protest music remained confined to the television. The music of St. Jude and other suburban parishes reflected the need for a controlled and familiar modern culture.

S T. JUDE'S CHURCH was designed to provide a safe, comfortable, and informal environment for those Catholics who lived in what city planners call "exurbia." In the exurbs, residents do not commute into the heart of the city as they do in the suburbs. People live on the periphery of an urban area, often holding jobs in offices also located on the outskirts of the city. Although residents might travel into the city for a special meal or to a cultural or sporting event, most of their lives are spent in semi-rural areas.

Throughout the West, exurbs were growing. In the decade between 1960 and 1970, Jefferson County experienced an 80 percent population increase. During a period when riots occurred in cities across the country, Americans were moving in greater numbers to the detached and self-contained exurbs.

Parishioners of St. Jude's were similar to those Americans living in ex-urbs across the country: educated, white, and mobile. For them, a church—Protestant or Catholic—was often the center of their social as well as religious lives. Like Margaret, exurb dwellers had no extended family in the immediate area. Many had children who were now in high school, requiring less parental involvement. They looked to their churches to provide a sense of belonging, tradition, and meaning in a world dominated by newly built housing divisions.

The families that came to St. Jude's had little organic connection with one another during the day. Although Father Bill did his best to cultivate a friendly and spiritually open environment at church, he recognized that this only went so far in creating a Catholic community. His large parish of eighteen square miles and 1,400 households would not be able to develop a participatory form of Catholicism without finding a way to deepen their spiritual lives outside the church. The spirit of Vatican II motivated Father Bill to think of new ways to stimulate and realign the ways in which his "exurban Catholics" practiced their religion.

To solidify the Church in the lives of his parishioners, Father Bill de-veloped a system of "Little Parishes." Taking his cue from Jesus, who gathered small groups of people around him, Father Bill divided the parish into small neighborhood units. For each unit, Father Bill asked a couple to coordinate monthly meetings that included prayer, religious discussion, and informal socializing. Nancy and Roger Frenette remem-ber being tagged for this by Father Bill. The weekend before their first Little Parish meeting, the couple quickly painted their basement walls and borrowed folding chairs from the church. "A lot of people came," Roger recalled, "our basement was chock-full. There wasn't hardly any air to breathe." The success of the early meetings stimulated more parish interest.

Little Parishes centered on engaging the questioning, adult Catholic. In the words of the St. Jude's parish bulletin, they helped parishioners who wondered, "Where can a conscientious Catholic who is yearning for both information about his or her faith and for some milieu in which his or her faith can grow and deepen find a suitable environment?" Father Bill's goal was to make St. Jude's "an alive, concerned community of faith."

To cultivate a mature relationship with God, the Little Parishes of-fered learning experiences in theology, Scripture, liturgy, and social justice. "Father Bill was really big on education," Mur Hiltenbrand reflected. "He wanted the people to know what was going on in church so we could be informed. He was really big on everyone being active and involved; he hooked us."

Beyond merely providing adult education, the Little Parishes were designed to support, sustain, and deepen the parishioners' spiritual lives. Lead couples arranged the monthly meetings and picked the Bible readings, hymns, and prayers. The success of each Little Parish depended on its ability to combine religious education, spiritual uplift, and sociability. The active participation that the Council called for would be modeled in these lay-driven, small-scale, Christian communities.

Once or twice a year, Father Bill or one of his assistant priests would come to a Little Parish and say a home Mass. Before attending St. Jude, Margaret had never experienced such a Mass. The theologians of *ressourcement* who had influenced the Council's documents on the liturgy looked to the early Church for inspiration on what the Mass should look like. At the birth of Christianity, worship was often held in houses. Liturgical specialists believed that the nature of the Mass as a communal meal could be underscored if it were celebrated in a more domestic setting. At a Little Parish Mass, the priest would lay a white cloth on a dining room table and start the liturgy. Rather than give a sermon, he sat down with everyone and discussed the Scriptural readings. People sang without a leader or even music. The hosting family baked the bread that the priest consecrated.

At the home Masses, spiritual feelings and personal hopes came out in the open. For Margaret, home Masses were beautifully intimate and full of meaning. They solidified the notion that Christ came to his followers in an intense way during the celebration of a meal. Mur Hiltenbrand found her Little Parish to be so meaningful that she had Father Bill baptize two of her children during their monthly meetings.

The Little Parishes attempted to get couples who rarely spoke of serious religious topics to think "big thoughts." "That was a little frightening to some of us," Bill Campbell wrote in 1973. "It meant something else piled on top of a busy schedule. It meant that we would have to try and remember a bunch of new names and faces (even if we couldn't remember the names) if we saw them at church or the store or the neighborhood streets. It meant we had to do something that we weren't sure at all that we were going to like." For many parishioners, the Little Parishes not only let neighbors meet each other, but it also encouraged them to speak candidly and expose their feelings without fear of embarrassment.

Margaret and Ken's Little Parish echoed the rosary circle that Margaret went to in Monterey Park. People met without a priest and prayed and talked. At Little Parishes, however, women shared a part of their domestic religion with men. Men who typically were more comfortable raising money were now being asked to discuss their religious feelings. The devotional side of Catholicism that had been associated with women and the theological side that was the domain of men were being merged. The laity as well as the clergy were being asked to reflect with focused discipline on the contours of their faith.

Unlike the Monterey Park rosary group, where religious and social intimacy was cultivated as an alternative to the impersonal space of the church, the Little Parishes were continuations of the relaxed environment of St. Jude's. During her years in Denver, Margaret did not meet with other women to say the rosary. This is not because this devotion became less important to her; rather, other practices in her church community were adding more religious dimensions to her spiritual life.

THE LITTLE PARISHES were particularly important at St. Jude's because Father Bill had decided not to build a parochial school. Prior to deciding on a design for the church, Father Bill traveled with three other priests to seven different states in four days ("I'll never do that again," he reflected). These men were to head up four new parishes in the corners of the archdiocese, and they were looking at newly built Catholic communities. "What did we learn?" Bill recalled. "Schools were ending; there were none. Parishes were starting up, but they were not building; schools. I came back to the parish and got up in the pulpit and said, 'We will never have a Catholic school.'"

American parishes established in the years after the Council built churches first and often never a school. As early as 1964 Mary Perkins Ryan, a mother of five boys from Chicago, published *Are Parochial Schools the Answer?* In it she connected the dots between the religious philosophy being discussed at the Second Vatican Council and America's vast network of Catholic schools. Although she wrote her book as a series of questions to consider, her conclusions were obvious enough: The halcyon days of the Catholic school were over.

With the Council encouraging Catholics to be open to modern culture, the old ghettoized, school-centered Catholic culture was dead. Schools no longer needed to inoculate Catholics against a diseased world. In the United States, several generations of Catholic immigrant children had already been educated. Protestants no longer printed slanted versions of history in school textbooks. Continuing to prop up a vast and unnecessary educational system only drained money and personnel from other Catholic services.

For Father Bill, the decision not to build a Catholic school was an obvious choice. Not only did parochial education tend to separate Catholics from the non-Catholic world, but schools were also getting increasingly more expensive. Parents demanded high levels of educational achievement from their children. Catholic schools were keeping up in religion and the humanities, but excellence in science was flagging. Furthermore, it had become clear that the federal government was not going to come to their rescue with aid from taxes.

The system was beginning to collapse. "The parishes that had schools," Father Sievers reflected, "had to hire lay people and struggle to keep the schools open." Schools were hiring lay people because, unlike in the early sixties when Mary Perkins Ryan was doing her research, the number of teaching sisters was drying up. "What built our Catholic faith in this nation?" Bill Sievers asked rhetorically. "Catholic schools. What happened to the Catholic schools? We lost the free labor of all the nuns."

In 1960 there were 168,527 Catholic sisters in the United States. The numbers increased, year after year, until 1966, when there were a total of 181,421 women in religious orders. After that point, there was a rapid decrease in the numbers of young women entering the novitiate and an increase of older women asking to be released from their vows. By 1976 the total number of Catholic sisters had declined to 130,995—a 28 percent decrease in the decade since 1966.[6] The Belgian Sister Sourire herself had left the Dominicans in 1966. The American Sister Corita, who had become famous for her mod art and creative Mary's Days, left the Immaculate Heart Sisters in 1968.

Sisters left their orders for many reasons. Holy Names Sisters who taught at St. Stephen's had gone through six years of thinking about the meaning of their religious lives. Like many sisters at the time, they had designed and redesigned their habit, eventually abandoning it entirely. Their rulebook assumed a dramatic new look in 1973. Sisters were leaving schools and starting new jobs in social work and in parishes. The constant change was unbearable for many of them.

For other women the convents were not changing quickly enough. From their perspective, a backward-looking Vatican Curia, hostile parish pastors, and old-fashioned mother superiors were all dragging their feet. In 1970, after going back and forth for years with the Archdiocese of Los Angeles and Rome about their new rule, the Immaculate Heart Sisters lost their struggle to determine their own religious lives. Father Edward Heston, secretary of the Congregation of Religious, explained to *Time* magazine reporters why the Vatican refused to give in: "When it became obvious that these ladies no longer wanted to operate within the framework of the religious community, there was nothing else to do but permit them to get out."[7] A third of the Immaculate Hearts left the order entirely, a third formed their own lay community, and a third stayed in the order. Religious orders of women, who wanted to seriously alter their devotional life and how they interacted with the world, would have to be cagey in how they articulated their new visions.

For generations, joining a convent had been a way for many American women to pursue spiritual and professional goals with family and community support. Many parents proudly boasted that they had a nun in the family. By the early seventies, however, women across the country were being told that they no longer had to sacrifice having a husband and children in order to have a career. The women's movement was fighting to end discrimination in the workplace. New history books recognized the past achievements of the nation's wives, mothers, and daughters. Social critics were pointing out the sexist assumptions not only in the middle-class home but even in liberal associations like the Civil Rights movement.

For young Catholic women, professional opportunities that did not require the heroic act of celibacy were slowly opening up. Although women had been entering the workforce in increasing numbers since the early twenties, by the seventies they were paid better and given more respect. A Catholic girl could now dream about being a full-time teacher or nurse or social worker without having to become a nun.

Although the vast majority of Council Fathers had no interest in directly expanding the role of women in the Church, women theologians and Catholic sisters quickly combined the ideas of the feminist movement with their own spiritual longings. The feminist movement also enabled women in parishes to demand equality with the men in the parish. Women as well as men should be active participants in their faith. If the Church was trying to integrate the divine into the world and not isolate religion from modern culture, then why opt for a life in a convent? Couldn't women pursue spiritual perfection outside the convent without sacrificing marriage, sex, and children?

And, then, of course, there was love. Even before sisters exchanged their habits for little veils and shorter skirts, their everyday interactions with priests and the laity had greatly increased. After decades of being told not to express their personal feelings, to hide every curve of their bodies, and to flee from "particular friendships," sisters were being encouraged to cultivate their personal freedom. In order for a deep spirituality to be cultivated, women were told that they needed to recognize their authentic feelings about God, their fellow human beings, and themselves. For many women, this meant admitting that they could not manage the generalized love required of the communal, celibate life.

Women left their orders at such a rapid rate that convent leaders had no time to prepare a thoughtful response to what was happening. Initially, orders fell back on the time-honored way of dealing with a sister who left: Ignore her. The numbers became so large, however, that those who remained felt like rats on a sinking ship. "There were a lot of misunderstandings," Sister Benedicta of the Holy Names remembered. "It was hard for people like us who were staying to watch people we had known for years leave. Especially the young ones, they were our future. It was a difficult time." As a young superior, she was barely older than those nuns she oversaw. "You had first vow sisters or novices and you watched them leave after a year, with different reasons for going. It wasn't easy. It wasn't easy." A far-reaching crisis was occurring. Sisters were leaving the convents, and those who remained were exploring new forms of Christian service.

This was no time, Father Bill rightly concluded, to be starting a Catholic school. But the question remained: Who was going to prepare children to become adult Catholics? If sisters were not going to get the second graders ready for their First Holy Communion, then who would?

In 1971 parishioner Bud Schroeder answered those questions by articulating a philosophy of education for St. Jude's that reflected the conclusion of many parishes across the country: "The religious formation of the child belonged primarily to the parents and the home. St. Jude's would assist the parents but would never substitute for them with a school."[8] Each week the Sunday bulletin informed parents that *they* were to prepare their own first and second graders for their First Holy Communion. "The child," it laconically explained, "must be able to distinguish the difference between ordinary bread and the Eucharist."

Starting in the early seventies, Catholic parents were expected to educate their children in the faith. Children were to receive their First Holy Communion together with their families at a Sunday Mass, not with their peers in a special ceremony. Communion should be given to young children, but confession should wait until they were older. Only older children could truly understand the more complicated notions of sin that the Council had promulgated.

The transference of religious education from Catholic sisters to Catholic parents was a radical change in the American Church. The Council documents had stressed the importance of laymen and -women in ministering to the world. They also emphasized the importance of parents in ministering to their children. Catholic concern for the "domestic church" and "family values" was stimulated by the Second Vatican Council. Even before the decline in the numbers of American sisters during the late sixties and seventies, parents were told that they—and not the clergy—were the foundation on which their family's faith resided. At St. Jude's the first layperson who Father Bill hired was a coordinator of religious education. John Peto organized 150 parents to teach Sunday school to the parish's 1,100 children.

With parents now responsible for their own children's religious education, it became all the more imperative that the adults of the parish have a firm grasp of the history and beliefs of their faith. The Little Parishes, dialogue sermons, archdiocesan workshops, and retreats by the

Dominicans were all geared to offer adults a sophisticated understanding of what it meant to be a Christian in the modern world.

The challenge to parishes after the Second Vatican Council was to convince Catholic adults that they were responsible for understanding just why it was that they were Catholic and what it meant to be a Catholic. If parents didn't understand why children should go to Communion with their families and postpone their first confession, then the next generation would be confused about the whole affair. Sisters were no longer in charge.

S OME CATHOLICS resisted these changes. Father Bill remembered that the day he announced that the parish would not build a school, many parishioners came up to him and told him that they would be leaving St. Jude's. They wanted their children to go to Catholic school, and his promise to subsidize the existing parochial schools did not satisfy them. Driving was a way of life in the exurbs, so these Catholics would simply travel to another Catholic church for Mass. The spirit of Vatican II emphasized the importance of serious religious reflection and the God-given right of conscience. Catholics who did not like the reforms were empowered to speak out, and unlike earlier generations, they expected to be heard. The days of Catholics being confined to a geographical parish because that was the rule were over.

It was not only the lack of a Catholic school that motivated parishioners of St. Jude to move to a different parish or even to rethink their commitment to Catholicism. The very environment that drove Mur Hiltenbrand to depict her church as "so vibrant, so alive" and Mary Clydesdale to recall with pride how the services were "fresh and new" repulsed others. No one knew more intimately how controversial the changes were than the pastors who enacted them.

Forty years later, Bill Sievers has not forgotten the disgruntled Catholics who hated what he treasured most in the Church. Shortly after the Council was over, Sievers had gone to Baltimore to visit his brother. After saying Mass at his brother's church, he remembers bragging just a bit to some of the parishioners about how different and progressive things were in Denver. The response was not positive. "You're

the reason my father left the Church" came the reply from one Baltimore Catholic.

There was also the time a visiting priest from Venezuela said a mariachi Mass at St. Jude's. "He's up there saying Mass," Bill reported with a
smile, "and we've got trumpets blasting, violins, the whole schmear." Afterward a man walked up to Father Bill and said, "Am I to think that I
have been to a Mass?" Without missing a beat, the priest parried, "Well,
he's got the same orders that I do. He's an ordained priest just like I am."
The parishioner handed his pastor his offering envelope and said, "Take
me off the parish list."

Parishes struggled to communicate with those who were discon-
tented. In May 1977 St. Jude's hosted a meeting focused on bringing inac-
tive Catholics back into the Church. They advertised the gathering in the
local newspaper, explaining that the organizers hoped people would
move toward reconciliation if they could "voice their problems, questions, curiosity or dissatisfaction with where the Catholic Church is in relation to themselves as individuals." Not surprisingly, several of the
people who came specifically complained about the liturgical changes.
One woman explained that she looked around the church and wondered
where the tabernacle and sanctuary light were and what happened to
the words of the Consecration. "The church has changed," she observed
critically, "I don't recognize it. There is no life, just a vast empty hall."

Associate pastor Father John Burton tried to reassure her that none
of the essentials had changed. He pointed out the tabernacle on the wall
with its three sanctuary lights. The Eucharist was still the center of
Catholic worship, and the familiar light symbolizing the Real Presence
remained. But then another woman objected to the guitar Masses and
regretted the loss of hymns, statues, and novenas. She voiced a sentiment heard throughout the country at the time: The church had been
"Protestantized." St. Jude's, of course, still had its statues and hymns, and
no one had been saying novenas since Roosevelt was in office, but no
matter.

Complaints about Vatican II's reforms were everywhere. The popular
press reported that Catholics grumbled about the end of meatless Fridays and that nuns were wearing miniskirts. Even committed St. Jude's
parishioners like Susan Clarke reflected that, "It was hard for me to give
up some of those traditions, even though I was excited about more par-

ticipation. It was difficult to give up what had been engrained in me from the time I was five years old."

From the time of the Council, a few conservative leaders snubbed all attempts at renewal. In Europe, Archbishop Marcel Lefebvre, the superior general of the Holy Ghost Fathers, rejected the Second Vatican Council documents. Calling Pope Paul VI a traitor and the new liturgy a "bastard Mass," he started the Society of St. Pius X to train priests in the Tridentine Mass and scholastic theology.[9] Father Gommar DePauw, a former Canon Law professor at a seminary in Maryland, secured in 1966 the favors of Cardinal Alfredo Ottaviani and established a center for traditionalist Catholics in Long Island, New York. During the seventies, however, these organized traditionalist groups remained weak voices within the American Church.

Margaret could have been caught up in the traditionalist movement that was slowly growing in the country after the Second Vatican Council, but that didn't happen. She voted Republican, shook her head with consternation over students who protested the Vietnam War, and found the Beatles' music to be so much noise. However, through her church, Margaret experienced something of the positive optimism of the countercultural sixties. Parish life at St. Jude's mediated many of the changes that were occurring in the wider American culture. Just as social critics rejected the dehumanizing character of "the system" and looked to alternative work and living experiences, so Margaret found meaning in the new physical intimacy of St. Jude's. Although she never would have listened to contemporary music on the radio, she was willing to try to sing Beatles tunes at church because the teen choir was so enthusiastic. Modern architecture and art as well as modern Catholicism had become a part of everyday life for Margaret.

Many suburban Catholics like Margaret, who were detached from the rebellious sixties and seventies, welcomed the changes in their Church because they functioned to deepen their spiritual commitments. When bishops and pastors worked hard to explain the Council reforms, parishioners experienced the positive and constructive excitement of a renewed Catholicism. At St. Jude's, the Little Parishes did not attempt to instill dispassionate knowledge of Catholic history and theology but rather sought to make Catholics more confident in their own personal relationship with Jesus. Around the country, lay Catholics were being

placed at the center of the reforms, and many of them began to experience a deeper spirituality. An accessible, small-scale religiosity that
scorned the abstract and monumental was being encouraged in
parishes. The predictability that had marked Catholicism a generation
earlier was being replaced by the spontaneous and fragmentary.

As the Council reforms became more institutionalized in American
parishes, more and more laypeople assumed new ritual roles within their
churches. Catholics came to experience God in ways that made sense to
them, and they began to generate their own religious truth. The religious
conventions that Margaret had lived with for decades had been replaced
with others—ones she found more meaningful, authentic, and uplifting.
Women in particular were empowered by their expanding presence on
the altar. Their newfound religious confidence would soon place them
on a collision course with those who felt more comfortable with older
models of Church authority.

chapter seven

A DECIDING PEOPLE

Margaret and Ken had always been involved with the parishes they attended. In Toledo, Margaret had served as president of the Altar and Rosary society. In Monterey Park, she helped raise money for the school. Before the Council, parishioners and clergy both assumed that lay people would financially support their parish while leaving the major decisions up to the pastor. Rituals that took place in the church involved the priests and their assistants. Women presided over devotions in their homes but not in the public space of the church.

What was different after the Council was that the laity assumed roles in the leadership and ritual life of their parishes. Father Bill, like many reform-oriented priests across the country, transferred spiritual as well as practical power to his parishioners. Catholics were asked to reflect, decide, and act. Through her parish, Margaret began to understand the world in a new way.

As soon as he became their pastor, Bill Sievers appointed a group of parishioners to help him run the new Catholic community. By 1969 members of the St. Jude's parish council were elected rather than appointed. Men and women on the council didn't merely raise funds for the parish; instead, they were expected to oversee and coordinate all parish activities. Ken remembers, "We worked together on everything." Decisions had to be made about whether or not young people needed their own space for recreation, whether to buy a house for a rectory or to build one, which committees should be formed, and who should be hired to work in the parish. Council representatives were assigned to stand in the vestibule after Mass to answer questions and field complaints. Being a member of the parish council was an honor. Forty years later, Ken still has the metal name tag that parish council members wore.

Parish councils relied on the voluntary spirit of their members, but increasingly, laymen and -women were being paid for the time they contributed to St. Jude's. In 1970 the parish had four paid positions: three priests and a deacon. This was typical of a pre-Vatican II parish: priests aided by an advanced seminarian—a "priest-in-training." After the Council, however, barriers were lowered against the modern world. Professional expertise became less suspect. As American parishes sought to be more relevant to educated, middle-class Americans, pastors saw that paying for expertise improved their congregations.

The staff at St. Jude's doubled from four to eight by 1974. There were still only three priests who said Mass, but now there were two secretaries coordinating the growing parish, a business manager helping free the pastor from financial woes, and a couple serving as youth ministers. By 1978 the paid staff numbered sixteen. Three priests were joined by a sister and two deacons. In addition to the business manager, there now were five secretaries and a director of communications. Two youth ministers and a liturgical director rounded out the pastoral team.

By multiplying the various ways that people could participate in the religious and leadership life of the parish, Father Bill hoped to increase their understanding of their faith and their commitment to Christ and each other. Parishioner Helen Hurt remembered that even though the parish was eager for financial support, "we didn't put names on plaques when people donated. We were a whole community and we didn't want individuals to be set apart and above. Christ made us all equal; we all own a part of the Church. We didn't want a royalty in the parish; we wanted to stress that we were all in this together."

As priests introduced a managerial mode to their parishes, they simultaneously introduced a new set of problems. Parishes had always had leading families who shaped how the church would be run. Their influence, however, was not institutionalized and it was always balanced by the pastor. After the Council, parishioners held new powers that permitted them to clash not only with the priests but also with each other. Even if a parish hoped for an end to "royalty," preventing the unavoidable envy, resentment, competition for recognition, and jockeying for influence that these positions engendered was not always easy. For every individual elected to the parish council, there were inevitably several candidates who were not. The spirit of Vatican II did not introduce laypeople to parish power politics, but it did legitimize and thereby complicate their influence.

Innovative parish activities across the country were increasingly led by a "new" Catholic woman. Although Ken had been transferred out of Colorado by 1978, he and Margaret would not have been surprised to learn that by that date, half of St. Jude's pastoral team was composed of women. These women possessed a serious commitment to their faith in addition to having secretarial or professional training. Unlike the laywomen of an earlier era who volunteered in the church office or the sister who worked selflessly in the school, these women expected to have their training and talents recognized and compensated. Women like Helen Marie Hurt, who became St. Jude's first director of liturgy, received a serious voice in parish affairs.

Each week at St. Jude's, Father Bill called together his pastoral team and, in addition to getting updates on their own activities, asked for help on his Sunday sermons. What ideas did they think evolved out of the day's gospel readings? Increasingly, women were influencing the day-to-day activities of their churches by being elected to parish councils and remunerated for their professional talents.

At times, women took on duties at St. Jude's that had not been approved by the Vatican. In 1972 Pope Paul VI issued *Ministeria Quaedam*, an apostolic letter laying out changes in the "minor orders." Among those ministries that *Ministeria Quaedam* clarified were that of reader and acolyte. Readers would have the privilege of reading from the epistles and psalms at Mass. Only reading from the gospels would remain a clerical responsibility. Acolytes would assist at Mass not unlike altar boys, but they could also distribute Communion as a "special minister" if a priest was unavailable or if the number of communicants was large. Women, however, would be ineligible for either of these new ministries: "In accordance with the ancient tradition of the Church," *Ministeria Quaedam* explained, "the ministries of reader and acolyte [are] reserved to men."

Embedded within *Ministeria Quaedam* is the ambivalence that Pope Paul VI brought to all his writing after the Second Vatican Council. On the one hand is the strong desire to bring men and women closer to the ritual life of the Church. What better way to excite Catholics about the importance of the Bible than by letting them read from it to those gathered at Mass? On the other hand, *Ministeria Quaedam* reveals the Pope's reluctance to detach any of the ritual functions of the Mass from the priesthood. Historically, holding "minor orders" (such as the offices of porter, reader, exorcist, and acolyte) was part of the training for Holy Orders. One way to make sure that these new ministers were accorded the seriousness once due to the minor orders was to limit them to men. In this way a distinction could still be made between priests and laypeople.

To pay Helen Hurt to be a "liturgical minister" while prohibiting women from reading the epistles to the congregation made little sense. Increasingly, Catholics who approved of the changing Church got the feeling that the Vatican was backpedaling. Pope Paul VI seemed to be wishy-washy about embracing what was good about the modern world. Conservatives like Cardinal Ottaviani, who was the powerful head of the Sacred Congregation for the Doctrine of the Faith, consistently pressured the pope to limit liturgical change. Deciding that women could not be readers or acolytes seemed to demonstrate that the Vatican preferred to look backward to the "ancient tradition of the Church" rather than forward into a future of equality between the sexes. This was disappointing to many reformers.

Both the pastor of St. Jude's and the leaders of the Archdiocese of Denver had to walk a thin line between reform and the preservation of "the ancient tradition." In 1970, two years before *Ministeria Quaedam*, the Archdiocese of Denver had initiated a program for "special ministers of the Eucharist." Council documents had stressed the centrality of the Eucharist to Catholic life, so more people were receiving Communion at Sunday Mass. To help the priests accommodate the larger number of communicants, men and women were trained to distribute Holy Communion. Eucharistic ministers also took Communion to people who were home sick or in the hospital. On the day he was installed as a "special minister," Ken recalled feeling a new closeness to Jesus. "We civilians passed out Communion to the priests and nuns," who had attended their celebratory first Mass, "That's pretty classy."

Three years later, the Vatican issued guidelines regarding such special Eucharistic ministers. *Immensae Caritatis* (1973) made it clear that
lay Catholics might be made special ministers only if no "reader, major
seminarian, man religious, woman religious, or catechist" could be
found. The Vatican sought to preserve a distinction between those
people who had been installed in a particular ministry and ordinary
Catholics. *Immensae Caritatis*, however, had given bishops permission to
adapt the guidelines to fit their local needs. Denver's Archbishop James
Casey exercised "prudent discretion" and eliminated the Vatican's order
of preference. In Denver, laywomen were considered worthy to function
as Eucharistic ministers in and of themselves not simply because men or
nuns were unavailable.

Likewise at St. Jude's, Father Bill decided that women should be able
to read from the Bible at Mass just like men did. Rather than formally install only men as readers per *Ministeria Quaedam*, he simply asked for
volunteers who were willing to read the epistle at Mass as lectors. Margaret and the other female lectors were unaware of the technical differences that permitted them to be active on the altar without impinging
on the authority of the male priesthood. Father Bill quietly compromised
the letter of the law with what he understood to be the spirit of the Second Vatican Council.

For many of the women who participated in the new Catholic liturgy,
the Council enabled them to draw closer to God's word and sacrament.
Before her time at St. Jude's, Margaret did not think much about what
was in the Scriptures. She knew Bible stories but was not familiar with
the text itself.

Because reading from the Bible at Mass had become an important
part of the service, Margaret now spent time rehearsing the weekly texts.
Practicing meant that she looked more closely at what was actually written in the Bible. Her engagement with the Scriptures was exactly what
the Council Fathers hoped would happen when Catholics became more
involved in the Mass.

Margaret had been raised in a Church where children were taught an
elaborate etiquette for approaching and receiving the consecrated host.
Consequently, seeing her husband and women friends on the altar took
some getting used to. The priest and his special ministers handed the host
to the communicant, and eventually they would also offer the chalice filled

with Christ's blood. But just as Margaret mastered her nerves in order to stand up and read at Mass, she came to feel comfortable with the new way of receiving Communion. Rather than diminish the importance of the sacrament, it took on a new intimacy and relevance.

MARGARET WAS SATISFIED with her lector role, and she was unaware of the negotiation that had to be accomplished for her to be given that responsibility. As she neared her fiftieth birthday, she was participating in the Mass in ways that she never would have imagined as a young woman. Margaret saw women distributing Communion, being paid for working with church committees, and organizing St. Jude's music. She thought: How far we have come. Other women looked at the same activities and wondered: Why can't we do more?

New forms of Catholic leadership continually raised the issue of women's place in renewal. In 1975 a married man, Gene Mooneyham, joined the staff at St. Jude's as a permanent deacon. The Council Fathers established the office of permanent deacon, and since 1968, the U.S. bishops had permitted deacons to take on many priestly duties. Permanent deacons could officiate at Baptisms and funerals. They could bless marriages, preach, conduct worship services based on Scripture, and assume a variety of other tasks in the parish. That year Mooneyham was one of twenty-four permanent deacons in Denver and one of eight hundred serving across the country. Throughout the world, dioceses were rapidly ordaining married men as deacons.

When Mooneyham was welcomed in the St. Jude's parish newsletter, the article explained that "wives of candidates are closely screened and interviewed. Heavy emphasis is placed on the wife's assent to her husband's new role in the Church. Doris Mooneyham has attended all except two of the classes with her husband in the past two years."[1] The newsletter described how Doris participated in the parish's Light of God prayer group and traveled with her husband to Rome for the International Catholic Charismatic conference. Doris had also raised the couple's five children. Increasingly, Catholics in the United States were asking why couldn't women like Doris become permanent deacons? Or, for that matter, why couldn't they become priests?

The idea that women might be ordained priests was not so foreign to graduates of Catholic schools. Margaret in particular had learned from smart, well-spoken Catholic nuns. Even in the midseventies, when many sisters had exchanged their habits for civilian clothes, Margaret never questioned their dedication to Catholicism. For Catholics who had had positive parochial school experiences, nuns already seemed to function as female Catholic clergy by modeling intelligence, self-sacrifice, and holiness. They were theologically and ritually knowledgeable, so it seemed reasonable to offer them—and, for that matter, all women—full theological education and sacramental authority.

Younger Catholics were also under the influence of the women's movement. Dr. Elizabeth Farians, a Catholic who headed the Ecumenical Task Force on Women and Religion formed by the National Organization of Women (NOW), summed it up this way: "It's alright if women come to church with cake in their hands," she observed, "but if they come with an idea in their heads they're not welcome."[2]

Across the country, women were demanding full equality in their religious communities. Protestant women pushed to be included in the ritual and leadership life of their congregations. They argued for inclusive language in prayer books, for hiring women on seminary faculties, and for including women's stories in their congregational histories. Feminist writings such as Betty Friedan's *Feminine Mystique* and Kate Millett's *Sexual Politics* heavily influenced the writings of Christian thinkers, including the ideas of Catholic theologians like Rosemary Radford Reuther, Elizabeth Schüssler Fiorenza, and Mary Daly.

By the midseventies, Methodists, Presbyterians, and Lutherans were already ordaining women to the ministry. The first female reformed Jewish rabbi was ordained in 1972. Episcopalian women who were illegally ordained in 1974 were officially ordained two years later. In 1975 two thousand Catholics gathered in Detroit for the first Women's Ordination Conference, demanding that women be permitted to become deacons and priests. A year later, at a conference called by the U.S. Conference of Bishops, over 1,300 Catholic lay delegates representing dioceses around the country called for the ordination of women.

When the Second Vatican Council met in the sixties, it was easy to ignore Archbishop Paul Hallinan's suggestion that women be given equal consideration in the schema on the Church in the modern world. By the seventies, however, the pressure to eliminate sex discrimination was being felt around the globe. Consequently, in 1973 a papal commission was established to explore the role of women in society and in Catholicism. Three years later the Sacred Congregation for the Doctrine of the Faith issued a Declaration on the Question of Admission of Women to the Ministerial Priesthood (also known as *Inter Insigniores*), hoping to clarify the Church's stance on female ordination.

The text began with Pope John XXIII's historic observation that women taking part in public life was a positive mark of our present age. It went on to note that the Second Vatican Council stated in *Gaudium et Spes* that discrimination based on one's sex was something "which must be overcome and eliminated as being contrary to God's plan." After citing several of the great women of the Church and acknowledging that many Protestant communities ordained women, it concluded that "the Church, in fidelity to the example of the Lord, does not consider herself authorized to admit women to priestly ordination."

Inter Insigniores laid out the scriptural and theological reasons for this decision. Christ did not call any woman to be one of his twelve apostles and neither did the apostles after the death of Judas. Even Mary, Jesus's mother, "was not invested with the apostolic ministry." When a priest acts in his ministry, he acts in the place of Christ. Because Jesus was a man, there must also be a "natural resemblance" between Christ and his minister. Biblical and theological ideas relied on gendered symbols to reflect the mystery of the Church. Such images were rooted in divine truth.

In conclusion, as if to remind Catholics that the modern trend toward flattening distinctions between people has limits, *Inter Insigniores* stated that "equality is in no way identity, for the Church is a differentiated body, in which each individual has his or her role. The roles are distinct, and must not be confused."

For many Catholics, the Vatican's argument for not ordaining women seemed to be in stark contrast to its support of human rights and the dignity of all persons stressed at the Council. In 1967 Pope Paul VI published the encyclical *Populorum Progressio*, which he had begun after returning from a 1964 trip to India. The encyclical sought to shift Catholic attention away from the East/West, communist/capitalist divide and toward the North/South, developed/undeveloped gap. *Populorum Progressio* warned that economic and social dislocation would produce dangerous "public upheavals, civil insurrection, [and] the drift toward totalitarian ideologies." Although past missionary work had made certain contributions, it was now up to "the concerted effort of everyone" to remedy poverty and social ills while increasing education and culture.

Paul VI was particularly harsh on the subject of rich nations who used the right of private property and free trade to secure their own wealth while depriving others of their basic livelihood. Economics should benefit the whole world, he argued, not simply a small group of individuals. "Continuing avarice on their part," *Populorum Progressio* concluded, "will arouse the judgment of God and the wrath of the poor, with consequences no one can foresee. If prosperous nations continue to be jealous of their own advantage alone, they will jeopardize their highest values, sacrificing the pursuit of excellence to the acquisition of possessions."

Richer nations, therefore, must not only aid developing countries financially, but they must also make sure that their trade relations are just. Only by approaching global problems politically, economically, and spiritually can "a more humane world community" be built "where the progress of some is not bought at the expense of others."

Traveling in 1968 to Medellín, Colombia, the pope met with Latin American bishops who agreed that the way to secure peace, social justice, and human rights was to create a preferential option for the poor and to decouple Catholicism from violent political regimes. The 1971 Synod of Bishops called for the Church as well as the world to examine whether or not it served as an "authentic witness on behalf of justice." From scholars crafting liberation theology that investigated the relationship between economics and Christianity to base communities of the poor trying to apply the Bible to their everyday lives, social justice became a Catholic rallying cry. Papal statements made in 1971 (*Octogesima Adveniens*) and in 1975 (*Evangelii Nuntiandi*) continued to analyze social and economic injustices as well as issue calls for action.

In Denver the connection between economic, social, and religious justice was clearly articulated by Archbishop James Casey's auxiliary bishop, George Evans. Many American bishops caught up in the liturgical changes initiated by the Council concentrated on clergy training and church renovation. Conversely, Evans took seriously the Council's statement in *Gaudium et Spes* that the Church's "solitary goal" was to "carry forward the work of Christ" who "entered this world to give witness to the truth, to rescue and not to sit in judgment, to serve and not to be served."

Throughout his career as second-in-command in Denver, Evans worked ceaselessly to further the rights of the disadvantaged, end the war in Vietnam, and establish equality between the sexes. In 1968 he organized Catholic businessmen to build low-cost housing for the urban poor. When one complex was finished, he moved into one of its one-bedroom apartments so he could better understand "the problems of the people who live in our projects."[3]

Evans lobbied the Colorado legislature on behalf of the poor, the elderly, and the homeless. He also took positions on controversial issues. In 1972 it was the auxiliary bishop who addressed a crowd of thirty thousand who had gathered on the state capitol lawn for an "Evening of Peace" in support of U.S. withdrawal from Vietnam. When several Sisters of Loretto were arrested for trespassing at the Rocky Flats nuclear weapons plant, Evans accompanied them to their court hearings. Traveling to California, Evans marched and picketed in solidarity with César Chávez and migrant laborers.

George Evans was also one of the few Catholic bishops who spoke out in favor of passing the Equal Rights Amendment in the early seventies. First introduced into Congress in 1923 by suffragist Alice Paul, the amendment simply stated that "equality of rights under the law shall not be denied or abridged by the United States or by any state on account of sex." The amendment passed the House and Senate in 1972 and was sent to the state legislatures for ratification. Colorado was one of twenty-two states that immediately ratified the amendment. The state also introduced similar language on gender equality into its own constitution.

In contrast to another Catholic, Phyllis Schlafly, who was instrumental in ensuring that the amendment did not acquire its requisite number of state ratifications (thirty-five of the required thirty-eight states ratified the amendment, and five of those later voted to rescind their ratification), Evans saw the equality of women as yet another social justice issue that the Church needed to support. For Evans, "the role of the church should be that of the conscience of our society, alerting it to problems and providing examples for their solution."[4]

Evans's stances on hot-button political issues most likely prevented his promotion. He remained an auxiliary bishop in Denver until he died in 1985. Not surprisingly, at one point, when Denver's Archbishop James Casey traveled to Rome to report on the state of his diocese, the pope told him in no uncertain terms to tell his auxiliary bishop to stop publicly supporting the ordination of women.[5]

Bishop Evans believed that both his activities on behalf of the poor and his criticism of the Vietnam War were fully supported by the documents of the Second Vatican Council. Parishes like St. Jude's also responded to the Council's call to "serve and not to be served." In 1973 Father Bill formed a commission to "educate through reflection and action, the people of the parish to their responsibilities as Catholics to minister to the physical, economic, and social needs of others."[6] Among a number of parishioners there was a growing awareness that their plush homes, trimmed lawns, and safe streets had lulled Catholics into forgetting the American reality of urban decay and rural poverty.

St. Jude's Social Justice Commission intended to address community needs by funneling money from the collection baskets of St. Jude's into deserving social service agencies. In 1976 St. Jude's sent 5 percent of its total offertory collection to organizations such as the Cenikor drug rehabilitation community, the Denver Indian Center, and César Chávez's United Farm Workers Union. Although some money sustained specific Catholic efforts—like funding an inner-city parish to hire a pastoral assistant to work with the African American community—most did not. Over thirty local and national groups were supported by the parish. The Social Justice Commission inserted pleas in the parish bulletin that said "BOYCOTT LETTUCE support Farm Workers by buying Almaden wine & not Gallo." Little Parishes were asked to explore topics like "Liberty & Justice for All" or "How Do Men and Women View the Women's Role in Society Today?" Parish youth did volunteer work. The Social Justice Commission set out boxes in the church's vestibule to collect canned goods for local food banks.

In 1975 St. Jude's responded to the disintegrating situation in Southeast Asia by sponsoring a Vietnamese refugee family. When the family of eight arrived, Roger Frenette presented them to the congregation at Sunday Mass. "The parish responded hugely, unbelievably," Roger remembered. The parishioners helped the newly arrived family navigate their new, complicated life in the suburbs by finding them housing and jobs, giving them English lessons, and teaching them how to drive. Eventually

St. Jude sponsored two other Vietnamese families, caring for a total of twenty adults and seventeen children.

Sponsoring a Vietnamese family or collecting canned goods for a food bank was not that different from the forms of charity that Catholics practiced before the Council. What was different, however, was that many lay Catholics, priests, and nuns as well as a few bishops were turning away from their decades-long preoccupation with communism and instead looking at other forms of economic and social exploitation. Through her parish was how Margaret became aware of the exploitive conditions of migrant workers in California and the displacement of Vietnamese boat people. Visiting priests and nuns who had direct contact with the poor in Appalachia or Latin America outlined how our own government and economy was complicit in the making of poverty. Just as contemporary music and art were brought into many American parishes after the Council, so were contemporary social justice issues.

There were, nevertheless, distinct limits to how far the parishioners of St. Jude's would listen to the Church's analysis of the modern world. Bishop Evans and the Sisters of Loretto saw a connection between the military industrial complex that profited from the bombs dropped in Vietnam and the boat people who came to Denver as refugees. But Jefferson County was also the home to the Martin Marietta Corporation, which made missiles and missile components. At the other end of the county, Dow Chemical Company produced plutonium trigger components for nuclear bombs at their Rocky Flats plant. This was the same company that had manufactured the napalm and Agent Orange used to deforest the Vietnamese landscape. Employment with these companies not only secured families a middle-class lifestyle, but it also enabled Denver's Catholics to pay for their churches, which included the salaries of the outspoken Bishop Evans and the Sisters of Loretto.

St. Jude's staff introduced parishioners to causes that Catholics were fighting for around the world, but parishioners made their own decisions whether or not to support them. Just because their Church directed attention to certain issues did not mean that all agreed. Roger Frenette knew that some parishioners sincerely asked themselves, "Is this what Christ would do? Would he make bombs?" Margaret and Ken still believed that dropping the bomb on Japan saved American lives, so they had little sympathy for *Gaudium et Spes*'s conclusion that the arms race is "not a safe way to preserve a steady peace." Like many of their neighbors, they supported America's strong defense stance. Margaret did not approve of Bishop Evans's antiwar activities, but through her church she learned that reasonable Catholics—not just unwashed hippies— could be against America's involvement overseas.

Through the Social Justice Commission at St. Jude's, Margaret confronted a broader range of social justice positions. Although she chose not to boycott nonunion grapes and lettuce, she did begin a long relationship with an order of priests who worked among the poor in Appalachia. For Margaret and for many of her generation who were critical of liberal protests, the parish served as a trusted interpreter of world culture and politics.

O N A SWELTERING summer day on the last Sunday of July 1968, Margaret and her family had finished up their first year in Jefferson County and were adapting to the bleachers they had to sit on at "St. Alameda's." As Father Bill was finishing up Mass with the list of announcements, he looked out at his uncomfortable flock. "Well ... regarding ... ," and then came a pause and a smile: "Big Daddy says no!"

Nancy Frenette never forgot the moment. "The place roared and everyone clapped and laughed," she reported. Pope Paul VI had just announced that artificial birth control would still be off limits. "That was the sign of the times," Nancy observed, that so few at St. Jude's took the pontiff's conclusion seriously that day.

Catholics had not always found sex so funny. Sometime during the 1920s, Catholic priests noticed that the status of women had undergone a dramatic change and that families were getting smaller. "Birth control is now a practice with Catholics," an influential article warned, "and it is on the increase."[7]

Catholic immigrant families had always been large, but more and more Catholic households were starting to resemble those of their non-Catholic neighbors. Margaret's German-born grandmother had been one of ten children, but Margaret's mother had only two children. Social scientific descriptions of this trend are spotty, but a 1935 study of Wisconsin showed that there was a decline in the fertility rate of Catholics between 1919 and 1933 and that the Catholic birth rate was falling faster than the rate of non-Catholics.[8] Contraception was becoming more available, less shameful, and more effective.

By the late twenties, American Catholic bishops and theologians had launched a vigorous campaign to promote the Church's opposition to birth control. Priests who ran "missions," which are a type of Catholic revival meeting, were expected to ask the married who went to confession about contraception. Fictional stories about the glories of large families appeared in Catholic magazines and newspapers. Pastors delivered sermons condemning declining birth rates by euphemistically warning against modern sensuality and selfishness.

In 1930 Pope Pius XI issued an encyclical on Christian marriage that enthusiastically reaffirmed the Church's opposition to contraception. *Casti Conubii* restated a Victorian perspective on gender, one that had been under attack by modern thinkers, doctors, and couples: "For if the man is the head," it pronounced, "the woman is the heart, and as he occupies the chief place in ruling, so she may and ought to claim for herself the chief place in love." Marriage was instituted not by man but by God, and as such, the family had to reflect a higher order. The pope condemned divorce and said that "the bond of marriage cannot be loosed even on account of the sin of adultery."

The argument against contraception hinged on an argument for procreation over pleasure. "Since, therefore, the conjugal act," *Casti Conubii* explained, "is destined primarily by nature for the begetting of children, those who in exercising it deliberately frustrate its natural power and purpose sin against nature and commit a deed which is shameful and intrinsically vicious." In other words, sexual intercourse is essentially for making babies. Those who ignore its fundamental purpose and use contraceptives transgress against how life is meant to be. Their act is wicked.

Clarifications of *Casti Conubii* stated that all forms of contraception—mechanical or chemical—were intrinsically immoral. This meant that they could never be justified by any mitigating circumstances or factors. Any form of sterilization undertaken to terminate fertility was also equally wrong. The *New York Times* printed the encyclical, and it was read aloud in place of a sermon in the 450 parishes of the New York archdiocese.

Casti Conubii stimulated a Catholic rhetoric on marital morality that was only slightly less fiery than postwar anticommunism. The use of birth control would inevitably lead to materialism, divorce, and the devaluation of the family. Popular Catholic literature presented sex as a problem that was easy to handle if couples only exercised proper discipline. The general argument was that babies were a gift from God, who would never give a couple anything they could not manage. Bishops across the country worked to defeat legislation that legalized the promotion and distribution of contraceptives. In 1953 in Toledo, Catholics successfully waged a campaign to remove condom vending machines from taverns.[9] Dioceses across the country adopted premarriage forms that stated Catholic opposition to birth control and asked engaged couples to promise to lead a married life in conformity to Church teachings.

During the fifties, large families were treated as the mark of being a true Catholic. Sociologists calculated that for the marriage cohort of 1951–1955, Catholics women at the end of their childbearing years had an average of four children, with non-Catholics having three. This was a change from the decade earlier when Catholics had an average of 3.13 children and non-Catholics had 2.91—only a slight divergence between the groups. From the peak of fertility in the fifties, the numbers began to decline for all women. Still, as late as the 1961–1965 cohort, Catholics had 20 percent more babies than white non-Catholics.[10]

Although Catholics had larger families than non-Catholics, this was not necessarily always intentional. In 1951 the Church had approved the "rhythm method" of birth control for couples who had serious reasons for either spacing their children or limiting births. Sex could be confined to the periods of a woman's "natural sterility," with abstention during fertile times. Employing the rhythm method required careful monitoring of a woman's cervical mucus and checking one's anal temperature before beginning each day. Euphemisms about marital morality soon gave way to gynecological realism.

Couples who found the rhythm method either unpalatable or ineffectual looked to illicit forms of contraception. After deciding their families were large enough, women agreed to hysterectomies or sought tubal ligations. When the birth control pill was released for general use in 1960, a conversation began about its appropriateness for Catholics. One of its developers, Catholic gynecologist John Rock, argued that the Pill was similar to the approved rhythm method and so should be acceptable. Although theologians disagreed, Rock took his case to the public through his many articles published in the popular press. By the time of the Second Vatican Council, sociologists estimated that half of all Catholics practiced some type of birth control, and a third was using the Pill.[11] Catholic fertility was on the decline, and by the midseventies it equaled that of non-Catholics.

As we have seen, Pope Paul VI withdrew specific consideration of birth control from the Council's agenda just prior to the third session. Not surprisingly, conservative Council Fathers did not relish a public discussion of sexuality. The majority of Council Fathers felt that a discussion of contraceptives would distract from important deliberations on the meanings of marriage. Birth control, however, was on the minds of those Fathers who came from developing countries, where high birth rates were not being matched by increased economic production. The United Nations and other global governmental agencies promoted birth control as an alternative to starvation and death. Fertility had become a social justice concern and would somehow have to be addressed.

During the Council, Pope Paul VI expanded an earlier commission set up to examine the question of birth control. American Catholics who hoped that the Church would approve contraceptives were pleased to see that the Birth Control Commission included not only bishops and theologians but sociologists, gynecologists, demographers, economists, members of government agencies, and even married couples. Americans Patty and Pat Crowley had brought to the Commission their polling of members of the Christian Family Movement. They had asked their members to write letters reflecting on their experience with the rhythm method. The vast majority who responded told tales of frustration and disillusionment. Patty Crowley was convinced that her articulation of their experiences had hit a chord with the celibate members of the Commission.

Indeed, in 1966 the New York Times reported that trustworthy sources in Rome let it be known that "the majority of the theologians on the advisory commission believe there is no insuperable theological barrier against the Church changing its present position, which holds that periodic abstinence (the rhythm method) is the only moral means open to Roman Catholic families who wish to limit the number of their children." A year later in 1967, the final report was finished. It soon became public that the majority of the Birth Control Commission had concluded that the Church *could* change its teachings on birth control while maintaining the necessity for marital love and responsible parenthood.[12] Only four of the Commission's fifty-five members had rejected the final report.

Those who hoped for change would be disappointed. In issuing *Humanae Vitae* in July of 1968, Pope Paul VI went against the recommendation of his Birth Control Commission. The prohibition of contraception continued. The pope justified his conclusion by observing in *Humanae Vitae* that both the moral and natural order was created by God, including the biology of men and women. Human beings do not have "unlimited dominion" over their bodies or their sexual faculties. If one frustrates the natural law of the body as God designed it, then one "contradicts the will of the Author of life." God intended for sexual organs to be, by their very nature, focused on the generation of life. Likewise, marital love is a divine gift. If one denies it by depriving the marriage act of its reproductive role, then one is in opposition to the plan of God. *Humanae Vitae* insists that "each and every marital act must of necessity retain its intrinsic relationship to the procreation of human life."

Humanae Vitae, however, recognizes that there are natural periods of time when a woman cannot become pregnant. In addition, it acknowledges that "responsible parenthood" might require the limiting of family size. Consequently, "the Church teaches that married people may then take advantage of the natural cycles immanent in the reproductive system and engage in marital intercourse only during those times that are infertile, thus controlling birth in a way which does not in the least offend the moral principles." This awareness of the natural order of sexuality and the "ordering of births" will demand reason and mastery as well as self-denial. Rather than hindering love, however, such "shining witness to the chastity of husband and wife" will enrich the couple spiritually, thus bringing the family "abundant fruits of tranquility and peace." Thoughtfulness and consideration will expand while "inordinate self-love" will contract.

The reception of such insights was not positive. When, in 1968, the Pope issued *Humanae Vitae* and summaries of its negative position on contraceptives appeared in the newspapers, Margaret remembers thinking, "We can't accept that." Margaret had had serious problems with childbearing, and now at the age of forty-two, birth control was no longer a personal issue. Her issues with the decision were not personal;

instead, what was at stake for her was the credibility of her Church to speak intelligently about human sexuality and marriage.

The pope's encyclical relied on an understanding of natural law that made little sense to her or to many other Catholics. Although *Humanae Vitae* took a holistic and spiritual approach to reproduction and eliminated the Victorian sex roles found in *Casti Conubii*, Margaret and many Americans understood it simply as a statement that said "no." Whatever contribution *Humanae Vitae* might have made to the discussion of family life was lost because Margaret concluded that the pope had refused to respect the decisions of thoughtful Catholic couples. Paul VI had ignored the counsel of a commission that he himself had appointed. With his promulgation of *Humanae Vitae*, Pope Paul VI became the "birth control pope" for Margaret. "Nobody liked Paul VI," she reflected on the era. "John XXIII was the pope of the Second Vatican Council."

Because a copy of *Humanae Vitae* had been leaked to a set of American theologians at Catholic University before its official announcement, pro–birth control reformers had an immediate and succinct response to the papal decision. Within days, eighty-seven U.S. theologians concluded that Paul's encyclical was not infallible and that Catholics could dissent from it if they had good reasons. Couples should decide for themselves to use birth control if it was "necessary to preserve and foster the values and sacredness of their marriage."[13]

Soon after, eighty-five additional theologians joined the original group and signed a fuller statement. They acknowledged the teaching role of the Church (as the "magisterium") but also insisted that it was their duty as theologians to reflect and evaluate papal statements. From the perspective of theologians like Charles Curran, who had signed the statement, *Humanae Vitae* assumed an ahistorical approach in its evaluation of contraception. Curran argued that because other Church positions, such as supporting slavery and condemning lending money for interest, had been judged erroneous, the changing historical context might also merit a new response to birth control.[14] Critics also hoped that the pope would take into consideration evolving notions of individuality and freedom. In the Declaration on Religious Freedom (*Dignitatis Humanae Personae*), the Council Fathers had agreed that the conscience cannot be forced to believe the truth. Freedom of religion, once a condemned value, was now shown to be grounded in the dignity of every human person.

This was not to say, however, that theologians dissenting from the claims of *Humanae Vitae* assumed that all Church pronouncements should be decided by individuals. Curran explained that individuals were often wrong, so their conscience could not be the final judge. *Humanae Vitae* needed to be evaluated on the ultimate moral criterion of truth. That truth was to be discovered by examining the insights of the whole People of God—from the scientist to the theologian to the person in the pew.

Theologians also argued that *Humanae Vitae* ignored modern notions of biology and, in fact, focused too exclusively on the reproductive role of the sexual act. Rather than imagining the benefits that regulating world population might bring, *Humanae Vitae* reintroduced the fear of unbridled sexual expression that would result in a loss of respect for women. Like much of Catholic theological writing prior to the Second Vatican Council, the encyclical assumed the worst about human nature. *Humanae Vitae* fell back on theological reflections—like natural law— that made little sense in the modern world. Critics could not see how the encyclical addressed the real lives of men and women.

Dissenting theologians in the United States looked to liberal European bishops to support their arguments. In the Netherlands, Dutch bishops sent out a letter to all parish priests explaining that the pope's encyclical was not infallible and that although such an authoritative pronouncement must be taken seriously, it should be used along with other considerations by couples. The Dutch bishops seemed particularly piqued at the fact that the report of the Birth Control Commission held so little influence on the pope.

This interpretation of the encyclical did not hold sway everywhere, however. For the most part, bishops in the United States did not follow the path set by their liberal colleagues in the Netherlands. The harshest critic of dissent was Cardinal Patrick O'Boyle, head of the Archdiocese of Washington, D.C. Even before *Humanae Vitae* had been published, Boyle sent a letter to his priests telling them not to vacillate from the Church's position on contraceptives. In response, forty-two of the clergy signed an open letter in defiance: "Many of your priests cannot in conscience follow this directive because it gives no room for either probable opinion regarding the practice of contraception or the right of conscience so clearly enunciated in the documents of Vatican II."[15] After the encyclical was published, the cardinal called on all his priests to unequivocally follow the Church's teachings. This time, fifty-two Washington priests signed a "statement of conscience" supporting the position of the dissenting theologians.

Liberal Catholics in Washington, D.C. were caught off guard by the response of their cardinal. Over the years, Patrick O'Boyle had earned a reputation as a progressive on social justice issues. In 1950 he had desegregated the archdiocesan parochial schools, long before Washington public schools were debating the possibility. When Martin Luther King Jr. brought thousands of poor black people to the Lincoln Memorial for a March on Washington for Jobs and Freedom, O'Boyle delivered the invocation immediately before Marian Anderson sang "The Star-Spangled Banner."

But Cardinal O'Boyle's support of such protests did not extend to Catholics who challenged the Church's teachings. In response to the Catholic University theologians' statement that there was a "right to dissent" from authoritative, nonfallible teachings, O'Boyle pointed out that the theologians offered "no evidence that the Catholic Church ever tolerated dissent of the sort that they are carrying out and even instigating."[16] American bishops had all agreed that racial discrimination was wrong; they just differed on what should be done to end those immoral practices. Supporting Martin Luther King Jr.'s protests could be understood as paralleling the Church's condemnation of racial prejudice; however, supporting priests who refused to acknowledge the wisdom of *Humanae Vitae* could not be justified.

A month after *Humanae Vitae* was issued, Cardinal O'Boyle had a statement read from every pulpit in his archdiocese that commanded Catholics to follow the restrictions against artificial birth control. When the cardinal read his letter from his pulpit at St. Matthew's Cathedral, two hundred Catholics stood up and walked out. Their act of defiance was unprecedented in Washington, D.C. history and "perhaps in the world," according to the *New York Times*.[17] Equally impressive was the gesture of the remaining twelve hundred individuals who stood up and applauded the cardinal for a full minute. The cardinal went on to call into his office each dissenting priest and individually question him about his position on the encyclical. Those who did not recant were suspended from preaching, teaching, and hearing confessions. Some were removed from their parishes and others had their salaries canceled.

Catholics have always disagreed with their clergy and their Church. At times they have been severely punished for their dissent, as when the bishop of Erie placed an interdict on St. Joseph's parish because parishioners refused to support a diocesan cemetery. In individual cases of disagreement with a Church law, a dispensation could ease the difference between the ideal and the reality. Both Margaret and her mother received dispensations to marry Protestants. In postwar America, Catholics ignored their priests and watched movies that were condemned, used condoms to avoid pregnancy, and refused to desegregate their neighborhoods. Whenever an organization has a system of rules, people develop ways to get around them.

What was different in 1968 was that Catholics were no longer satisfied with quietly circumventing the rules. Educated lay Catholics voiced their criticism in a multitude of venues. Catholics who disagreed with *Humanae Vitae* brought their dissent into the public by talking to *Time* and *Newsweek* reporters. Theologians published their positive perspectives on contraceptives, and priests signed statements that urged Catholics to follow their own consciences in the matter of birth control. Although Cardinal O'Boyle's response was unique in its ferocity, other priests found that they could support without retribution their parishioners who decided to go against *Humanae Vitae*. Those who rejected the encyclical decided they wanted to stay Catholic. The Vatican did not have a monopoly on God.

The humorous announcement by Father Bill and the spontaneous response by the parishioners at St. Jude's was eventually transformed into a more thoughtful reflection on the issue of contraceptives. At a 1977 open forum designed to address questions that people had about Catholicism, two of St. Jude's priests discussed birth control and sexual relations. Father Slattery cited a theological principle that "conscience is the proximate norm of the law and so one should ask, What does *my* conscience say regarding this rule? The Church encourages individuals to make responsible decisions, decisions they are willing to submit to God's judgment." During the decade after *Humanae Vitae*, priests felt comfortable laying the decision about birth control at the feet of individual Catholics. Father John Burton stated the principle more forcefully: "It is the Christian's moral obligation to interpret every law."

Consequently, the rejection of artificial birth control by Pope Paul VI forced married Catholics to evaluate the authority of the pope in defining behaviors that were not religious *per se*. Parishioner Bill Campbell speculated that the controversy over *Humanae Vitae* "might have been the beginning of people forming their own conscience." Catholics who had experienced the spirit of Vatican II did not feel like they were committing a sin by using contraception. Using birth control was one of many ways that Catholics were practicing spiritual and social empowerment.

Although Margaret and her friends were shy about discussing sexual matters, they were not insecure about their importance within "the Body of Christ." Vatican II had given them not only a new set of responsibilities within the parish, but it also gave them the language with which to assert their rights as a People of God. As suburban mothers, Margaret and her friends did not approve of the sexual revolution spinning around them, but they also did not think that a celibate male clergy should be defining when they could have sex. Thoughtful Catholics were discussing, thinking, and even praying over the matter of birth control. They then made their *own* decision.

O N MARCH 16, 1976, a small notice appeared in the *Rocky Mountain News*, one of Denver's two newspapers: "Father William Sievers resigned from the church and is leaving the priesthood, it was announced at Mass Sunday." The article briefly noted that his resignation was for personal reasons.

Two days earlier, Father John F. X. Burton had faced the congregation at St. Jude's and announced with no elaboration that Father Bill had left and would not be coming back. Until a new pastor could be appointed, he would remain in charge of the church. Nothing more was said from the pulpit about the departure—ever.

The parishioners were dumbstruck. Many of them had counted their pastor as a personal friend. They had no inkling that he was unhappy with his vocation. They discussed the situation with the other priests at St. Jude, but no one had any insights into why Father Sievers had quit.

William Sievers had been the pastor of St. Jude's for almost ten years and had strongly shaped the parish. Although parishioners did not know any of the details about why he decided to leave the priesthood, they did know that if priests could disappear so easily, both their parish and the larger Church were entering into a new era.

Reflecting on his resignation over thirty years later, Bill Sievers continued to hold his reasons close to his heart. "I burned out," he explained. "I got drinking, becoming an alcoholic. Got fooling around. So I left the ministry." The pressures of the parish were great and the expectations were high. There were seven thousand people at St. Jude's. "How do you minister to all those people?" Bill sighed. "One weekend I had twelve weddings. You need lots of services to handle them, so we'd have ten or eleven Masses on the holidays. How do you get to know all those people? I don't consider handing out Communion to people I didn't know to be a particularly meaningful ministry." When pushed to clarify those feelings of long ago, Bill answered with another, larger question: Do we ever know the reasons for why we do what we do?

Eventually Bill Sievers married and lived with his wife for twenty years before she died. He worked for nonprofit agencies, and when he got too sick to live by himself, he moved into the senior center on whose governing board he had served. Finances are increasingly an issue because former priests cannot claim a retirement from their dioceses or religious orders. Although Bill no longer worked as a priest, he continued to link his spiritual life to Catholicism. "I still say my priest's Office every day," he recounted. His home has statues of Mary and the saints. Attending Mass is still meaningful, but so are the services that his Protestant minister friends conduct at the senior center.

Although the parishioners at St. Jude's were taken off guard by the departure of their pastor, the departure of priests from parishes was in itself no longer a surprise to anyone. The year Bill Sievers left, an estimated 258 diocesan priests resigned their positions. [18] This number was significantly lower than the peak year of 1969, when 750 priests had left. *Time* magazine signaled the alarm with a 1970 cover story: "The Catholic Exodus: Why Nuns and Priests Are Leaving." During a short span of three years, from 1966 to 1969, the number of men who left the priesthood increased almost fourfold. Furthermore, young men were not entering the seminary and becoming ordained. The peak year for American ordinations was

1967, when 1,062 men became priests. By 1976 that number had declined to 700.

Priestly resignations and a declining number of seminarians were all the more frightening because of the increasing ratio of people to priests. During the Depression years, Catholic growth was only 6 percent, but the number of clergy grew by 26 percent. Consequently, by 1942 there was a reasonable ratio of one priest per 617 Catholics. The Baby Boom of the fifties and the expansion of immigration in the midsixties increased the Catholic population, but it did so without a concomitant rise in the number of men entering the priesthood. By 1975 for every priest there were 1,100 Catholics. If we count only diocesan priests (the ones most likely to be working in parishes), the ratio increases to 1 to 1,819.[19]

This worsening Catholic exodus prompted the first large-scale survey of the state of American priesthood. In 1967 the Catholic Conference of Bishops, taking its cue from the Second Vatican Council's encouragement of modern scholarship, commissioned a group of scholar-priests to undertake studies on various aspects of the priesthood. The initial results were presented at the spring 1971 meeting of the nation's bishops. Historical, sociological, and psychological reports described the current state of the priestly life, and a theological study was intended to provide a set of religious ideas useful in evaluating the other reports. The sociological report alone would survey five thousand active priests, one thousand men who had left the active ministry, and 250 bishops.

The bishops were not pleased with the results of their $500,000 study. Jesuit Carl Armbruster, who headed the group of priests working on the theological report, stressed the importance of the priest's service role, "who like Christ responds to the needs of men," and criticized the historical significance given to the priest's cultic powers to conduct the sacraments.[20] The theological report concluded that no scriptural or dogmatic grounds existed for forbidding either a married priesthood or the ordination of women. At a later meeting in 1972, the American bishops decided to forego publishing the theological study.

The historical, sociological, and psychological studies were eventually published, although not without igniting controversy of their own. Because they attempted to reflect existing realities through interviews and questionnaires rather than to discover the true meaning of priesthood through theological reflection, it was more difficult for the bishops

to quarrel with the studies' results. The social scientific reports in particular revealed that serious internal problems motivated priestly resignation. Sociologist-priest Andrew Greeley concluded that many priests
were lonely and isolated. They were frustrated with their superiors and
angered by the ways the Church exercised authority. Sixty percent rejected the artificial birth control prohibition. Looking for friendship, they
formed relationships with women that often led them to rethink their
vows of celibacy. Of the men he studied, 56 percent believed that priests
should be free to marry.[21] Pope Paul VI's encyclical *Sacerdotalis Caeliba-
tus* (1967), which upheld clerical celibacy as a "brilliant jewel," had not
convinced American priests otherwise.

A study conducted by a Georgetown University social research group
in 1970 concurred with Greeley.[22] Although the majority of priests were
staying in the priesthood, many of those were unhappy and in conflict.
Priests told interviewers that they sensed little true affection from their
fellow priests, parishioners, or superiors. Even with the changes adopted
after Vatican II, priests felt a lack of independence. They believed their
achievements were not recognized.

After the Council, priests were continually being asked to alter both
their leadership styles and their ritual activities without guidance from
their bishops. Because few men were ever fired from the priesthood, the
indulgence of dysfunctional, malcontent, and lazy priests lowered the
morale of competent clergy. Men tended to enter the seminary early,
some even before high school. They had never honestly evaluated what a
lifetime of celibacy would entail. Sociologists warned of a serious crisis of
personal and religious identity.

Throughout the country, priests also faced a major disconnect between the values they wanted to practice in their parish and those that
were upheld by their clerical superiors. Priests like Bill Sievers took seriously the biblical call to Christian community. Sievers in particular
wanted to cultivate a religious environment of mutual care and spiritual
depth. Reform-oriented priests felt that collegiality and equality should
be the basis of religious life. However, the reality was that the ideals of
openness, charity, and connectedness they sought to practice in their
parishes were frequently met with secrecy, authority, and distance at
higher Church levels. The institutional Church—in the diocesan
chancery office or in Rome—was a complex, impersonal system that was

structured around tradition, loyalty, and obedience. Many priests felt that they were caught between the ideals of the spirit of Vatican II and the harsh realities of the Vatican itself.

Although Bill Sievers would never point a finger at his own parishioners, they also contributed to the burn-out that he experienced. After the Council, laymen and -women not only voiced their opinions to their clergy but also expected the clergy to respond to their needs. Priests should preach better sermons and organize more meaningful associations. With the benefit of professional business managers, directors of liturgy, and youth ministers, the laity concluded that their priests should now have the time to produce uplifting religious services and counseling sessions. Men less self-confident than Bill Sievers might have felt that demanding lay leaders diminished their authority as priests. Even if a priest was not threatened by the women and men running his parish, the sheer number of people to organize was daunting.

Catholic priests were not the only clergy who were deserting their congregations. Protestant ministers and Jewish rabbis were also finding new jobs, although not at the same rate as their celibate brothers. During the sixties and seventies, religion—in the same way as the government, the military, industry, and the university—was presented as a part of "the system" that beat down creativity and innovation. The system was considered to be a monolith that had its own life, which was unchangeable by any mere individual. True reform of society could come only from outside the system. Clergy were not immune to skepticism about their own system. Many left because they believed that religion merely preserved a false, totalizing truth. "Organized religion," explained one former rabbi, "kills the enthusiasm of religion."[23] Tired of attending to the everyday worries of his congregants, he left to take an organizing job to improve race relations.

In addition, the popular media encouraged Americans to get real and find their authentic selves. Like their secular male counterparts, priests trained in the forties and fifties had learned how to cultivate a calm, detached, controlled demeanor. The culture of the sixties, however, asked men to share their feelings and deal with conflict out in the open. The silent, stoic, self-sacrificing male of the fifties, who worked two jobs so his family could afford the house in the suburbs, was no longer the model of masculinity. American popular culture valorized the individualist who "tuned in, turned on, and dropped out." Healthy individuals were honest with themselves and expressed even disruptive feelings. Sexual expression was to be relished rather than repressed. At the very least, men were supposed to reflect seriously on the lives they were leading. Men and women were both expected to ask themselves: "Do I really want to do this?"

CLERGY WERE NOT the only ones asking themselves, "Do I want to do this?" Before World War II, on any given week, only one third of the adult population had attended a religious service.[24] Then, during the fifties, the numbers went up. Participating in religion became a mark of being a good American, a strong parent, and a contributing citizen. In 1955 and 1958, almost half of all American adults told pollsters that they went to either a church or synagogue in the past week. A year later in 1959, the numbers began to decline. People were deciding not to go to church. By 1968 slightly more than a third (38 percent) of all Protestants claimed they attended church that week. For all the same reasons that people were skeptical of the system, they became critical of their religions.

Catholics had always gone to church more frequently than Protestants or Jews, but now their numbers were slipping. In the peak year of 1958, a Gallup Poll reported that 74 percent of all Catholics had attended Mass within the week. Each subsequent year, however, Catholics went to church less often.

Vatican II did not cause the decline in Mass attendance, but it also did not stop it. Just before the Council began in 1961, the number had fallen to 71 percent. In 1966, long before the reforms were widespread, pollsters reported a decline to 68 percent. Between 1958 and 1969, Catholics stopped going to church at a rate twice that of Protestants. During that decade of uneven acceptance of Catholic reform, Mass attendance had fallen to 55 percent. When the Vatican II era ended with the death of Pope Paul VI in 1978, the percentage of people who attended weekly Mass had declined to slightly over half (52 percent) of those who self-identified as Catholic.

Sociologist Father Andrew Greeley concluded, after his studies of the seventies, that the decline in Mass attendance was primarily due to the disastrous response to *Humanae Vitae*.[25] Catholics, he argued, fully approved of the Council's reforms. However, their disappointment with the way that birth control had been handled was what motivated many of them to stop going to Mass—or, more precisely, to go to Mass less frequently. More than a decade after the encyclical in the eighties, Greeley cited polls that showed that declining church attendance had stopped. Weekly attendance at Mass was holding steady at about 50 percent of the Catholic population. Following his earlier appraisal, Greeley then concluded that once those frustrated with a conservative Vatican response to sexuality left, the remainder of Catholics continued to find weekly church attendance meaningful.

Deciding to not go to Mass, however, was a much more complicated decision. By the early seventies, most of the women of Margaret's generation were beyond worrying about whether or not to use birth control. They were, however, making the decision to stop going to church for other reasons. In Toledo, Margaret's coworker Harriet had divorced after her marriage had fallen apart. A civil divorce, however, did not alter Harriet's married status in the Church's eyes. Every time she had sex with her new husband, she was sinning and thus was not in the proper state to receive the Eucharist.

In 1977 Pope Paul VI had ended automatic excommunication for the divorced and remarried, but Catholics who remarried were still denied the Eucharist. Increasingly, Catholics were securing annulments, but Harriet thought that annulments were too often used simply as a means to move on to a new relationship. The Church was being hypocritical about divorce. Harriet decided there was no room for her in such a religion. The newly married couple joined the United Methodist Church.

In California, Margaret's friend Sue had also stopped going to Mass. Sue had been a faithful participant at the neighborhood rosary circle and had been active in the Church since she was a small child in Boston. But not long after she became a grandmother, her grandson became quite sick and eventually died. During his illness, Sue felt that the nuns and priests who should have been caring for the child abandoned him. She saw no evidence of Christian charity in their behavior toward the grieving family. God continued to be there for her, but Catholic leaders had failed her. There was no more reason to go to church.

MARGARET HEARD ABOUT Father Bill's departure from her friends who still resided in Colorado. Three years earlier, in 1973, she and her family had moved to Morgantown, West Virginia. In 1969 a new federal prison had been opened there for young offenders, and for the first time in the nation's history, it was named after a person: Robert J. Kennedy. Ken was asked to head an institution named after the attorney general who had stimulated federal prison reform and inspired Ken's own governmental service. As always, it was difficult for Margaret to leave, but she knew that her husband had struggled to stay in Colorado for six years. Now he was being promoted to warden, so it was time to pack once again.

Harriet and Sue had faced serious challenges in their lives that were not eased by their participation in a parish community. Margaret, however, was among the half of all Catholics who continued to feel that the Mass, the sacraments, and the clergy enriched her life. On a social level, the parish provided a ready-made community for a family that moved back and forth across the United States. St. Jude's parish had functioned to interpret the changes of the sixties in ways that made sense to this couple from the Greatest Generation. The Second Vatican Council had mediated intense cultural change, thereby allowing Margaret to slowly adapt to a more open, informal, and skeptical America. The English Mass, with its priest who faced the people, brought her closer to the mystery of her faith. Standing near the altar and reading from the Bible helped Margaret understand the connection of the Catholic sacraments to the biblical message. Many people who Margaret respected had decided to alter their relationship with Catholicism, but she did not. For her entire life, her parishes had been slowly changing. Catholicism paralleled and sustained her own growth as a woman and as a religious person.

FIVE YEARS AFTER Margaret and Ken arrived in West Virginia, the era of the Second Vatican Council came to an end. On August 6, 1978, Pope Paul VI died at the age of eighty-one. Although he had not opened the Council, he had supported its continuance through three sessions. Unlike the charismatic Pope John XXIII, he had the daunting task of implementing the documents—compromises often written in a poetical language. The Council Fathers had returned home, but the pope remained with a powerful, bureaucratic Curia that was far less enthusiastic about enacting change. The constitutions, declarations, and decrees of the Council had to be put into action by the very people who consistently resisted renewal.

Paul started a reform of the Curia in 1967—a daunting task that would be met with only partial success.

The acceptance of the truly global nature of Catholicism was solidified through the pope's leadership. The voices of African, Latin American, and Asian Catholics who were first heard at the Council continued to be heard by the Vatican. Through his travels to the Middle East, India, Colombia, the Philippines, Australia, and Africa, Paul made it clear that the future of Catholicism lay outside the traditional West. Global social justice included warmer relations between religions, and the pope made both symbolic and practical gestures toward Orthodox Christians and Anglicans. Following the progressives of the Council, Paul stressed what religions shared in common rather than what divided them.

Under the leadership of Pope Paul VI, the Eucharistic celebration did ultimately become the central focus of parish life. Participation in the sacraments drew parishioners closer to the biblical text. Margaret was among the majority of American Catholics who deeply appreciated making the Mass more understandable and less intimidating. For those Catholics who continued to come to Mass, more and more took Communion. The very intensity that Catholics felt in their connection to God permitted many of them to reject some of the pope's pronouncements while remaining strong in their faith. For Margaret, the Second Vatican Council had succeeded in deepening her religious life while providing her the means to experience the cultural changes of the era. The flow of energy coming from the Council had been positive and invigorating.

In the later years of his life, Pope Paul VI had questioned whether opening the windows during the Council era had let in an invigorating breeze or a destructive wind. His anxiety over the great cultural changes that were sweeping the globe made him more open to the conservative voices in the Vatican. In 1976 the pope turned his back on Annibale Bugnini, the powerful curial cardinal who had supported liturgical reform and served as secretary of the Congregation for Divine Worship, by appointing him papal nuncio to Iran. Stronger centralization of authority in Rome with less shared responsibility by the world's bishops challenged the Council's value of collegiality. Conservative claims that empowering the laity had merely led to frivolous rituals and priests who catered to the whims of their parishioners were being accorded more respect and attention. A reform of the reform became inevitable.

chapter eight

LEGACIES

Margaret moves slowly these days. She's had heart bypass surgery and a hip replacement. Still, each Sunday she puts on one of her best dresses and makes sure that Ken doesn't wear the pair of pants with the stain on them. The drive to Blessed Trinity Church is not very long, but they do have to hurry: If they are running late, they might not get one of the handicap parking spots. Ken drops Margaret at the foot of the stairs that lead up to the porch of the church. By the time he parks the car and gets to her, she is almost to the opened door. Taking her arm, the couple says hello to Father Pat Sheedy, who greets his congregation as they arrive for eleven o'clock Mass. A large banner over the entrance proclaims, "Welcome Home."

Much has changed since the end of the Vatican II era in 1978. The collapse of communism, the rise of economic globalization, and the prominence of religious fundamentalisms have altered the flow of political power. A charismatic Polish pope with a traditional outlook on Catholicism extended an open hand toward conservative movements within the Church. Throughout the Catholic world, a sex abuse crisis not only exposed the crimes of individual priests, but it also challenged the integrity of Church authorities at the highest levels. Bishops closed parishes and schools as populations shifted, urban churches became too expensive to maintain, and the number of clergy and sisters continued to dwindle. Disgusted with the un-Christian behaviors of the world and the hierarchy, Catholics took solace in their parishes.

After leaving Colorado in 1973, over the next eight years Ken was appointed as warden at prisons in West Virginia, California, and Texas. Then, in 1981, at the age of fifty-seven, he retired. In the federal government, working in a prison is considered hazardous duty and therefore carries a mandatory retirement age. Having moved twelve times since leaving Erie, where the couple would finally settle was unclear. They decided on Ocala, a small city in central Florida. Friends from the Bureau of Prisons had lured them there with reports of year-round golf and quiet living.

Although the town of Ocala was established in 1846, it remained a frontier outpost until the 1890s, when phosphate, a mineral used for making fertilizers, was discovered nearby. The phosphate produced luscious grass that, combined with the weather, made the area perfect for raising horses. Thoroughbred racehorse farms soon dotted the countryside. The horse farms eventually drew Spanish-speaking immigrants who were willing to muck out the stables. By 1983, when Margaret and Ken moved into their newly built ranch-style home, Ocala had a population of 38,636.[1]

After a life of constant movement, Margaret has now lived in Florida longer than any other state—considerably longer than she lived in her birth state of Pennsylvania. She and Ken have watched as horse breeders sold their farms to housing speculators, and shopping centers with names like Paddock Mall took the place of the open fields. Light industry developed in Marion County, and the area became a regional medical center. By 2008 Ocala's population had grown to 53,587.

Between 2000 and 2007, Marion County experienced a 25 percent growth spurt. Before the 2008 recession and the implosion of Florida's housing market, demographers were predicting that the state's population would almost double between 2000 and 2030.[2] Ken cusses out the retired "snowbirds" who clog the streets during the winter months, but 75 percent of the county's residents are under sixty-five. Margaret and Ken ended up retiring in a town that came to resemble their former residences in Monterey Park and Jefferson County: an expanding residential area with the character of a suburb.

Like the county itself, Blessed Trinity parish has steadily grown since its founding in 1892. It has become a diverse religious community composed of Filipina nurses who work in the city's hospitals, Mexican grooms who care for the county's thoroughbreds, retired teachers from Michigan on tight budgets, and teenagers who have never been outside of Florida.

The parish began with a wooden-frame church that was replaced in 1922 with a brick one. At that point only 135 Catholics lived in the Protestant town so the 350-seat church seemed spacious. By the sixties, however, 900 families were members. The diocese purchased seventeen acres of land a few miles from downtown, and the fundraising for a larger facility began. In 1961 Blessed Trinity parishioners dedicated a new school building and convent for the sisters who would teach there. As with Margaret's parish in Toledo, a temporary church that seated 700 was assembled on the top floor of the school. During the week, 200 pupils ate in the cafeteria at the rear of the church.

From the sixties through the eighties, when Catholics across the nation were skipping Mass on Sunday or not going to church at all, Blessed Trinity was experiencing unprecedented growth. Catholic retirees from the Frostbelt were moving south, and Catholic immigrants from around the globe came to central Florida for jobs and affordable housing. Between 1971 and 1979, weekly attendance at Mass doubled. By 1974 two thousand parishioners were attending Mass each Sunday at Blessed Trinity, and many of them had to stand during the service. Ten years after the temporary church was dedicated, parishioners had to take action to cope with the overcrowding. They voted to build a new church.

The pastor at that time, Father Francis X. J. Smith, was particularly in tune with the *aggiornamento* of Vatican II. He had served as diocesan director of the liturgical commission that implemented the New Order of the Mass. A new church would enable him to accommodate his growing parish while physically representing the values of the Council. Father Smith leaned toward a modernist-style church that concentrated attention on the Mass. Blessed Trinity's building committee and parish council eventually approved designs by parishioner and architect, Berry Walker. A Vatican II–style church was dedicated on April 21, 1974.

At its dedication, Blessed Trinity was a poster child of modernist Catholicism: abstraction, simplicity, emptiness, and informality encouraged all to focus on the Mass and the assembled congregation. As with St. Jude's Church in Colorado, the new Blessed Trinity Church was built in a fan shape with the pews arranged in a semicircle so all worshippers could see each other. Four narrow strips of stained-glass windows with abstract symbols representing the Scriptures divided a vast expanse of white wall. Bright orange carpet drew the congregation's attention to a slightly raised, spacious altar area. Rather than having any fixed artwork behind the altar, a projector was set up to show slides of religious paintings during Mass to illustrate the theme of the day's liturgy.

By the time Margaret and Ken arrived in Florida, Blessed Trinity was already losing its look of Vatican II modernism. Over the course of a decade, priests and parishioners had slowly filled the sanctuary with an array of objects and images. During the Christmas and Easter seasons, parishioners softened the stark sanctuary by decorating it with wreaths, plants, banners, and bowers of greenery. A liturgical committee brought in a small crucifix and a statue of Mary. The music minister placed a piano and set of pews for the choir up toward the altar.

Just like a home that gets increasingly cluttered over the years, Blessed Trinity's emptiness slowly disappeared. The parishioners grew tired of Vatican II–era modernism. Notes from a 1983 staff meeting critically observed that "Everything looks like boxes and the stone is too heavy." So new art was commissioned. A bronze bas-relief of a Risen Christ covered the screen where art slides were once shown. A baptismal font that looked not unlike a marble backyard hot tub was purchased and a mosaic of the Trinity symbol was mounted near it. Stands for candles and for the Bible were placed near the altar. The orange carpet was torn out and a new one of unremarkable beige installed. Because the parish was still rapidly expanding, an upper balcony was added to expand the church's seating capacity.

Obviously, no one at Trinity particularly liked the Vatican II aesthetic of simplicity nor Father Smith's fondness for late-sixties modernism. Still, it was the very cluttering of the altar area over thirty years that began to cause problems for something that everyone *did* like about the Vatican II era: the active participation of parishioners in church rituals.

Then, the arrival of a new pastor stimulated a rethinking of the design of the sanctuary. In 1988 Father Patrick Sheedy became head of Blessed Trinity. Like Father Smith, he was fully committed to Vatican II's vision of a people-led Church. He routinely asked extended families who gathered for Baptisms and weddings to join the priest close to the altar. At the Easter Vigil, sometimes as many as thirty-five new converts stood in the sanctuary to be formally welcomed into the Church. Families and special groups brought the bread and wine to the altar during Offertory processions. Each Sunday, as many as twelve Eucharistic ministers offered the Eucharist in its forms of bread and wine to hundreds of parishioners.

By the new millennia, Blessed Trinity was again bursting at the seams. The central Florida parish was a "megachurch," made up of over 3,500 families. Since the church's dedication in 1974, it had modified its space to adjust to the real liturgical and aesthetic needs of the People of God. However, when the sanctuary space filled up, physically accommodating those very people was difficult. Father Pat and the parish council decided that the sanctuary area needed to be enlarged.

Many American parishes that emptied their churches during the sixties and seventies have undertaken renovations that reintroduce crucifixes, statues, ranks of candles, Stations of the Cross, small chapels, and pipe organs. Building committees composed of parishioners have opted for church designs that include distinct Catholic images while still creating a warm and inviting atmosphere. Across the country, parishes have modified the Second Vatican Council's preference for noble simplicity with a post-Council fondness for traditional Catholic symbols.

Now when Margaret and Ken slip into one of the back pews at Blessed Trinity for Sunday Mass, they experience a "post-Vatican II" church. A renovation in 2005 made precious space available in the sanctuary while erasing the hard edges of Vatican II modernism. The new visual centerpiece was a dramatic life-size crucifix hanging behind the altar in a blue-painted niche that is stenciled with gold relief. Columns and arches in dark wood draw attention to the white body on the cross. The Risen Christ bronze has been moved from the center and placed near a new baptistery, where running water flows from a small basin for babies into a larger one that can be entered for immersion Baptisms. On each side of the sanctuary are two ranks of pipes for the new organ and colorful statues of the Virgin Mary and St. Patrick. Along the walls of the church are the fourteen Stations of the Cross with descriptive plaques. The days of folk masses, vacant white walls, and orange carpeting are over at Blessed Trinity.

Blessed Trinity's classical columns were suggested by one parishioner and another painted the Byzantine-styled icons that lead up to the balcony. Thomas Glisson, a former parishioner who works in New York City as a liturgical artist and who had designed the Risen Christ bas relief, made the new crucifix. At St. Jude's parish in Colorado, a recent renovation also placed a life-sized crucifix behind the altar. The two statues of St. Joseph and the Virgin Mary, which previously were near the pews and faced the altar along with the congregation, have been moved to the front of the church. The statues now face the people.

THERE WERE A NUMBER of reasons for reintroducing images back into parish churches. For many Catholics, sparsely decorated churches never seemed very Catholic in the first place. They continued to have lively devotions to the saints in their homes, say the rosary before going to bed, and criticize the perceived "wreck-o-vation" of Catholic spaces. For others, especially those born after the Council, religious identity in the modern world was tightly bound to a distinctive set of practices and objects: Evangelicals dressed in "witness T-shirts," Mormons bought CTR rings, and Jews wore yarmulkes. Catholics knew that they had at least as many artifacts to identify themselves as other religious groups, but somehow it all had vanished. As the country became more institutionally religious in the eighties, young Catholics became receptive to moral and doctrinal certainty and to their religious tradition's cultural heritage. They also wanted to *see* their faith just as early generations of Catholics had.

At the same time, parish pastors became more sensitive to the voices of their own congregations—a stance encouraged by the Council. Many priests agreed with Father Sheedy and supported the liturgical, theological, and social changes brought about by Vatican II, though they had little taste for Catholic asceticism. The spirit of Vatican II had convinced many priests that church design and even rituals could reflect the changing taste and style of the people. Americans in general were more conservative, so parishes had to adapt. As churches aged and required renovations or even new structures, empty spaces were filled.

On a more academic level, theologians, liturgists, and younger Catholic thinkers had been reconsidering the role of ritual, symbol, and design in parish life. Although they acknowledged the importance of the new theology that was so influential in revitalizing worship, they argued that the theologians of the sixties had missed important aspects of religious life. Influenced by anthropologists, ritual studies experts, and contemporary theologians—as well as their own sense of discomfort with how the Council reforms played out in parishes—revisionists have promoted a "reform of the reform."

Critics argue that images, symbols, and rituals function in very complicated and ambiguous ways. They are not easily controlled and managed. Something is lost by shifting emphasis from ritual to moral lessons and a comfortable environment. By simplifying Catholic practices and spaces, a deep and vital power was cut off. Ceremony served to bring together people who, in their daily lives, had little in common with each other. Public worship in a space that reflected beauty enabled Catholics to acknowledge the glory, grandeur, and majesty of the divine mystery. All periods of Catholic history—not merely the early Church—contain profound truths and thus could inspire Church arts and architecture.

Critics of both the plain style of church design and the ritual experimentation of the Vatican II era gained ascendency in 1978 with the death of Pope Paul VI and the election of John Paul II. Karol Józef Wojtyła became the head of the Catholic Church after Pope John Paul I died, who had presided at the Vatican for only thirty-three days.

Born in 1920 in Wadowice, Poland, John Paul II was the first non-Italian pope in 455 years. The new pope's spiritual orientation was cultivated during the brutality of World War II and the harsh political climate of communist Eastern Europe. John Paul II is remembered for his warm smile and extensive travels, but his piety also had a darker dimension that was shaped in his youth. Like many Poles, he possessed a deep and mystical attraction to the Virgin Mary. As pontiff, he visited apparition sites around the world. He believed that God *did* intervene in the world in miraculous ways. Throughout his pontificate, John Paul II encouraged Catholics to recover the devotions that they practiced prior to the Second Vatican Council. In particular, he believed that images showing Mary as a loving mother and Christ as the suffering servant stimulated the desire for salvation.

John Paul II and his bishops believed that the spirit of Vatican II had caused many Catholics to disregard the truths actually contained in the Council documents. As bishop and then archbishop of Kraków, Wojtyła had attended the Council. His book *Love and Responsibility* is credited with influencing the ideas in *Humanae Vitae*, Pope Paul VI's encyclical prohibiting contraception.[3] Although in 1959 Pope John XXIII established a papal commission to revise the 1917 Canon Law, it would be under John

Paul II that the changes of Vatican II were consolidated into a new set of ecclesiastical norms and regulations.

The pope interpreted the documents of Vatican II in ways that disappointed liberal Catholics. Following the Council's promotion of ecumenism, John Paul II made unprecedented overtures of friendship to Jews and other non-Christians, though he refused to broaden power-sharing with the world's bishops. He called for the equality of men and women, but he made certain that girl acolytes were not present at his Masses (although after 1994, bishops could allow girl servers in their dioceses).[4] Nuns were to wear suitable habits. The poor should be loved and cared for, but the political activism of priests was condemned. John Paul II had an abiding love of young people, but he often revealed a profound distaste for pop culture and modern lifestyles. As he aged, the pope increasingly insisted on a strict adherence to a set of moral, doctrinal, and ritual certainties, with punishment meted out to those who dissented.

John Paul II's travels throughout the world underscored the global nature of Catholicism. A charismatic speaker, he gained the love and respect of many inside and outside of the Church. At the same time, his appointment in 1981 of the theologian Joseph Ratzinger as head of the Congregation for the Doctrine of the Faith signaled that John Paul II would enforce doctrinal conformity. Ratzinger (called "God's Rottweiler" by both admirers and opponents) shared with the new pope the conviction that the spirit of Vatican II had distorted the real meaning of the Council documents.

Born in 1927, Ratzinger grew up in a small village in Catholic Bavaria and experienced life under the totalitarian regime of Nazi Germany. After his ordination, he completed graduate studies and became a noted theologian. During the Second Vatican Council he served as a *peritus* for the cardinal of Cologne, joining with other progressive German theologians in calling for reform. During the tumultuous years of the sixties, however, he became fearful that change had gotten out of hand. Germany seemed to be leaning toward revolution, anarchy, and the return of totalitarianism. More than ever, the Church must stand as a bulwark to keep the modern world from tearing itself apart. His university activities and writings showed an increasingly conservative bent.

As head of the Congregation for the Doctrine of the Faith, Ratzinger was responsible for promoting and safeguarding Catholic belief. The old-

est of the Curia's nine congregations, the organization was founded in
1542 to defend the Church from heresy. For twenty-four years, Ratzinger
sought to discipline what he understood to be the experimentation and
distortion of Catholic ritual, morality, and beliefs that occurred after the
Second Vatican Council. Under his leadership, theologians were silenced
and suspended from teaching at Catholic institutions, bishops were
chastised, and tradition was promoted over innovation.

In his writings, Ratzinger rejected what he called the "new icono-
clasm" of the Second Vatican Council. He preferred the visually dynamic
baroque church, which he called "a unique kind of *fortissimo* of joy, an Al-
leluia in visual form." Twentieth-century liturgical and artistic reformers
did manage to sweep away "kitsch and unworthy art," Ratzinger wrote,
but their efforts resulted in "a void, the wretchedness of which we are
now experiencing in a truly acute way."[5]

Just prior to the renovations at Blessed Trinity, Catholic leaders published two documents that reflected changing attitudes about ritual, the
arts, and architecture. In 2000 the U.S. Conference of Catholic Bishops
approved the publication of *Built of Living Stones: Art, Architecture, and
Worship*, which replaced a similar statement on design from 1978. Two
years later in 2002, the *General Instruction of the Roman Missal* was issued from the Vatican. It stipulated how the Mass and sacraments
should be performed, and it replaced the General Instructions from
1975. Both of these documents were a response to perceived misunderstandings and errors that cropped up after the Council. They sought to
clarify ambiguities that had risen after the period of experimentation.

For instance, although the 1975 General Instructions required
churches simply to have a "cross clearly visible either on the altar or near
it," the 2002 instructions specifically stated that the cross was to have
"the figure of Christ crucified upon it." In 1975 it was acceptable for a
cross without the corpus to be carried into the sanctuary during the entrance procession, remain during Mass, and then be removed at the recessional. In the 2002 instruction, priests were explicitly reminded that
because the crucifix "calls to mind for the faithful the saving Passion of
the Lord," it should "remain near the altar even outside of liturgical celebrations." The large crucifixes pastors and parish building committees
introduced into churches reinforced the sacrificial nature of the Mass,
which conservatives felt had been downplayed after the Council.

FOR MANY CATHOLICS who lived half their lives before the reforms of Vatican II, crucifixes were as much a vivid reminder of Catholic identity as they were a symbol of Christian salvation. The new, life-sized crucifix that was placed in the sanctuary at Blessed Trinity in 2005 not only met the requirements of the General Instructions, but it also dramatically asserted the special character of Catholic devotion. For Margaret, crucifixes are so connected to Catholicism that initially she hadn't noticed that the bronze Risen Christ had been moved aside.

Over her eighty-plus years as a Catholic, Margaret has seen church interiors move from high Victorian frippery to pragmatic suburban to austere modernism and then back again. Her travels across the country have taught her that maintaining an inner faith and a commitment to the mystery of the Eucharist is better than fussing about where statues should be set up or whether a church should have them. Debates over where to place the baptistery or tabernacle, which concern liturgy experts and building committees, hold no interest for Margaret.

But not all Catholics are so easygoing. Margaret's friend Mary Ann Haggerty was "very crushed and disappointed" when the crucifix was added to Blessed Trinity. "It's not that I don't want to have a cross in the church," she explained, but "it's just too big." Mary Ann felt that she understood the significance of the cross in Christianity. She knew it was the act by which Jesus redeemed mankind from sin, but she also knew that three days later he rose from the dead. It was the Resurrection, and thus the image of the Risen Christ, that she preferred to see when she knelt to pray at Mass.

The current preference for realistic depictions of the life of Christ and the bodies of the saints also worries her. Literal representations seemed to limit the mystery of faith. "When I think about the birth of Christ," she reflected, "I don't think of shepherds and a stable and Mary with a veil on. I think of Jesus coming into the world as our Savior and Redeemer." The crucifix, because it attempted to represent an unknowable historical act, served to distract people from the more important end result: the eternal life promised in the Gospels. For Mary Ann, theology is embodied in the arts, and their current direction is troublesome.

The 2002 General Instructions on the Roman Missal also sought to rectify Catholic understanding of the Eucharist and other sacraments. For forty years since the Council, critics warned that the Mass had become too dependent on the personality and character of individual priests and parishioners. Home Masses, weddings outside of churches, liturgies in which first names were given at Communion time—all were gestures shaped by the inclination of individuals. The Mass and the sacraments seemed more like private, family functions than symbolizing Church unity. Conservatives complained that Catholics had exchanged solemnity and beauty for experimentation and triviality. Churchgoers were forgetting that the Eucharist was the real body and blood of Christ.

Changes in the Roman Missal sought to reinforce the real presence of Jesus in Communion by introducing more rituals of respect into the Mass. In the 1975 General Instruction, priest and acolytes were required simply to give a "sign of reverence" when they came to the foot of the sanctuary at the beginning of Mass. In the 2002 revision, this gesture was changed to a "profound bow," a bow from the waist. The new General Instruction called for bowing throughout the Mass: At the part of the Creed that mentioned the Incarnation, Catholics were to bow their heads. They were to bow before they received the Eucharist, and then again when the priest blessed them at the end of Mass.

Margaret still hasn't got the hang of when to bow at Mass. For her and many of the seniors who attend church at Blessed Trinity, the nuances of ritual movements have little significance. Margaret tries to remember to bow before taking the host and cup, but only because she has been told to do so.

Such gestures hold more significance to Mur Hiltenbrand and Helen Marie Hurt, women from St. Jude's parish. Fifteen years younger than Margaret and more attuned to the theology behind liturgical etiquette, they resent the shift in the understanding of the Mass. They argue that the increase in the amount of bowing and kneeling has introduced a formality to the service that diminishes understanding the Mass as a reenactment of the Last Supper, when Jesus shared a meal with his friends. In this point in our history, they observe, bowing and kneeling are foreign movements that occur at royal courts. Did Jesus come to be a king or to be a servant? A full understanding of the Eucharist comes from the heart and the mind, not the body. For Mur, the current pastor at St. Jude's takes the prescription for bowing too seriously. "You'd think the pope was Japanese," she joked.

Proponents of the "reform of the reform" endorse the move toward bowing. These are the same individuals who have also pushed parishes to offer Latin Masses, purchase elaborate vestments for their priests, train their choirs in Gregorian Chant, and advance the cult of the saints. Supporters look to Pope Benedict XVI (the former Cardinal Joseph Ratzinger) for encouragement. His 2007 *motu proprio*, for example, permitted priests to say the pre-Vatican II 1962, Latin Mass when so requested by their parishioners. Priests celebrating the Latin Mass face the altar rather than the people.

Although accepting the Latin Mass began in the eighties with Pope John Paul II, since the summer of 2008 Pope Benedict XVI has also requested that those who receive Communion from him at papal Masses kneel and receive the host on the tongue. In *The Spirit of the Liturgy*, he argued that kneeling was an element of Christian culture with deep spiritual meaning. The papal master of ceremonies, Monsignor Guido Marini, explains that that posture underscores "the truth of the Real Presence [of Christ] in the Eucharist, helps the devotion of the faithful, and introduces the sense of mystery more easily."[6]

Although Blessed Trinity parishioners might debate the relevance of bowing and kneeling, neither Margaret nor her friends want to see the return of the Latin Mass. Another parish in Ocala, Our Lady Queen of Peace, has a priest who says a Latin Mass, but Margaret has no interest in attending. Margaret feels the power of the words of the Mass precisely because she can understand what they mean.

Furthermore, she disagrees that there should be a more solemn atmosphere on Sunday. Although she rarely goes to Sunday evening Mass—where electric guitars and a drum set provide the beat for singing—nevertheless, she agrees it's a good idea to engage young people. In any case, for her, kneeling is too difficult to do for long periods. She can understand how some might not understand the concept of the "real presence," but that is a problem with teaching, not with the Mass itself. At Blessed Trinity at Communion time, even non-Catholics and children walk with their families to the sanctuary to receive a blessing from the priest or Eucharistic ministers. That, for her, is a sign of what going to church is all about.

Along with the reinvigoration of Catholic material culture and a more formal Mass, additional religious practices have been introduced into

Blessed Trinity and other American parishes. Some of these rituals were widely practiced by Catholics before the Second Vatican Council: the communal saying of the rosary, Benediction, Stations of the Cross, Crowning of Mary in May, Eucharistic Adoration, and First Fridays. These practices have been streamlined and given a modern theological spin. Other devotions are new since Vatican II. At various times during the year, parishioners at Blessed Trinity can attend a Divine Mercy novena, a St. Peregrine Mass for a cure for cancer, or Easter Processional devotions. At the parish's mission church, La Guadalupana, devotions are conducted in Spanish.

Adjacent to the parish office, there is a discreet entrance that opens up into a minichurch. On a plain altar in the chapel, a golden monstrance holds a large consecrated host—the body of Christ. A parishioner sits facing the altar, praying the rosary. After her hour, another person shows up. He reads from his Bible and glances at some religious pamphlets scattered on the pews. After his hour, another person shows up. And then another. And another, around the clock, twenty-four hours a day, seven days a week.

In 1993 Father Martin Lucia, founder of the Apostolate for Perpetual Eucharistic Adoration from Mt. Clements, Michigan, spoke at Blessed Trinity Church. He had been inspired by Pope John Paul II's desire that "perpetual adoration" (continual prayers in front of the exposed Eucharist) be started in every parish. Eucharistic adoration, especially for discrete periods of time (known as the Forty Hours) had been a fixture in pre-Vatican II Catholicism. However, because the devotion began in the seventeenth century and has no roots in the early Church, it fell out of favor after the Council.

Parishioners at Blessed Trinity responded to the call of the pope and Father Lucia's enthusiasm. They transformed an office into a chapel and explained the importance of the devotion. Mary Ann Haggerty (the one who does not care for the new crucifix) coordinates 168 individuals who promise to stay for an hour a week and the two hundred substitutes who will come when needed. She explains that although it can be frustrating to find someone to take the slot from three to four in the morning, the pews have been filled continuously since the devotion began fifteen years ago. She thanks her husband for the computer program that helps her schedule the "adorers," and she herself finds the "time with Jesus" to be centering and renewing. In the intimate and quiet space of the chapel, she has time to meditate in the presence of the "Most Blessed Sacrament."

Blessed Trinity has also reintroduced the blessings of homes, animals on St. Francis's feast day, and Easter foods. Some of these rites, like the blessing of Easter foods, had been previously practiced by specific ethnic groups. Now, all parishioners are encouraged to take part in linking the material, ordinary world with the spiritual. "The blessing does not take long," the bulletin explains, "and does not require any special preparation on your part."

Although a priest is needed to consecrate the host that is exposed for Perpetual Adoration, at Blessed Trinity laymen and -women conduct the blessings. Volunteers are specially appointed to pray with other parishioners and then bless their homes and family. (The priests enjoy blessing the pets on St. Francis's feast day). Although the practice of blessing is firmly rooted in pre-Vatican II Catholicism, the involvement of the laity in the ritual reflects the changes of the Council. Blessings, as with Perpetual Adoration, are organized and sustained by parishioners.

THE REINVIGORATION of Catholic devotional life also has its political dimensions. In 1973 Roe v. Wade legalized abortion throughout the United States. Although the Catholic Church has long spoken out against birth control and abortion, the Second Vatican Council's openness to Protestants enabled American Catholics to broaden their involvement in contemporary social movements. During the sixties and seventies, Catholics marched with Baptists against segregation, burned draft cards with Episcopalians to protest the Vietnam War, and worked with Mennonites to fight world hunger.

By the eighties, evangelical Protestants were joining with Catholics in their struggle against abortion. At the same time, the Catholic hierarchy clamped down on any theologians, priests, nuns, and politicians who took pro-choice positions. Pre-Vatican II public condemnation of birth control was transformed into post-Vatican II public condemnation of abortion. Although abortion rates have been gradually declining since 1990, American women still have almost twice the rate of abortions (21 per 1,000 women of childbearing age) as women in Western Europe (12 per 1,000). Our very religious country has three times the abortion rate as does the secular Netherlands. In spite of generations of condemnations, Catholics are as likely as other Americans to have an abortion.[7]

To integrate anti-abortion activities into the liturgical calendar, the U.S. Conference of Catholic Bishops designated October to be Respect Life month. October 5 is Respect Life Sunday—a date close enough to the November elections to remind citizens in the pews who they should vote for. The anniversary of the Supreme Court decision on January 22 is observed as "a particular day of penance for violations to the dignity of the human person through acts of abortion and of prayer for the full restoration of the legal guarantee to the right to life."[8] Mass is celebrated that day in purple vestments, the same color that is worn during Lent.

At Blessed Trinity, just outside the church under a monumental oak tree draped in Spanish moss, parishioners have placed a grave marker with the inscription, "In prayerful memory of our millions of unwanted babies. No one cared. Conceived—Aborted—."

T HE FORCE BEHIND the spiritual life of Blessed Trinity Church, Patrick Sheedy, is very much a priest of the Second Vatican Council. Born in 1940, he was ordained in Cooraclare, County Clare, Ireland in 1965, the year the Council ended. The fourth of twelve children, he and a brother had decided to leave the family farm and enter the priesthood. Although his brother remained in Ireland, after his seminary studies Sheedy came to the United States. Father Pat was ordained specifically to minister in Florida. First in St. Augustine and then in the newly formed diocese of Orlando, he worked as a priest, teacher, and director of Catholic Charities. In 1988 he was appointed pastor of Blessed Trinity. Father Pat's ties to Ireland are still strong. He frequently visits his family there in the summers and enjoys bringing his Irish humor into American southern culture. The mascot of the Trinity Catholic High School is a fighting Irishman, and the students' uniforms are green and white. The church's new statue of St. Patrick was paid for with gift money given for the fortieth anniversary of his ordination.

All the priests and sisters who work at Blessed Trinity were born outside the United States. Retired priest Father Michael O'Keeffe was ordained for the diocese of Savannah, Georgia, after studying in a seminary in Waterford, Ireland. In 2009 Father Roy Eco, originally from the Philippines, joined the parish. Father Alphonso Cely, another associate priest who runs La Guadalupana, was born in Colombia. Recent associate priests were born in Haiti and in the Republic of Congo. In 2000 Father Pat sponsored three Sisters of the Immaculate Heart of Mary Reparatrix to come from Uganda to serve in the parish. Several years later, Father Alphonso arranged for three Colombian nuns to come to Ocala to provide religious education, spiritual counseling, and advice on liturgies for the Spanish-speaking parishioners. Blessed Trinity built them a convent and funds their activities. All the sisters wear habits.

The international character of the American parish is neither new nor unique. As vocations have fallen in the United States, the number of foreign-born priests and nuns has necessarily increased. Even during the peak vocation years of the first half of the century, dioceses in Florida and California were forced to import priests from foreign countries. Monsignor O'Carroll, who was the pastor at St. Stephen's in Monterey Park for thirty-two years, had been ordained in 1922 in Ireland to work for the Archdiocese of Los Angeles. In the early twentieth century, many of the priests who staffed Erie's national parishes were born in countries like Slovakia or Hungary. Although the Sisters of St. Joseph who taught Margaret at Sacred Heart School were born in Pennsylvania, many of the Sisters of the Holy Family of Nazareth who taught her friends at St. Stanislaus were born in Poland. The Catholic Church in the United States has always been an immigrant Church.

The multinational staff at Blessed Trinity reflects a new direction in immigrant Catholicism: All the younger priests and sisters are from the southern hemisphere. The First Vatican Council of 1870 was dominated by Europeans, with Americans present but not influential. Almost a hundred years later at the Second Vatican Council, Americans were responsible for the important discussions on religious liberty. Council Fathers from Africa, Asia, and Latin America also made substantive contributions to interventions concerning languages, rituals, marriage, and social justice. Their insights into the postcolonial world enabled the Council Fathers from Western countries to see that the vernacular—as both a language and a cultural style—could be a meaningful way to worship. The Second Vatican Council modeled a culturally diverse, global Catholicism that set the stage for a truly transnational Catholicism.

Nowadays at Blessed Trinity, Ugandan Sister Mary Concepta wins awards in Ocala's chili cook-off contests. She offers tastes of her concoctions at parish suppers, where the music and entertainment is offered by the Filipino community. Margaret and Ken rarely miss a church potluck because the food is so impressive. When Margaret had her surgeries and couldn't get to Mass, Sister Juliet Ateenyi Nakalema was the one who brought her Holy Communion. She is in charge of the Ministry to the Sick, and in 2009 she coordinated eighty-seven men and women who bring Communion to sixty-five shut-ins, patients in two hospitals, and the residents of sixteen senior care facilities. For many Catholics of Margaret's age, Sister Juliet and her ministers are the face of the Church.

Negotiating cultural differences between immigrant communities and "native" Americans rarely goes smoothly. It has always caused what church leaders now euphemistically call "challenges." As we have seen in Erie, German-born congregations were not shy in confronting their Irish-born bishop. Even when hostilities did not break out, deciding what was an ethnic custom and what was a Catholic practice was no easy task. More than any other religious group in the United States, Catholics have long struggled to worship peacefully and productively with people from different places.

When Margaret and Ken first arrived in Florida, they attended church at Our Lady of the Springs. Their new home was located within the boundary of this parish. For several years they enjoyed the company of Father Michael Farrell, who was born in Ireland and took particular pleasure in joking with Ken. When Father Mike was transferred, a less amiable pastor was appointed. Eventually Margaret and Ken "adopted" the parish's young associate priest, who was born in Tanzania. When his mother came for a visit, Margaret fixed supper for the pair. Father Deus Byabato had a gentle manner and what Margaret felt to be a deep spirituality.

Other parishioners, however, were less enthusiastic about the African priest. They claimed to find his English difficult to understand and his ways disorganized. As Ken tells it, when Father Deus took over as temporary pastor, the "old people in the parish" revolted. Not long after, Father Deus asked for a transfer and eventually became a hospital chaplain in Illinois where his uncle was a priest. Margaret still gets upset when she recalls his treatment: "They didn't like him because he was a black man, and that's the absolute truth." Ken was so disgusted that he insisted the couple move their church membership to Blessed Trinity. Each year Father Deus and Margaret exchange Christmas cards. He writes that he is well suited for his work with the sick and much happier now that his mother lives with him. When he came for a conference in Orlando, he drove up and visited. His picture is posted on Margaret's refrigerator door.

Language and cultural differences between immigrant priests and parishioners echo throughout American Catholic history. In the years since the Council, Catholics have become more aware of the hidden costs of the importation of foreign priests. Ireland, for instance, no longer exports priests because it has a greater need than the United States for clergy. In 2007 only seven men were ordained in the entire country. The situation for religious women was even worse, with only two making their final vows that year.[9]

Although the statistics are a bit shaky, there is no question that the ratio of priest to parishioners is better in the United States than in the continents of the southern hemisphere. In Africa, for every priest, there are 4,694 Catholics to minister to; in South America the number rises to 7,138. These numbers compare to 1 priest for every 1,375 Catholics in the United States.[10] Should Catholics participate in the "brain drain" of the talented from developing countries? Are these new missionaries truly contributing to the globalization of Catholicism or merely supplying labor for the "spiritual consumerism" of the wealthy living in the northern hemisphere?

The United States would probably not have such a shortage of priests if bishops ordained women and married men. The success of the permanent diaconate in the United States clearly indicates that American Catholics are willing to take on spiritual leadership roles in their parishes. At the end of the Vatican II era, there were approximately 800 married men serving as deacons around the country. By 1995 that number had risen to 11,371, and in 2007 there were 15,027 permanent deacons. Blessed Trinity has three deacons, one of whom works exclusively with Spanish-speaking parishioners. The United States has more deacons than all the countries of the rest of the world combined. While women still cannot be ordained deacons, they dominate the lay ministries that are open to them. In 1999 almost 30,000 lay ministers worked in parishes—a number that is up 36 percent from 1992—and 75 percent of those were women.[11] Since the Second Vatican Council, American men and women have not shied away from serving their God and their religious community.

B LESSED TRINITY benefits from a tremendous commitment from its laity. The priests and sisters, of course, have played a crucial role in leading and motivating that commitment. In 1991 the parish council decided to adopt a parish model called "The Stewardship Way of Life." The goal was to intensify parishioners' commitment to God and their faith community. It asked parishioners to put God first in their lives, and in gratitude and thanksgiving return a portion of their "time, talent, and treasure" to him. The Stewardship Way of Life stresses the tight interweaving of personal piety, volunteering, and the financial support of the parish.

At Blessed Trinity, all new church members attend a Stewardship 101 meeting that lays out these ideas. They then commit in writing to a series of promises: to worship at Mass as a family every weekend, to volunteer for one of the various parish ministries, and to offer 10 percent of their gross family income to God, 8 percent to the parish, and 2 percent to a charity of their own choice. In return, families could participate—at no cost—in most of the ministries maintained by the parish, including Blessed Trinity's grade school and the diocesan high school.

Almost everything at Blessed Trinity is run by volunteers. With the exception of its schoolteachers and a paid church staff of sixteen, parishioners do everything from plumbing to serving lunches at funerals to working at Habitat for Humanity. They help with a prison ministry and drive trucks to pick up used furniture for their thrift shop. A year-round soup kitchen provides daily meals to the hungry. The parish has a volunteer public relations person, photographer, and webmaster. Families agree to clean and decorate the islands in the parking lot, festooning them with plastic flowers and colored stone. They make rosary beads, run marriage preparation classes, and distribute ashes on Ash Wednesday There is an equally long list of ministries available for Spanish speakers.

Father Pat believes that getting everyone involved in the parish and avoiding "parish gurus" who run everything is important. He rarely pays for any good or service: He asks and people give.

Yet, typically, American Catholics are more likely *not* to give. Protestants donate twice as much as Catholics to their churches. The numbers get even worse when we compare Catholics with conservative Protestants: Baptists give three times more, and members of the Assemblies of God more than four times more. In a 2002 survey of Catholics, those living in Florida gave slightly more than the national average of 1.04 percent of the median household income. Sociologists who study church finances find that as churches get larger, people give less. Catholic parishes are typically eight times larger than mainline Protestant congregations, and Blessed Trinity is large for a Catholic church. Still, approximately a third of the families at Blessed Trinity follow the "Stewardship Way of Life."[12]

Enough parishioners tithe to enable Blessed Trinity to finance an extensive Catholic educational system. From September to June, a long line of SUVs snake around the campus of Blessed Trinity. With their motors on and their windows rolled up to keep the AC inside, the parents are waiting to pick up their children. In 1964, at the peak of the era of Catholic schools, Blessed Trinity had 326 children enrolled. In 2009, when parochial schools around the nation had closed, it had 700 students and a waiting list. Father Pat wants to build a second school across town. Trinity Catholic High School, which is administered by Christian Brothers for the Diocese of Orlando, was completed in 2002. It has thirty-two classrooms, a media center with a television studio, computer labs, gym, cafeteria, chapel, music rooms, and an assortment of sports fields.

The South has long supported private schooling—support that intensified after the desegregation of public schools and the Supreme Court's decision on school prayer. Ocala has six parochial schools, whose affiliations range from Baptist to Episcopalian to Seventh-day Adventist. Local parents want schools to provide religious instruction for their children, school prayers, and discipline along with basic education. Consequently, the success of Blessed Trinity schools is partially due to their location in a growing area that supports private education.

Nevertheless, success is not simply a matter of demographics. Father Pat and church leaders work hard to link together a spiritual commitment to God, the financial support of the parish community, and the benefits of a Catholic education. Although parochial education only became a common feature of American Catholic life in the twentieth century, it holds an important place in marking Catholic identity. Even Catholics like Margaret, whose children are long out of school, are willing to support the parish school because it is so closely tied to "being Catholic." Schools are a significant resource for the congregation, but they also require the continual and enthusiastic involvement of parishioners and parish leaders.

ONE OF THE WORRIES of Catholic reformers after the Council was that a sophisticated parochial school system would direct funds and personnel to middle-class suburban neighborhoods at the expense of fostering a just and equitable social order. If Catholics were preoccupied with their children's uniforms and books, how could they face the realities of global poverty, racism, and war? Wouldn't schools—not unlike sentimental devotions to the Virgin Mary—encourage Catholics to look inward rather than outward into the hard world?

Shortly after Sister Juliet arrived in 2000 from Uganda, her mother died. When she returned to Ocala from the funeral, she brought back a snapshot of the church that served as her family's parish. In passing, Sister Juliet showed the picture to one of the teachers at the school who in turn asked if she could bring the photograph to her class. The children were surprised that anyone could go to Mass in a mud hut built of sticks. They decided to fundraise for a new church. Blessed Trinity already sent money to Belize, Honduras, Guatemala, and the Dominican Republic. Ten percent of the church's yearly income was earmarked for domestic and foreign charities. There was something special, however, about this church: It was the church of Sister Juliet's family.

Seeing the dedication of the elementary students, Father Pat contacted the bishop of the diocese of Hoima and asked about the feasibility and cost of building a church in the village of Nalweyo. An hour by unpaved roads from the Ugandan capital, Kampala, Nalweyo has no electricity, running water, or sewage system. Villagers are subsistence farmers who raise sweet potatoes, cassava, bananas, and beans on small family plots. Almost all of the Nalweyo's residents are Catholic, as are about half of those who live in the surrounding area. With the support of

Bishop Deogratis Byabazaire, Blessed Trinity began raising money for a church. In 2003 Catholics in Ocala and Nalweyo decided to form a partnership together.

A year later, Father Pat, Sister Juliet, and fourteen parishioners from Blessed Trinity traveled to Uganda to participate in the dedication of Blessed Trinity Nalweyo. The parishioners had secured a $15,000 grant from the Koch Foundation and raised the remainder of the money needed to build and furnish a $125,000 brick church, complete with stained glass windows and wooden pews. In their suitcases they brought an array of chalices, altar linens, vestments, holy water fonts, and candle lighters. They marveled at how they managed to get all of those items as well as two monstrances, a standing crucifix, and five hundred scapulars through customs. Those who were not carrying church supplies were loaded down with school materials: encyclopedias, soccer balls, paint brushes, pencils, construction paper, and on and on.

Once in Uganda, the travelers were welcomed with dancing and songs. They visited orphanages, heard Mass at the Shrine of the Ugandan Martyrs, and received an overview of African politics from the American Embassy.

The trip to Uganda sparked an even stronger commitment of Blessed Trinity to the people of Nalweyo. One parish couple, Jack and Barbara Spencer, spent several six-month periods helping the community with building projects. A teacher stayed for five weeks. Joyce Lemek, a local tax accountant, helped organize in Nalweyo a co-op for the men to manage, which included a piggery, beehive, and a set of animals. She remembers how a Presbyterian farmer gave her money for the beehive, a pharmacist friend paid for a cow, and in three weeks she collected over a thousand packs of vegetable seeds in Ocala. Other parishioners took yearly summer trips. During one visit, Father Pat baptized forty-eight babies in the new church. Bishop Byabazaire flew to Ocala for the celebration of Blessed Trinity's completed 2005 renovation.

Within seven years the Ocala parish had helped the Nalweyo parish build a church, a parish hall, find and pay for a full-time priest, and provide him a rectory. The two communities constructed an eight-classroom school room, outfitted the students in used Blessed Trinity uniforms, and hired and supported six teachers. The Florida parishioners, along with friends across the country, "adopted" individual Nalweyo schoolchildren with their $200 donations to the project. The stream of school supplies continued in the visitors' suitcases. The two sister parishes arranged for three nuns from Sister Juliet's order to stay in the village, building them a convent. A young professional couple donated $80,000 to help complete a retirement home in Kampala for the order's older nuns. Even Ocala's brides gave their gently used wedding gowns to be sent to Africa.

Blessed Trinity parishioners' enthusiasm for Nalweyo soon outgrew the size of their missionaries' suitcases. During the spring of 2009, Joyce Lemek helped organize the filling of a forty-foot shipping container to be sent to Nalweyo. A local recycling company volunteered to help with logistics, and a farmer donated a 72-horsepower tractor and other farm implements to be shipped to Nalweyo. The 140 acres of land that the co-op bought had never been plowed, and the village only had machetes to clear weeds. Margaret participated in "Barefoot Sunday," leaving her shoes at the altar to be sent to Africa. Two thousand pairs were stuffed in the container. Munroe Regional Medical Center donated six baby incubators, and wheelchairs were packed up for the elderly nuns. More than five hundred boxes of clothing, medical supplies, and school equipment made the two-month trip over the oceans to be distributed in and around Nalweyo.

A steady stream of parishioners from Ocala now makes the long trip to Uganda every year. Some work for months, and others are guests only for a few days. Evaluating what long-term impact their donations and labor will have on the complicated village life of an east African nation is difficult. Father Pat sees self-sufficiency as the goal, and all the Blessed Trinity parishioners who have been to Nalweyo know that patience and perseverance cannot be overstressed. They are well aware that six baby incubators may have little impact in a nation where the primary cause of death is malaria. Still, they see their investment in the education of village children to bode well for their futures.

Unlike other aid workers in Africa, the Catholics of Ocala share with the Catholics of Nalweyo a set of deeply held spiritual beliefs, the participation in an elaborate ritual system, an acknowledgement of a worldwide authority structure, and even the assent to a common religious history. They might disagree over whether Mass should be fit into an hour or wander over three, but they both agree that a transformation has occurred among both of their parishes because of their partnership. In this case, middle-class Catholics have not simply drained the talent from a developing country, nor have they allowed traditional devotions to direct their attention relentlessly inward. The two parishes' mutual trust that the spirit of God will guide them is what allows both communities to put aside their suspicions and work toward a more just and equitable world.

As soon as she gets fingerprinted—a new diocesan requirement for volunteering since the sex abuse scandals—Margaret hopes to spend a couple of hours every week at Blessed Trinity's elder care facility. In addition to Mass, she also attends a weekly women's circle that studies the Bible. For the "civic generation," who grew up belonging to Army units, unions, PTA organizations, and bowling leagues, continued involvement in religious communities late in life is no surprise.

Every study on healthy aging stresses the importance of maintaining social networks that work against the isolation that comes with age. Going to church or synagogue is the number one form of organizational activity among the elderly. Sociologists have shown that the more women attend religious services and know other members of the congregation, the less physically disabled or depressed they are likely to be.[13] Congregational life provides social support and relationships. It offers seniors a chance to sit next to a younger person at a group dinner and to hear assuring words from religious leaders that every individual has value and worth.

For Margaret, Catholicism provides the means to create a positive response to aging, illness, and, eventually, death. God has put her on earth to know, love, and serve him and, when he decides the time, he will call her home. In the meantime, her parish provides her with spiritual and social sustenance. The stress on the active participation of the laity, social justice, ecumenism, and global awareness that were stimulated by the Second Vatican Council has worked to keep Margaret attached to both the supernatural and the communal activities of her religion.

The openness that the Council created empowered her to look for parishes that exemplified what she understands to be real Christian values. The spirit of Vatican II supported a critical perspective on the

Church's pronouncements. If she were younger, she'd use birth control, and she thinks women should be able to be priests. Critics complain that this is a form of "cafeteria Catholicism" that allows diners to pick and choose only what they like to eat from an array of abundant, but taste-less, options. A better analogy may be that Margaret's Catholicism is like a Sunday dinner at grandmother's house, where all the food is familiar and hearty. If you don't want to eat something, you put a little on your plate, swirl it around a bit, feed some to the dog, and then compliment Granny on how wonderful the apple pie is. Margaret's is a polite genera-tion, and she was taught not to make a fuss. Still, Margaret doesn't eat what she doesn't want to.

Margaret likes to plan ahead. She and Ken have attended a workshop at Blessed Trinity about Alzheimer's disease and the symptoms of senile dementia. They have their living wills made out and have already paid for their funerals. Some of their friends have arranged for burials in their hometowns, but Ken decided to take advantage of the free plots for vet-erans at the Florida National Cemetery just south of them in Bushnell. After all, the war was what pushed the couple to marry, and GI Bill bene-fits are what enabled them to change their lives. And since the Second Vatican Council, they are no longer required to be buried in a Catholic cemetery. Before ending in the earth, however, there will be the Mass of the Resurrection at Blessed Trinity.

The priest will dress in white and gold vestments that celebrate eter-nal life rather than the black of death, as would have been the case before the Council. Afterward everyone will adjourn to the community center, where the bereavement committee will serve lunch, prepared by other volunteers. There will be people and food, together with a nod to the glory to come—a suitable ending for a long Catholic life.

ACKNOWLEDGMENTS

In researching this book, I relied on the hospitality of many individuals. I visited each parish that I wrote about, beginning with my family's ancestral villages in Germany. There, Maria Froess helped piece together what life was like in Bechenheim, and Franz Pfadt provided valuable genealogical aid in Leimersheim. Bernhard Lang traveled from Paderborn to help with translation. Danke!

In Erie, pastors at St. Joseph's, St. John's, St. Mary's, and Sacred Heart let me poke around in their basements and storage rooms. Sister Ann Loretta Urmann guided me through the archives of the Sisters of St. Joseph of Northwestern Pennsylvania. Mary Grace Lewis connected me with Francis Froess, in whose attic I found wonderful material about the schools my mother attended. As with all the cities I visited, librarians in the local history sections of the public library graciously assisted this curious Utah visitor.

Charlotte Troke, my mother's friend, organized seniors for me to interview about postwar Catholic America in Toledo, Ohio. The parish staff at Christ the King patiently brought me year after year of church bulletins, and the "Over Fifty Group" filled in many important details. Father Michael O. Brown lent me his parish history. Sister Mary Anton introduced me to retired Sisters of Notre Dame, whose memories were crisp and thoughtful. Pete Ueberroth, archivist at the Catholic Diocese of Toledo, steered me toward a cache of statistical material. I am grateful for all of their kindness and their commitment to preserving history.

In California, both north and south, the Sisters of the Holy Names of Jesus and Mary cannot be thanked enough. Sister Joan Doyle connected me with many sisters who had worked in southern California during the sixties and seventies. Karen Kinzey from the Holy Names Heritage Center in Oregon permitted me to tag along during her interviews of senior sisters at the Los Gatos convent. The Immaculate Heart Community allowed me access to their archives housed at the wonderful Corita Art Center in Los Angeles. At St. Stephen's, it turned out that Father Larry Estrada and I had been students in the parish's school at about the same time. It's just impossible to keep criminals away from the scene of the crime. A final thank you goes to Kevin Feeney at the Los Angeles Archdiocesan Archives.

The chapters on St. Jude's Church would not have been possible without the reflections of Bill Sievers. I hope that I have captured his warmth, candidness, and gentle humor. Past and present members of the parish also welcomed me into their homes. A special thank you goes to Mur Hiltenbrand and Helen Marie Hurt. The staff at St. Jude's, as with the other parishes, patiently let me look at what they have collected over the years. Father Dennis Grabrian, who was an associate pastor during the early seventies, commented on the chapters, making them stronger and more nuanced. The Archdiocese of Denver has significantly changed since the Vatican II era, but archivist Karyl Klein made my task of recovery much easier.

My parents' current parish, Blessed Trinity in Ocala, Florida, truly is an amazing faith community. Its pastor, Father Patrick Sheedy, supported this project in every way. Music director Richard E. Saalfeld shared with me his own research on the renovation of the church and looked over the chapter. Sister Juliet Ateenyi Nakalema took time away from her many duties to help me understand what she sees as important in the parish. Marilyn Curron helped me navigate the church archives, and Jannet Walsh clued me in on what it means to be Catholic in Florida. Many parishioners, especially those mentioned in the chapter, willingly shared their thoughts on their changing church.

A year-long sabbatical from the University of Utah and funding from the University Research Committee allowed me to travel to parishes and archives. Particularly helpful was the semester we lived in Washington, D.C., where I had access to the superb resources of the Catholic University of America and Georgetown University.

My own colleagues in the study of American religions graciously read drafts and made insightful comments. My appreciation goes out to Jim Fisher, Peggy Fletcher-Stack, Timothy Kelly, Patricia O'Connell Killen, Paul Lakeland, and Judith Weisenfeld. Lara Heimert, my editor at Basic Books, kept both my ideas and prose on the straight-and-narrow path of lucidity. Lara's keen eye and my agent Michelle Tessler's encouragement have supported me throughout this project.

Attempting to integrate family history with scholarship is not for the faint of heart. Luckily I had the continued support of my husband, John Hurdle, who I actually first met in junior high in 1967. Our daughter, Brigit, is now about the same age as we were then. Their love and forbearance created a home environment for which I am immensely grateful.

As I began this book in 2007, my mother was recuperating from open heart surgery. It became quite clear to me that for those of the Greatest Generation,

life is profoundly fragile. Change comes swiftly and often with sorrow. Consequently, I want to thank all of the seniors—and especially my parents—who
were willing to trust me with their memories.

One of the things that impressed me as I worked on this book was how my
mother maintained friendships with women throughout her long life. I was able
to interview fellow classmates from Sacred Heart elementary school, neighbors
she knew as a young wife, and individuals whose company she now enjoys in
Florida. Although she and my father moved frequently, my mother kept up correspondence with a rich array of women friends. Following this tradition, I dedi-
cate *The Spirit of Vatican II* to four special women: Linda Jansen, Lillian
Wondrack, Dianne Ashton, and Margaret Toscano. I thank them for their enduring friendship and continuous support, for their wisdom, and for the many years
of sparkling conversation.

NOTES

Introduction

1. Klaus Wittstadt, "On the Eve of the Second Vatican Council," in *History of Vatican II*, ed. Giuseppe Alberigo, (Maryknoll, NY: Orbis Press, 1995), 494.

Chapter One: Catholic Neighborhoods

1. Colman J. Barry, *The Catholic Church and German America* (Milwaukee, WI: Bruce Publishing Company, 1953), 4.

2. Barry, *Catholic Church and German Americans*, 8.

3. H. C. W. Wienker, *Saint Joseph's Parish, Erie, Pennsylvania, 1867–1992*, a privately published commemorative volume.

4. Wienker, *Saint Joseph's Parish*, 10.

5. *Quanta Cura* (Condemning Current Errors), para. 1.

6. *Quanta Cura*, para. 4.

7. *Dei Filius*, ch. 3:11.

8. James Gibbons, *Acta et Decreta Concilii Plenarii Baltimorensis* (1886), Decrees of the Third Plenary Council of Baltimore, nos. 127 and 124, Available at www.archive.org/details/actaetdecretacooogibbgoog.

9. Wienker, *Saint Joseph's Parish*, 11.

10. Godfrey Schlachter, *The Forbidden Marriages* (Collegeville, IN: Messenger Print, 1917).

11. [Servite Fathers], *Conducting the Perpetual Novena in Honor of Our Sorrowful Mother* (Chicago: Our Sorrowful Mother Novena, 1941), np.

12. Syllabus of Errors (1864), 45, 47, 48; Instruction of the Propaganda Fide Concerning Catholic School Children in American Public Schools (November 1875); and Decrees of the Third Plenary Council of Baltimore (1884).

13. *School Manual for the Use of the Sisters of St. Joseph of Carondelet* (St. Louis: Carreras, 1884), 12–13.

14. *The Trumpet* [school annual], Villa Maria, 1930. Private collection of Mary Grace Lewis, Erie, PA.

Chapter Two: Postwar Suburbs

1. Wilfred Parsons, "No Lavender, No Old Lace," *Columbia* (July 1943), as cited in Gerald P. Fogarty, *The Vatican and the American Hierarchy, from 1870 to 1965* (Stuttgart: A. Hiersemann, 1982), 350.

2. James Hudnut-Beulmer, *Looking for God in the Suburbs* (New Brunswick, NJ: Rutgers University Press, 1994), 33.

3. Fogarty, *The Vatican and the American Hierarchy*, 356, quoting letter of Stritch to McNicholas, Chicago Archdiocesan Archives, 17 May 1947.

4. John Cogley, "Liturgy and Language," *Commonweal*, May 2, 1958, 127.

5. Joseph H. Fichter, *Dynamics of a City Church* (Chicago: University of Chicago Press, 1951), 138.

6. *Toledo Chronicle*, March 13, 1953 and March 20, 1953.

7. Dennis Castillo, "The Origin of the Priest Shortage: 1942–62," *America*, October 24, 1992, 303.

8. Joseph H. Fichter, *Priest and People* (New York: Sheed and Ward, 1965), 188. Although his book was published in 1965, the research was conducted in 1959.

9. Timothy Walch, *Parish School: American Catholic Parochial Education from Colonial Times to the Present* (New York: Crossroad, 1996), 176 and John T. McGreevy, *Parish Boundaries: The Catholic Encounter with Race in the Twentieth-century Urban North* (Chicago: University of Chicago Press, 1996), 236.

10. Walch, *Parish School*, 170.

11. Sally Cunneen, *Sex: Female; Religion: Catholic* (New York: Holt, Rinehart Winston, 1968), 17f.

Chapter Three: Gathering in Los Angeles and Rome

1. Archer Speers and Curtis G. Pepper, "John XXIII—The Man Himself," *Newsweek*, November 10, 1958, 38.

2. John F. Kennedy, Announcement for Candidacy for President, January 2, 1960.

3. John F. Kennedy, Inaugural Address, January 20, 1961.

4. Basing her conclusion on census materials, Claudia Goldin cites 29.8 percent of all white married women were working in 1960. See *Understanding the Gender Gap: An Economic History of American Women* (New York: Oxford University Press, 1990), 17.

5. Pope John XXIII, Opening Speech to the Second Vatican Council, October 11, 1962.

6. [Archdiocese of Los Angeles], *The Tidings*, October 12, 1962 and October 19, 1962.

Chapter Four: The Council and Its Decisions

1. Bishop not named. As quoted in *Newsweek*, December 16, 1963, 80.

2. I'd like to thank Paul Lakeland for his observation about the "palace revolution" of the first session.

3. Henri Fresquet, *The Drama of Vatican II: The Ecumenical Council June, 1962– December, 1965*, trans. Bernard Murchland (New York: Random House, 1967), 53.

4. [Archdiocese of Los Angeles], *The Tidings*, November 9, 1962.

5. Ralph M. Wiltgen, *The Rhine Flows into the Tiber: A History of Vatican II* (Devon, England: Augustine Publishing Company, 1978), 28.

6. James Cardinal McIntyre, October 23, 1962 intervention on the Dogmatic Constitution of the Sacred Liturgy, as cited in Vincent A. Yzermans, *American Participation in the Second Vatican Council* (New York: Sheed and Ward, 1967), 154.

7. Wiltgen, *The Rhine Flows into the Tiber*, 40.

8. Fresquet, *The Drama of Vatican II*, 182.

9. Floyd Anderson, ed., *Council Daybook: Vatican II Sessions 1–4* (Washington, D.C.: National Catholic Welfare Conference, 1965–1966), vol. 1, October 24, 1963, 212; Anderson, *Council Daybook*, vol. 1, October 18, 1963, 194.

10. Wiltgen, *The Rhine Flows into the Tiber*, 94.

11. John Courtney Murray, "The Crisis of Church-State Relationships in the U.S.A." (1950), as reproduced in Joseph A. Komonchak, John Courtney Murray, Samuel Cardinal Stritch, Francis J. Connell, "The Crisis of Church-State Relationships in the U.S.A.," *The Review of Politics* 61 (Autumn 1999): 675–714.

12. Anderson, *Council Daybook*, vol. 3, September 23, 1964, 37.

13. Anderson, *Council Daybook*, vol. 1, November 26, 1963, 305.

14. Joseph Blomjous, "Ecumenism in Africa: Reflections of a Bishop," *The Ecumenist* 2 (1964): 19, as quoted in Melissa J. Wilde, *Vatican II: A Sociological Analysis of Religious Change* (Princeton, NJ: Princeton University Press, 2007), 38.

15. Anderson, *Council Daybook*, vol. 4, November 15, 1965, 224.

16. Anderson, *Council Daybook*, vol. 3, October 28, 1964, 197.

17. Fresquet, *The Drama of Vatican II*, 634.

18. Fresquet, *The Drama of Vatican II*, 645.

19. Anderson, *Council Daybook*, vol. 3, September 29, 1965, 67; 69.

20. Anderson, *Council Daybook*, vol. 3, September 30, 1965, 76.

21. Anderson, *Council Daybook*, vol. 3, October 11, 1965, 115.

22. Anderson, *Council Daybook*, vol. 3, October 11, 1965, 119.

23. Anderson, *Council Daybook*, vol. 3, November 13, 1965, 219.

Chapter Five: Uneven Acceptance

1. Mary Gordon, *Final Payments* (New York: Random House, 1978), 89.

2. It should be made clear, however, that other dioceses on the West Coast were more open to reform. The Diocese of Oakland was a national leader in establishing priest councils and the Archdiocese of Portland was home to Oregon Catholic Press, which published widely used liturgical materials. Portland's archbishop worked closely with the laity and allowed significant parts of the Mass to be said in English well before the Council began. The first Mass performed facing the people occurred in Seattle. Seattle was also the home to the origins of what became the North American Forum on the Catechumenate, the dominant training forum for welcoming adults into the Church through the reinstituted Rite of Christian Initiation for Adults. I would like to thank Patricia Killen for this background.

3. Archdiocesan Liturgical Commissions to Priests, May 27, 1964, Archdiocese of Los Angeles Archives.

4. Interview by Bernard Galm of Sister Corita Kent for the Los Angeles Art Community Group Portrait, 1997, 30f. Typescript at the Corita Art Center of the Immaculate Heart Community, Los Angeles.

5. *Mary's Day 1964*, a film by Baylis Glascock, in DVD *Corita on Teaching and Celebration*. Unless otherwise noted, all quotes from Sister Corita in the proceeding paragraphs come from this film.

6. Ned O'Gorman, "In Celebration of Mary: Sing, March, Feast, Flower," *National Catholic Reporter*, November 11, 1964.

7. Julie Ault, *Come Alive! The Spirited Art of Sister Corita* (London: Four Corners Books, 2006), 37.

8. Martin W. Davis, *The Sisters as Campus Minister* (Washington, D.C.: The Center for Applied Research in the Apostolate, 1970), 7.

9. "The Nun: A Joyous Revolution," *Newsweek*, December 25, 1967, 46.

10. Recommendations of the Eighth General Chapter, July 1963, Immaculate Heart Community Archives, Los Angeles.

11. Circular Letters: Topic for Sermons for Fall, May 9, 1966; Traditional Devotions, October 26, 1966; *Versus Populum* and Altar Decorations, February 2, 1967, Los Angeles Archdiocesan Archives.

12. *National Catholic Reporter*, October 28, 1964; "M'Intyre Assailed by Another Priest," *New York Times*, June 14, 1964; "Negroes Rally Support to Critic of Cardinal," *New York Times*, 15, 1964; "Critic of Cardinal Transferred," *New York Times*, July 25, 1964. The *New York Times* was reporting on the controversy concerning Father William DuBay, who was an associate pastor at a predominately black parish in Compton. He had written Pope Paul VI asking for the removal of Cardinal McIntyre from office because of his failure to support the civil rights of minorities. After making his letter public, DuBay was relieved of his administrative duties in the parish.

13. "51,000 Coliseum Last Sunday Afternoon," *The Tidings*, May 8, 1964.

14. Announcement of Mary's Day, April 27, 1964 in Circular Letters, Los Angeles Archdiocesan Archives and "51,000 Coliseum Last Sunday Afternoon," *The Tidings*, May 8, 1964.

15. "To Archdiocesan Priests from Cardinal McIntyre," *The Tidings*, July 17, 1963. Circular Letters, Los Angeles Archdiocesan Archives.

16. Sister Corita, Galm interview, 34, 35; Don May, *Santa Ana Register*, May 20, 1965. Clipping at Corita Art Center.

17. These stories were all reported in the *National Catholic Reporter*: Altar girls, December 2, 1964; Dominican's removal, November 4, 1964; Epistle reading July 14, 1965; Seminarians, April 20, 1966; Sisters of Loretto, July 6, 1966; Glenmary Sisters, October 5, 1966; Hats, September 14, 1966.

Chapter Six: Design for Change

1. Letter to the editor, *Today's Parish*, Sept./Oct. 1971, 4.

2. "The First Instruction for the Proper Implementation of the Constitution on the Sacred Liturgy," *Inter Oecumenici*, September 26, 1964, Ch 5:91.

3. Episcopal Bulletin, September 8, 1964, Archdiocese of Denver Archives.

4. Episcopal Bulletin, August 25, 1964, Archdiocese of Denver Archives.

5. Robert S. Ellwood, *The Sixties Spiritual Awakening: American Religion Moving from Modern to Postmodern* (New Brunswick, NJ: Rutgers University Press, 1994), 108, 109.

6. Helen Rose Fuchs Ebaugh, *Out of the Cloister: A Study of Organizational Dilemmas* (Austin: University of Texas Press, 1977), 67.

7. "Religion: The Immaculate Heart Rebels," *Time*, February 16, 1970.

8. Parishioner memories recorded in 1992 in preparation for the parish's 25th Anniversary, unpublished manuscript, St. Jude's Catholic Church, Lakewood, Colorado.

9. Kenneth A. Briggs, "Ultratraditionalist Catholics Back a Prelate Opposed to Vatican II," *New York Times*, November 9, 1976.

Chapter Seven: A Deciding People

1. St. Jude's Monthly Newsletter, May 1, 1975.

2. Edward B. Fiske, "Women's Lib on the Marches in the Churches," *New York Times*, May 17, 1970.

3. Thomas J. Noel, *Colorado Catholicism and the Archdiocese of Denver, 1857–1989* (Boulder: University of Colorado Press, 1989), 186.

4. Noel, *Colorado Catholicism*, 186.

5. Thomas J. Reese, *Inside the Vatican: The Politics and Organization of the Catholic Church* (Cambridge, MA: Harvard University Press, 1998), 243.

6. This statement appeared in most St. Jude's parish bulletins in 1973.

7. Joseph V. Nevins, "Education to Catholic Marriage, Part II: Adverse Influences," *Ecclesiastical Review* 79, no. 6 (1928): 621, as cited in Leslie Woodcock Tentler, *Catholics and Conception: An American History* (Ithaca, NY: Cornell University Press, 2004), 43.

8. Samuel A. Stouffer, "Trends in the Fertility of Catholics and Non-Catholics," *The American Journal of Sociology* 41 (September 1935): 143–166; Charles F. Westoff and Elise F. Jones, "The End of 'Catholic' Fertility," *Demography* 16 (May 1979): 209–217.

9. Toledo *Chronicle*, June 26, 1953.

10. Westoff and Jones, "The End of 'Catholic' Fertility," 211, 216.

11. Raymond H. Potvin, Charles F. Westoff, and Norman B. Ryder, "Factors Affecting Catholic Wives' Conformity to Their Church Magisterium's Position on Birth Control," *Journal of Marriage and the Family* 30 (May 1968): 263–272; Melissa J. Wilde, *Vatican II: A Sociological Analysis of Religious Change* (Princeton, NJ: Princeton University Press), 120; Tentler, 5; and Westoff and Jones, 216.

12. John Cogley, "Rome Weighs Its Answer on Birth Control," *New York Times*, June 26, 1966. The birth control commission report was first leaked in Italy, but Vatican influence prevented its publication. Afterward, a copy was acquired by a Dutch priest, Leo Alting von Geusau, who eventually gave it to freelance writer Gary McEoin, who arranged for its publication on April 16, 1977 in the *National Catholic Reporter*; shortly after that, the *Tablet* published it in London.

13. Charles E. Curran, *Loyal Dissent: Memoir of a Catholic Theologian* (Washington, D.C.: Georgetown University Press, 2006), 52.

14. Curran, *Loyal Dissent*, 51.

15. "Priests in Capital Dispute Cardinal on Birth Control," *New York Times*, July 28, 1968.

16. Val Adams, "Cardinal Censures Priests in Encyclical Dispute," *New York Times*, August 24, 1968.

17. "200 Walk Out as Cardinal Backs Birth Edict," *New York Times*, September 23, 1968.

18. The exact number of priest resignations is not known. Even statistics during the sixties and seventies were collected by nonofficial groups. The following numbers are based on national estimates derived from a study of 89 dioceses assembled by scholars who were highly respected for their work on the declining number of priests: Richard A. Schoenherr, Lawrence A. Young, "Quitting the Clergy: Resignations in the Roman Catholic Priesthood," *Journal for the Scientific Study of Religion* 29 (December 1990): 463–481; "The Catholic Exodus: Why Nuns and Priests Are Leaving," *Time*, February 23, 1970.

19. Richard A. Schoenherr, Lawrence Alfred Young, Tsan-Yuang Cheng, *Full Pews and Empty Altars: Demographics of the Priest Shortage in United States Catholic Dioceses*, (Madison: University of Wisconsin Press, 1993), 302.

20. Edward B. Fiske, "Bishops Study Challenges Ban on Married Priests," *New York Times*, April 16, 1971.

21. Edward B. Fiske, "Most Priests Found to Oppose Birth Curb Ban," *New York Times*, April 15, 1971.

22. Willis E. Bartlett, ed. *Evolving Religious Careers* (Center for Applied Research in the Apostolate: Washington, D.C., 1970).

23. George Vescey, "Many Clerics Resigning to 'Get Involved'," *New York Times*, February 15, 1972.

24. These statistics and those in the following paragraph are drawn from "Poll Finds Church Attendance Is Down, but U. S. Holds Lead," *New York Times* December 22, 1968, and William V. D'Antonio, et al, *American Catholics: Gender, Generation, and Commitment* (Walnut Creek, CA: Altamira Press, 2001). Gallup Poll statistics on church attendance are routinely reported in national newspapers and used in surveys of religious America. Other sociologists argue that people notoriously overstate how often they attend their religious services. If as many people attended church as they said they did, the buildings would be overflowing on Sundays. Critics of the polls estimate that only half of adults who reported they went to church every week actually did go. What the polls actually are measuring, then, is religious identity, not actual churchgoing. See C. Kirk Hadaway, Penny Long Marler, and Mark Chaves, "What the Polls Don't Show: A Closer Look at U.S. Church Attendance," *American Sociological Review* 58 (December 1993): 741–752.

25. Andrew M. Greeley, *The American Catholic: A Social Portrait* (New York: Basic Books, 1977), 141–145, 147.

Chapter Eight: Legacies

1. City of Ocala, Planning Department.

2. U.S. Census Bureau, Ranking of Census 2000 and Projected 2030 State Population and Change, April 2005.

3. George Weigel, *Witness to Hope: The Biography of John Paul II* (New York: Harper Perennial, 1999), 207.

4. The Vatican Communication on Female Altar Servers issued by the Congregation for Divine Worship, March 15, 1994, stipulated that bishops had the option, but not the requirement, to permit girls to serve on the altar. However, following Canon 202, no. 3, this was to be understood as a temporary measure (known as *ex temporanea deputatione* in Latin) if circumstances ("for particular reasons," they state) merited it. The Committee on Divine Worship of the United States Conference of Catholic Bishops' current (2009) guidelines does not include this caveat. It does state that "No distinction should be made between the functions carried out in the sanctuary by men and boys and those carried out by women and girls." It does, however, reiterate that the decision is to be left up to the bishop. To eliminate the problem of only laymen being permitted to be acolytes, the term altar server should be used to refer to "those who carry out the functions of the instituted acolyte." See www.usccb.org/liturgy/current/servers.shtml.

5. Joseph Ratzinger, *The Spirit of the Liturgy* (San Francisco, CA: Ignatius, 2001), 130.

6. Carol Glatz, "Vatican: Receiving Eucharist Kneeling Will Be Norm at Papal Liturgies," *Catholic News Service*, June 26, 2008, available at www.catholicnews.com/data/stories/cns/0803381.htm.

7. World statistics based from 2003 were collected in a WHO and Guttmacher Institute study ("Abortion Worldwide: A Decade of Uneven Progress"). These findings were widely reported. See Elisabeth Rosenthal, "Legal or Not, Abortion Rates Similar," *New York Times*, October 11, 2007. The rate of 6.5 abortions per 1,000 childbearing-age women in the Netherlands is from 1996, cited by Stanley K. Henshaw, Susheela Singh, and Taylor Haas, "The Incidence of Abortion Worldwide," *International Family Planning Perspectives* 25 (1999), 30–38. On religious group differences, see Stanley K. Henshaw and Kathryn Kost, "Abortion Patients in 1994–1995: Characteristics and Contraceptive Use," *Family Planning Perspectives* 28 (1996): 140–147, 158, as reproduced online at www.guttmacher.org/pubs/journals/2814096.html; and R. K. Jones, J. E. Darroch, and S. K. Henshaw,

"Contraceptive Use Among U.S. Women Having Abortions in 2000–2001, *Perspectives on Sexual and Reproductive Health* 34 (2002): 294–303.

8. General Instruction of the Roman Missal, 2002, para. 373.

9. Cian Molloy, "Irish Directory Shows Ireland Heading Toward Major Priest Shortage," *Catholic News Service*, February 27, 2008, available at www.catholic news.com/data/stories/cns/0801105.htm.

10. The statistics are for 2002 and come from Dean R. Hoge and Aniedi Okure, *International Priests in America* (Collegeville, MN: Liturgical Press, 2006), 29.

11. Gail Besse, "Many Parishes Lay Led, Despite Vatican Reaffirming Priest's Role," *National Catholic Register*, June 14, 2006, available at www.catholic.org/ national/national_story.php?id=20205. In 1992 the American bishops asked Father Philip Murnion to conduct a study of lay ministries, and the results were published by the National Pastoral Life Center as *New Parish Ministers*. An update was conducted in 1999 and published as *Parishes and Parish Ministers: A Study in Parish Lay Ministry*. The statistics have been widely reproduced in books that discuss parish ministry.

12. Data on church finances come from "Financing Catholic Parishes," 2002, Georgetown University's Center for Applied Research on the Apostolate online, http://cara.georgetown.edu/pdfs/FinancingCatholicParishes.pdf; and from Blessed Trinity from their summary of the Stewardship Way of Life, located on their Web page, www.blessedtrinity.org.

13. Ellen Idler, "Religious Involvement and the Health of the Elderly: Some Hypotheses and an Initial Test," *Social Forces* 66 (1987): 236.

BIBLIOGRAPHICAL ESSAY

Chapter One: Catholic Neighborhoods

The family history of the Liebel and Froess family was constructed from census records, Erie city and business directories, and interviews in Pennsylvania and Germany. I would like to thank Ray Froess for his family history records. Maria Froess in Bechenheim, Germany, and Franz Pfadt in Leimersheim deepened my understanding of the European context. In Erie, Mercyhurst College provided hospitality; the librarians at the Erie Public Library their expertise; and the staff at the Sacred Heart, St. Joseph's, and St. John's parishes access to their archives.

For early Erie history, see Samuel P. Bates, *History of Erie County, Pennsylvania* (Chicago: Warner, Beers & Co., 1884) and Edward Herald Mott, *Between the Ocean and the Lakes: The Story of Erie* (New York: Ticker, 1908).

A recent survey of German immigration and cultural impact is Frank Trommler and Elliott Shore, *The German-American Encounter: Conflict and Co-operation between Two Cultures, 1800–2000* (New York: Berghahn Books, 2001). German American Catholic history is thinner than that of the Irish or Italians. Although I think he overstresses the difference between the two communities, the classic social history of the early period remains Jay Dolan, *The Immigrant Church: New York's Irish and German Catholics, 1815–1865* (Baltimore, MD: Johns Hopkins University Press, 1975). For a wider and more politically oriented history, see Colman J. Barry, *The Catholic Church and German Americans* (Milwaukee, WI: Bruce Publishing Company, 1953) as well as Reinhard R. Doerries, "Immigrants and the Church: German-Americans in Comparative Perspective," in *German-American Immigration and Ethnicity in Comparative Perspective*, ed. Wolfgang Johannes Helbich and Waren D. Kamphoefner, 3–18 (Madison, WI: Max Kade Institute for German-American Studies, 2004) and Philip Gleason, *Conservative Reformers: German-American Catholics and the Social Order* (Notre

Dame, IN: Notre Dame University Press, 1968). An excellent summary in English of recent German scholarship on the relationship between church and state in the nineteenth century is Oded Heilbronner's review article, "From Ghetto to Ghetto: The Place of German Catholic Society in Recent Historiography," *The Journal of Modern History* 72 (June 2000): 453–495. The works Heilbronner reviews support ideas developed in Ronald Ross, *The Failure of Bismark's Kulturkampf* (Washington, D.C.: Catholic University of American Press, 1998).

The story of the St. Joseph's cemetery dispute was narrated in their seventy-fifth anniversary parish history from 1918 and then reproduced in a 1992 commemorative volume, *Saint Joseph's Parish, Erie, Pennsylvania, 1867–1992*. This and other valuable materials on local Catholic life may be found at Catholic University in their American Catholic Pamphlets and Parish History Database.

The story of "Vatican I" comes from James J. Hennesey, *The First Council of the Vatican: The American Experience* (New York: Herder and Herder, 1963), but a more engaging account of the struggles between church and state that circled around the Council is David Kertzer, *Prisoner of the Vatican: The Pope's Secret Plot to Capture Rome from the New Italian State* (New York: Houghton Mifflin, 2004). For a general survey of European ideas and events that shaped modern Catholicism, see Michael Burleigh, *Earthly Powers: The Clash of Religion and Politics in Europe from the French Revolution to the Great War* (New York: Harper Perennial, 2005). For the theological, Raymond F. Bulman and Frederick J. Parrella, eds., *From Trent to Vatican II: Historical and Theological Investigations* (New York: Oxford University Press, 2006) as well as the wide-ranging set of essays edited by Darrell Jodock, *Roman Catholic Modernism and Anti-Modernism in Historical Context* (New York: Cambridge University Press, 2000). For the U.S. situation, see Thomas McAvoy, *The Americanist Heresy in Roman Catholicism, 1895–1900* (Notre Dame, IN: University of Notre Dame Press, 1963).

Many of the encyclicals and other papal documents have been placed online. See the links under "libraries" hosted by EWTN (Eternal Word Television Network) at www.ewtn.com and "Papal Encyclicals On-Line" at www.papal encyclicals.net.

I have described nineteenth-century Catholic life in several articles and books. See Colleen McDannell, *The Christian Home in Victorian America, 1840–1900* (Bloomington: Indiana University Press, 1986) for domestic devotions; "Going to the Ladies' Fair: New York's Irish Catholics," in *The New York Irish*, ed. Ronald Baylor and Timothy Meagher, 234–251(Baltimore, MD: Johns Hopkins Press, 1997) for female fundraising; and "Christian Kitsch and the Rhetoric of Bad Taste," in *Material Christianity: Religion and Popular Culture in America* (New Haven, CT: Yale University Press, 1998), 163–197 for church decorations and design. For the Erie situation, I used the diocesan newspaper, the *Lake Shore Visitor*. The advertisements for liturgical arts that companies added to *The*

Official Catholic Directory are invaluable for actually seeing what was considered to be good Catholic design.

Ann C. Rose argues that mixed marriages were agents of change in an American culture moving towards pluralism. See her *Beloved Strangers: Interfaith Families in Nineteenth Century America* (Cambridge, MA: Harvard University Press, 2001). The Diocesan Archives of Erie contain many letters of requests for dispensations for interfaith couples.

The inner life of those involved in Catholic devotions before World War II, which included attending novenas, is beautifully described in Robert Orsi, *Thank You St. Jude: Women's Devotions to the Patron Saint of Hopeless Causes* (New Haven, CT: Yale University Press, 1998). For a synthetic sketch, see James F. White, *Roman Catholic Worship from Trent to Today* (Collegeville, MN: Liturgical Press, 2003).

Statistics on churches and schools reproduced throughout this book are drawn from *The Official Catholic Directory* published yearly by P. J. Kenedy and Sons since 1817. On the Sisters of Saint Joseph, see *Centenary of the Sisters of St. Joseph of Northwestern Pennsylvania in the Diocese of Erie, 1860–1960*, privately published and located at the Catholic University of America, American Catholic Pamphlets and Parish History Database. Information on individual sisters and their teaching was collected from the Sisters of St. Joseph of Northwestern Pennsylvania from their Erie archives. Catholic proponents of parochial education published many statements of the problems with modern, secular education. For instance, see Thomas J. Jenkins, *The Judges of Faith and Godless Schools: A Compilation of Evidence Against Secular Schools the World Over Especially Against Common State Schools* (New York: New York Catholic Agency, 1882) and the Jesuit Paul L. Blakely's *May An American Oppose the Public Schools?* (New York: The American Press, 1937). I would like to thank Mary Grace Lewis for allowing me access to the attic of Francis Froess, who kept school materials from the 1920s and 1930s.

Chapter Two: Postwar Suburbs

The number of individual monographs on World War II battles is voluminous, but studies of how the war changed individuals are more limited. See Gerald F. Linderman, *The World Within War: America's Combat Experience in World War II* (New York: Free Press, 1997, Harvard University Press, 1999) and Lee Kennett, *G. I.: The American Soldier in World War II* (New York: Scribner, 1987). On the home front, see Emily Yellin, *Our Mothers' War: American Women at Home and at the Front During World War II* (New York: Free Press, 2004); Amy Bentley, *Eating for Victory: Food Rationing and the Politics of Domesticity* (Urbana: University of Illinois Press, 1998); Nancy Baker Wise and Christy Wise, *A Mouthful of Rivets:*

Women at Work in World War II (San Francisco: Jossey-Bass, 1994); John W. Jeffries, *Wartime America: The World War II Home Front* (Chicago: I. R. Dee, 1996); and Allan M. Winkler, *Home Front U.S.A.: America During World War II* (Arlington Heights, IL: H. Davidson, 1986).

The intersection between World War II, religion, and media is explored in Deborah Dash Moore, *GI Jews: How World War II Changed a Generation* (Cambridge, MA: Harvard University Press, 2004) and in the chapters on *Song of Bernadette* and *Going My Way* in Colleen McDannell, ed. *Catholics in the Movies* (New York: Oxford University Press, 2007). On Bernadette and Lourdes, see also John T. McGreevey, "Bronx Miracle," *American Quarterly* 52, no. 3 (2000): 405–443. For discussion of war multiculturalism, see Gary Gerstle, *American Crucible: Race and Nation in the Twentieth Century* (Princeton, NJ: Princeton University Press, 2001).

For the GI Bill and its contribution to the "civic generation," see Suzanne Mettler, *Solders to Citizens: The GI-Bill and the Making of the Greatest Generation* (New York: Oxford, 2005). For a general survey that sees the Bill as a "Congressional success story," see Glenn Altschuler and Stuart Blumin, *The GI-Bill: The New Deal for Veterans* (New York: Oxford University Press, 2009). On the specific situation at Penn State, see Michael Bezilla, *Penn State: An Illustrated History* (University Park: Pennsylvania State University Press, 1985). Political scientist Robert D. Putnam popularized the notion of a "civic generation" in a 1995 article and expanded it in his book *Bowling Alone: The Collapse and Revival of American Community* (New York: Simon & Schuster, 2000), although in that book he was trying to understand those who were *not* civic minded.

The Catholic cult of pain in the postimmigration era is explored by Robert Orsi in *Thank You Saint Jude: Women's Devotion to the Patron Saint of Hopeless Causes* (New Haven, CT: Yale University Press, 1996) and "'Mildred, Is It Fun to Be a Cripple?' The Culture of Suffering in Mid-Twentieth Century American Catholicism" in *Between Heaven and Earth: The Religious Worlds People Make and the Scholars Who Study Them* (Princeton: Princeton University Press, 2005), 19–47. Based on her study of the prescriptive literature of the Catholic popular media, Paula Kane presents the contours of conservative Catholic womanhood in "Marian Devotion Since 1940: Continuity or Casualty?" in *Habits of Devotion: Catholic Practice in Twentieth-Century America*, ed. James M. O'Toole, 89–130 (Ithaca, NY: Cornell University Press, 2004). My own perspective on the loosening of the "offer it up" philosophy is shared by Timothy Kelly, "Our Lady of Perpetual Help, Gender Roles, and the Decline of Devotional Catholicism," *Journal of Social History* 32 (1998): 5–26.

On Toledo, see John Robinson Block et al., *Toledo: Our Life, Our Times,* vol. 2 1800 to 1960 (Toledo: The Blade, 2006) and *Growing Toledo: A Ten Year Comparison,* 1953–1963, prepared by the city budget office in 1964.

The religious revival of the 1950s has been well documented by historians of American religions. A good introduction includes Patrick Allitt, *Religion in America Since 1945: A History* (New York: Columbia University Press, 2003); James Hudnut-Beumler, *Looking for God in the Suburbs: The Religion of the American Dream and Its Critics* (New Brunswick, NJ: Rutgers University Press, 1994); and Charles H. Lippy, *Being Religious, American Style: A History of Popular Religiosity in the United States* (Westport, CT: Praeger, 1994). Mark Silk discusses the creation of a postwar "Judeo-Christian tradition" in *Spiritual Politics: Religion and America Since World War II* (New York: Simon and Schuster, 1988).

For Catholic popular culture, see Mark Massa, *Catholics and American Culture: Fulton Sheen, Dorothy Day, and the Notre Dame Football Team* (New York: Crossroad, 1999); and for Catholic involvement with Protestants to create "clean" literature, see Una M. Cadegan, "Guardians of Democracy or Cultural Storm Troopers? American Catholics and the Control of Popular Media, 1934–1966," *The Catholic Historical Review* 87 (2001): 252–282; and Catholic collaboration with Jews in Kevin M. Schultz, "'Favoritism Cannot Be Tolerated': Challenging Protestantism in America's Public Schools and Promoting the Neutral State," *American Quarterly* 59 (2007): 565–591. The anti-Catholicism of postwar intellectuals, of which Paul Blanshard is only the most well known, is astutely discussed by John T. McGreevy in "Thinking on One's Own: Catholicism in the American Intellectual Imagination, 1928–1960," *The Journal of American History* 84 (1997): 97–131.

Although he frequently criticizes writers on Catholicism as having few actual statistics to back up their assumptions and conclusions, Andrew M. Greeley's *The Church and The Suburbs* (New York: Sheed and Ward, 1959) relies mostly on generalizations rather than collected data and actually reflects very little on real life in the suburban parish. Other studies from the period include Gerhard Lenski, *The Religious Factor: A Sociological Study of Religion's Impact on Politics, Economics, and Family Life* (Garden City, NY: Doubleday, 1961), and the work of the priest-sociologist Joseph H. Fichter, *Priest and People* (New York: Sheed and Ward, 1965), *Social Relations in the Urban Parish* (Chicago: University of Chicago Press, 1954), and *Dynamics of a City Church* (Chicago: University of Chicago Press, 1951).

Statistical information on churches in Toledo, Ohio, are drawn from materials contained in the Diocesan Archives: *Official Year Book of the Diocese of Toledo*, *Diocese of Toledo Annual Report*, and the multivolume history of the diocese, written by Lawrence A. Mossing, *The Golden Era in the Diocese of Toledo*, vol. 8 (Diocese of Toledo, 1991). The Diocesan newspaper, *The Chronicle*, is available on microfilm at the Lucas County Library in Toledo.

Although the reception of the Eucharist is by far the most important ritual in the lives of Catholics, it has been studied primarily from a theological perspective.

For the rare social-historical approach, see Margaret M. McGuinness, "Let Us Go to the Altar: American Catholics and the Eucharist, 1926–1976," in James M. O'Toole, *Habits of Devotion*.

There are many books on the European side of the Liturgical Movement, but the only one that looks at it from the vantage point of the American parish is Keith F. Pecklers, *The Unread Vision: The Liturgical Movement in the United States of America: 1926–1955* (Collegeville, MN: The Liturgical Press, 1998). See also Louis Bouyer, *Liturgical Piety* (Notre Dame, IN: Notre Dame Press, 1955), the memoir of Bernard Botte, *From Silence to Participation: An Insider's View of Liturgical Renewal*, trans. John Sullivan (Washington, D.C.: Liturgical Press, 1988), and the introduction to the texts in R. Kevin Seasoltz, *The New Liturgy: A Documentation, 1903–1965* (New York: Herder and Herder, 1966). Reform in art is discussed in Susan White, *Art, Architecture, and Liturgical Reform: The Liturgical Arts Society, 1928–1972* (New York: Pueblo Pub. Co., 1990). The harsh perspective of liturgical reformers on the average parishioner appears frequently in liberal Catholic magazines of the period, especially *Commonweal* and *America*.

The relationship between domesticity and political containment is explored in Elaine May, *Homeward Bound: American Families in the Cold War Era* (New York: Basic Books, 1988). Although Catholic leaders and parishioners were involved as major producers and consumers of anticommunism publications, this history has not been fully analyzed. For a case study of one Cold War Catholic figure see, James T. Fisher, *Dr. America: The Lives of Thomas A. Dooley, 1927–1961* (Amherst: University of Massachusetts Press, 1997).

Because St. Agnes is no longer an active church, her Jubilee volume (1910–1985) may be found at the Lucas County Public Library. Christ the King parish has its fiftieth anniversary book written by Father Michael O. Brown as well as a complete set of bulletins and letters sent to parishioners from the establishment of the parish in 1954 through the end of Father Goes's pastorate in 1978. I would like to thank the senior parishioners of Christ the King parish who I interviewed as well as the retired Sisters of Notre Dame who graciously shared their memories of teaching at Christ the King.

Although the 1950s were a critical period for American Catholicism, there is not a comprehensive social history of the era. I have relied on Dennis Castillo, "The Origin of the Priest Shortage: 1942–62," *America* (October 24, 1992): 302–304 for the pre-Vatican II state of male vocations. The declining interest in mass displays of Catholic devotionalism is argued by Timothy Kelly in "Suburbanization and the Decline of Catholic Public Ritual in Pittsburgh" *Journal of Social History* 28 (1994): 311–330 and the first part of his *The Transformation of American Catholicism: The Pittsburgh Laity and the Second Vatican Council, 1950–1972* (Notre Dame, IN: Notre Dame University Press, 2009). On the history of Catholic schools, see Timothy Walch, *Parish School: American Catholic Parochial Education from Colonial Times to the Present*, (New York: Crossroad, 1996).

Chapter Three: Gathering in Los Angeles and Rome

The impact of Catholicism on the American culture and society of the fifties has been astutely chronicled by James T. Fisher. Beginning with his *The Catholic Counterculture in America, 1933–1962* (Chapel Hill: University of North Carolina Press, 1989), he considered Catholics as diverse as Jack Kerouac and Dorothy Day. This history of an era continued in a series of articles for the *U. S. Catholic Historian*: "Alternative Voices of Catholic Intellectual Vitality," 13 (Winter 1995): 81–94; "The Second Catholic President: Ngo Dinh Diem, John F. Kennedy, and the Vietnam Lobby, 1954–1963," 15 (Summer 1997): 119–137; and "John M. Corridan, S. J., and the Battle for the Soul of the Waterfront, 1948–1954," 16 (Fall 1998): 71–87. This last article was expanded into his *On the Irish Waterfront: The Crusader, the Movie and the Soul of the Port of New York* (Ithaca, NY: Cornell University Press, 2009). These books as well as his study of Tom Dooley clearly situate Catholics at the heart of postwar America.

Biographies of Pope John XXIII are multiple and take a variety of positions on the charismatic pontiff. The classic historical study is Peter Hebblethwaite, *John XXIII: Pope of the Century*, 2nd ed. (New York: Continuum, 2000); and a pithy recent biography is by Thomas Cahill, *Pope John XXIII* (New York: Penguin Books, 2002). More focused perspectives are Christine Feldman, *Pope John XXIII: A Spiritual Biography*, trans. Peter Heinegg (New York: Crossroad, 2000) and the pope's own reflections, *Journal of a Soul: The Autobiography of Pope John XXIII*, trans. Dorothy White (McGraw, 1965; New York: Image Books, 1999).

Likewise there are many biographies of John F. Kennedy, all of which deal to some extent with his Catholicism. Thomas J. Carty, *A Catholic in the White House?: Religion, Politics, and John F. Kennedy's Presidential Campaign* (New York: Palgrave Macmillan, 2004) and Shaun A. Casey, *The Making of a Catholic President: Kennedy v. Nixon, 1960* (New York: Oxford University Press, 2009) specifically explore the political implications of Kennedy's religion. Critic and peace activist Norman Cousins explored the connection of these powerful "Johns" in *The Improbable Triumvirate: John F. Kennedy, Pope John, Nikita Khrushchev* (New York: W. W. Norton, 1972) as did Garry Wills in *Bare Ruined Choirs* (New York: Doubleday, 1972).

The history of California is laid out by its state librarian, Kevin Starr, in multiple volumes. On the development of Monterey Park, see *The History of the City of Monterey Park: A Bicentennial Report* (np, 1976) and volume one of *The Historical Volume and Reference Works: Los Angeles County* (Los Angeles, CA: Historical Publishers, 1962).

Important works on the Second Vatican Council are cited in chapter 4 and on the sixties in chapters 5 and 6. However, on the Cuban Missile crisis, see Alice L. George, *Awaiting Armageddon: How Americans Faced the Cuban Missile Crisis* (Chapel Hill: University of North Carolina Press, 2003); Max Frankel, *High Noon in the Cold War: Kennedy, Khrushchev, and the Cuban Missile Crisis* (New York: Ballantine Books, 2004); and Sheldon M. Stern, *The Week the World Stood Still: Inside the Secret Cuban Missile Crisis* (Stanford, CA: Stanford University Press, 2005).

Chapter Four: The Council and Its Decisions

I have used Walter M. Abbott and Joseph Gallagher's edition of *The Documents of Vatican II* (New York: The American Press, 1966) and a slightly different translation available on-line from the Vatican Archives at www.vatican.va/archive/index.htm (accessed September 11, 2009). Monsignor Vincent A. Yzermans published the actual texts of 118 interventions by American bishops in *American Participation in the Second Vatican Council* (New York: Sheed and Ward, 1967).

The most accessible and insightful work on the Second Vatican Council is John W. O'Malley, *What Happened at Vatican II* (Cambridge, MA: Harvard University Press, 2008). This text not only details the events, characters, and theology of the Council, but it also sets them in historical context and provides their intellectual significance. The collection of scholarly articles in the five volume *History of Vatican II*, edited by Giuseppe Alberigo and Joseph Komonchak (Maryknoll, NY: Orbis Books /Leuven: Peeters, 1996–2006) is the most thorough study of the events and debates of Vatican II to date. The authors draw on the texts of the debates, diaries of the participants, and news reports to trace out the slow evolution of each of the documents. The volumes are Vol. I: *Announcement and Preparation of Vatican II* (1995); Vol. II: *The Formation of the Council's Identity: First Period & Intersession, October 1962–September 1963* (1998); Vol. III: *A Mature Council: The Second Period & Intersession, October 1963–September 1964* (2000); Vol. IV: *Church as Communion: Third Period & Intersession, October 1964– September 1965* (2004); Vol. V: *The Fourth Period and the End of Vatican II* (2006). These highly technical volumes have been condensed into one volume geared to the general reader: Giuseppe Alberigo, *A Brief History of Vatican II*, trans. Matthew Sherry (New York: Orbis, 2006).

The publication of the Giuseppe Alberigo and Joseph Komonchak volumes have provoked reflections on whether or not something "revolutionary" happened at the Council—for good or for bad—or if it simply was a continuation of Catholic theological development. A summary of that debate is provided in John W. O'Malley et al., *Vatican II: Did Anything Happen?* (New York: Continuum, 2007). For a nontheological, sociological interpretation of the Council that looks explicitly at the negotiations and compromises, see Melissa J. Wilde, *Vatican II: A*

Sociological Analysis of Religious Change (Princeton, NJ: Princeton University Press, 2007).

Good general introductions to the Council written at the time include Adrian Hastings, *A Concise Guide to the Documents of the Second Vatican Council* (London: Darton, Longman and Todd, 1968); Gary MacEoin, *What Happened at Rome? The Council and its Implications for the Modern World* (New York: Holt, Rinehart and Winston, 1966); and Ralph M. Wiltgen, *The Rhine Flows into the Tiber: A History of Vatican* II (Devon, England: Augustine Pub. Co., 1978). For a negative appraisal, see Michael Davies, *Pope John's Council* (New Rochelle, NY: Arlington House Publishers, 1977).

An excellent interpretation of the Council documents and their impact on world Catholicism by contemporary historians and theologians is Adrian Hastings, ed., *Modern Catholicism: Vatican II and After* (New York: Oxford University Press, 1991).

One of the many news agencies that covered the Council proceedings was the National Catholic Welfare Conference News Service. Under the auspices of the predecessor body to the U.S. Conference of Catholic Bishops, the NCWC News Service provided day-to-day coverage of Vatican II. That coverage, as well as English translations of some speeches, was reproduced in the three volumes of *Council Daybook* (Washington, D.C.: National Catholic Welfare Conference, 1965–1966).

A more controversial journalistic report, because of its clear support of the progressive agenda of the Council Fathers, are the books originally written by Redemptorist priest, Reverend Francis X. Murphy, under the pseudonym "Xavier Rynne." Initially Rynne/Murphy chronicled the Council for the *New Yorker*, but the popularity of his behind-the-scene reports motivated Farrar, Straus and Giroux to publish subsequent volumes on each session. These include *Letters from Vatican City: Vatican Council II (First Session): Background and Debates* (1963); *The Second Session: The Debates and Decrees of Vatican Council II, September 29 to December 4, 1963* (1964); *The Third Session: The Debates and Decrees of Vatican Council II, September 14 to November 21, 1964* (1965); *The Fourth Session: The Debates and Decrees of Vatican Council II, September 14 to December 8, 1965* (1966).

"Xavier Rynne's" American perspective can be broadened by a French one from journalist Henri Fesquet, who provided an almost daily reflection on the Council in *The Drama of Vatican II: The Ecumenical Council June, 1962–December, 1965*, trans. Bernard Murchland (New York: Random House, 1967).

Chapter Five: Uneven Acceptance

The various responses to the social and cultural changes of the sixties are described in Maurice Isserman and Michael Kazin, *America Divided: The Civil War of the 1960s*, 3rd ed. (New York: Oxford University Press, 2007). For the wider social, political, and economic context of the period, see John Morton Blum, *Years of Discord: American Politics and Society, 1961–1974* (New York: Norton, 1991) and Gerard J. DeGroot, *The Sixties Unplugged: A Kaleidoscopic History of a Disorderly Decade* (Cambridge, MA: Harvard University Press, 2008).

On Catholicism in the Midwest, see William Barnaby Faherty, *The St. Louis German Catholics* (St. Louis, MO: Reedy Press, 2004); Charles Shanabruch, *Chicago's Catholics: The Evolution of an American Identity* (Notre Dame, IN: University of Notre Dame Press, 1981); Steven Avella, *This Confident Church: Catholic Leadership and Life in Chicago, 1940–1965* (Notre Dame, IN: University of Notre Dame Press, 1981); Ellen Skerrett, Edward R. Kantowicz, and Steven M. Avella, *Catholicism, Chicago Style* (Chicago: Loyola University Press, 1993); Stephen J. Shaw, "The Cities and the Plains, a Home for God's People: A History of the Catholic Parish in the Midwest," in *The American Catholic Parish*, ed. Jay Dolan (New York: Paulist Press, 1987), 304–356.

Background on St. Stephen's parish and Msgr. O'Carroll is drawn from his obituary in *The Tidings*, January 16, 1987, interviews with Father Larry Estrada and the parishioners of St. Stephen's parish in March of 2008, the Seventy-Fifth Anniversary Bulletin of St. Stephen's (1996), and the "St. Stephen's" file at the Los Angeles Archdiocesan Archives.

Interviews of the Sisters of the Holy Names of Jesus and Mary were conducted in January 2008 at the Villa Holy Names in Los Gatos, California, and in the Los Angeles area in March 2008. I have altered the names of these sisters. A special thank you goes to the Holy Names Heritage Center in Lake Oswego, Oregon, for sending me rule books from the 1950s and 1970s.

The writing on sisters and nuns has expanded in the past two decades and includes scholarly monographs and journalistic appraisals. A good introduction to the history of women religious is Jo Ann Kay McNamara, *Sisters in Arms: Catholic Nuns Through Two Millennia* (Cambridge, MA: Harvard University Press, 1996) and in the United States in particular, John J. Fialka, *Sisters: Catholic Nuns and the Making of America* (New York: St. Martin's Griffin, 2003). An excellent reflection on how nuns were represented in the media and the impact that women religious had on evolving notions of feminism is Rebecca Sullivan, *Visual Habits: Nuns, Feminism, and American Postwar Popular Culture* (Toronto, Canada: University of Toronto Press, 2005). Other monographs on nuns in the American postwar period include Lora Ann Quinonez and Mary Daniel Turner, *The Transformation of American Catholic Sisters* (Philadelphia, PA: Temple University Press, 1992); Helen Rose Fuchs Ebaugh, *Women in the Vanishing Cloister: Organizational Decline in Catholic Religious Orders in the United States* (New Brunswick, NJ: Rutgers University Press, 1993); Marie Augusta Neal, *Catholic Sisters in Transition: From the 1960s to the 1980s* (Wilmington, DE: Michael Glazier,

1984); and Patricia Curran, *Grace Before Meals: Food Ritual and Body Discipline in Convent Culture* (Urbana: University of Illinois Press, 1989).

For sisters in the sixties, the classic statement is Léon Joseph Suenens, *The Nun in the World*, trans. Geoffrey Stevens (Westminster, MD: The Newman Press, 1963). Reflections by sisters of the era include Sister M. Charles Borromeo (Muckenhirn), *The New Nuns* (London: Sheed and Ward, 1968) and Sara Harris, *The Sisters: The Changing World of the American Nun* (Indianapolis, IN: Bobbs-Merrill, 1970). For an example of religious life just prior to the Vatican reforms, see Joan M. Lexau, ed., *Convent Life: Roman Catholic Religious Orders for Women in North America* (New York: Dial Press, 1964).

Sisters and former nuns are now publishing their memoirs that give more intimate glimpses into convent life. Of particular note are Deborah Larsen, *The Tulip and the Pope* (New York: Knopf, 2005); Mary Gilligan Wong, *Nun: A Memoir* (New York: Harcourt Brace Jovanovich, 1983); Sister Jane Kelly, *X-Rated Nun: Woman of Integrity* (New York: iUniverse, 2006); and from the same time in Australia, Cecilia Inglis, *Cecilia: An Ex-Nun's Extraordinary Journey* (New York: Penguin Books, 2003).

Some books by journalists filter the stories of sisters through their understanding of the larger Church. For sisters struggling because the Church is too conservative, see Kenneth Briggs, *Double Crossed: Uncovering the Catholic Church's Betrayal of American Nuns* (New York: Doubleday, 2006). For their problems being caused by a too liberal approach, see Ann Carey, *Sisters in Crisis: The Tragic Unraveling of Women's Religious Communities* (Huntington, IN: Our Sunday Visitor, 1997).

Although the Archdiocese of Los Angeles played a major role in the history of American Catholicism, scholarship on it is quite limited. The standard work is the two volume, *His Eminence of Los Angeles*, written by Monsignor Francis J. Weber, the archdiocesan archivist (Mission Hills, CA: St. Francis Historical Society, 1997). However, because Monsignor Weber limits scholarly access to the archives, his conclusions cannot be tested against the existing documentation. I was permitted to see only the "Circulars"—general letters sent from the Cardinal and various offices of the Archdiocese to the priests of the Archdiocese.

The discussion of Mary's Day is drawn from Julie Ault, *Come Alive! The Spirited Art of Sister Corita* (London: Four Corners Books, 2006); two films: *Primary Colors: The Story of Corita* (South Carolina Educational Television Network, 1990) and *Mary's Day 1964* (Baylis Glascock Films, 2007); and archival materials from the Corita Art Center of Immaculate Heart Community, Los Angeles.

Unfortunately, the story of the Immaculate Heart Sisters has been reduced to the conflict with Cardinal McIntyre. This story makes its way into most histories of American Catholic nuns. Those histories, however, are limited because Monsignor Francis J. Weber, the Los Angeles archdiocesan archivist, has closed

McIntyre's correspondence on the conflict. Weber's pro-cardinal telling is found in *His Eminence,* vol. II, pp. 416–441. For a contrasting view presented by the order's mother general of the time, see Anita M. Caspary, *Witness to Integrity: The Crisis of the Immaculate Heart Community of California* (Collegeville, MN: The Liturgical Press, 2003). Background on the order and its rules comes from the Immaculate Heart Community Archives, Los Angeles. Memoirs by former Immaculate Hearts also were helpful; see Midge Turk, *The Buried Life: A Nun's Journey* (New York: The World Publishing Company, 1971) and Jeanne Cordova, "My Immaculate Heart," in *Lesbian Nuns: Breaking Silence*, ed. Rosemary Curb and Nancy Manahan, (Tallahassee, FL: Naiad Press, 1985), 3–15.

On Proposition 14, see Thomas W. Casstevens, *Politics, Housing and Race Relations: California's Rumford Act and Proposition 14* (Berkeley, CA: Institute of Governmental Studies, 1967). Although the history of Catholics and race in California has yet to be written, a model for such a study is John T. McGreevy, *Parish Boundaries: The Catholic Encounter with Race in the Twentieth-Century Urban North* (Chicago: University of Chicago Press, 1998). On nuns and race relations, see Amy L. Koehlinger, *The New Nuns: Racial Justice and Religious Reform in the 1960s* (Cambridge, MA: Harvard University Press, 2007) and Suellen Hoy, *Good Hearts: Catholic Sisters in Chicago's Past* (Urbana: University of Illinois Press, 2006).

Chapter Six: Design for Change

For general surveys on religion in the sixties and early seventies, see Robert S. Ellwood, *The Sixties Spiritual Awakening: American Religion Moving from Modern to Postmodern* (New Brunswick, NJ: Rutgers University Press, 1994); Robert Wuthnow, *The Restructuring of American Religion: Society and Faith Since World War II* (Princeton, NJ: Princeton University Press, 1988); and Howard Brick, *Age of Contradiction: American Thought and Culture in the 1960s* (New York: Twayne, 1998). For the parallel countercultural movement among evangelical Protestants, see Preston Shires, *Hippies of the Religious Right* (Waco, TX: Baylor University Press, 2007). A more theoretical volume that places the era in a global perspective is Hugh McLeod, *The Religious Crisis of the 1960s* (New York: Oxford University Press, 2008).

As this book was going to press, Mark Massa published his summary of this tumultuous decade: *The American Catholic Revolution: How the '60s Changed the Church Forever* (New York: Oxford University Press, 2010). David Frum makes a persuasive case for the seventies' importance in *How We Got Here, The 70s, The Decade that Brought You Modern Life—For Better or For Worse* (New York: Basic Books, 2000). For histories with less ideological bent and more appreciation for the change the era wrought, see Peter Carroll, *It Seemed Like Nothing Happened: America in the 1970s* (New Brunswick, NJ: Rutgers University Press, 1990); Bruce

J. Schulman, *The Seventies: The Great Shift in American Culture, Society, and Politics* (New York: Free Press, 2001); Beth Bailey and David Farber, eds., *America in the Seventies* (Lawrence: University Press of Kansas, 2004); and Edward D. Berkowitz, *Something Happened: A Political and Cultural Overview of the Seventies* (New York: Columbia University Press, 2006).

I interviewed and worked with archival materials at St. Jude's parish in November of 2007 and September of 2008. In particular I would like to thank Susan and Fred Clarke, Bryon and Anne Finnefrock, Pat O'Connell, Bob Mueller, Arlene and Leo Schneider, Mur and Jim Hiltenbrand, Bill Campbell, Roger and Nancy Frenette, Helen Marie Hurt, Mary Clydesdale, Elaine and Bob Brennan, and William Sievers for their interviews. Steve Hickie, St. Jude's business administrator, graciously made available parish files, bulletins, histories, surveys, dedication booklets, "open forum" summaries, and newspaper clippings. A general history of St. Jude parish is found in *Saint Jude Church Lakewood, Colorado* (1970) and *Saint Jude Parish Directory* (1975).

Background on the Denver archdiocese is found in Thomas J. Noel's *Colorado Catholicism and the Archdiocese of Denver, 1957–1989* (Boulder: University of Colorado Press, 1989) and available online at www.archden.org/noel. The Archdiocese of Denver Archives has a set of Archbishop Vehr's scrapbooks, the "Liturgy Newsletter" from the early seventies, pastoral bulletins, and "circular letters" sent to archdiocesan priests. Papers from Archbishop Casey are thin because, according to archivist Karyl Klein, "the bulk of them were destroyed upon his death." The clipping file at the Denver Public Library contains articles on Catholic developments from the sixties and seventies.

A critical history of Catholic popular music in postwar America has not been written. Beginning efforts are Mark Oppenheimer, "Roman Catholics and the Folk Mass," in *Knocking on Heaven's Door: American Religion in the Age of Counterculture* (New Haven, CT: Yale University Press, 2003), 62–93, and Ken Canedo, *Keep the Fire Burning: The Folk Mass Revolution* (Portland, OR: The Pastoral Press, 2009). See also Miriam Therese Winter, *The Singer and the Song: An Autobiography of the Spirit* (Maryknoll, NY: Orbis Books, 1999) and *Why Sing? Toward a Theology of Catholic Church Music* (Portland, OR: The Pastoral Press, 1984). For the impact of the Council on music, see James J. Boyce, "Singing a New Song unto the Lord: Catholic Church Music," in *From Trent to Vatican II: Historical and Theological Investigations*, ed. Raymond F. Bulman and Frederick J. Parrella (Oxford: Oxford University Press, 2006) 137–159. The story of the "Singing Nun" is recounted in Rebecca Sullivan, *Visual Habits: Nuns, Feminism, and American Postwar Popular Culture* (Toronto, Canada: University of Toronto Press, 2005), 157–189. On the folk music revival, see Gillian Mitchell, *The North American Folk Music Revival: Nation and Identity in the United States and Canada, 1945–1980* (Aldershot, England: Ashgate, 2007); Dick Weissman and Ronald D. Cohen,

Which Side Are You On? An Inside History of the Folk Music Revival in America (New York: Continuum, 2005); Ronald D. Cohen, *Rainbow Quest: The Folk Music Revival and American Society, 1940–1970* (Amherst: University of Massachusetts Press, 2002); and Robert Cantwell, *When We Were Good: The Folk Revival* (Cambridge, MA: Harvard University Press, 1996).

For the expanding role of the laity, of which "little parishes" were a part, see sources listed in the next chapter.

Examples of warnings about declining Catholic schools include Mary Perkins Ryan, *Are Parochial Schools the Answer? Catholic Education in the Light of the Council* (New York: Holt, Rinehart and Winston, 1964); Reginald A. Neuwien, ed., *Catholic Schools in Action: A Report* (Notre Dame, IN: University of Notre Dame Press, 1966); Daniel Callahan, *Federal Aid and Catholic Schools* (Baltimore, MD: Helicon, 1964); C. Albert Koob and Russell Shaw, *S. O. S. for Catholic Schools* (New York: Holt, Rinehart and Winston, 1970); William E. Brown and Andrew M. Greeley, *Can Catholic Schools Survive?* (New York: Sheed and Ward, 1970); Frances Forde Plude, *The Flickering Light: What's Happening to Catholic schools?* (New York: W. H. Sadlier, 1974); and Andrew M. Greeley, William C. McCready, and Kathleen McCourt, *Catholic Schools in a Declining Church* (Kansas City, MO: Sheed and Ward, 1975).

For the declining number of women entering religious orders, see references on Catholics sisters and nuns listed in the previous chapter.

Every historian of twentieth-century Catholicism has noted that many Catholics rejected the changes of the Vatican Council, but there has not been an analytical survey of the contours of that rejection. Although not specifically focusing on "average" Catholics, Mary Jo Weaver and R. Scott Appleby's collection of essays, *Being Right: Conservative Catholics in America* (Bloomington: Indiana University Press, 1995) does lay out the varieties of ways Catholics rejected the liberal trends of the sixties and seventies. For an intellectual history, see Patrick Allitt, *Catholic Intellectuals and Conservative Politics in America, 1950–1985* (Ithaca, NY: Cornell University Press, 1993). For a concise description of alternative, anti-Vatican II Catholic organizations, see William D. Dinges, "Roman Catholic Traditionalism," in *America's Alternative Religions*, ed. Timothy Miller, 101–108 (Albany: SUNY Press, 1995) and his "We Are What You Were: Roman Catholic Traditionalism in America," in *Being Right*.

Criticism of the outcome of the Second Vatican Council was less pronounced during the seventies than in later years. Early criticism includes John Eppstein, *Has the Catholic Church Gone Mad?* (New Rochelle, NY: Arlington House, 1971); James Hitchcock, *The Recovery of the Sacred* (New York: Seabury, 1974); and the surveys of British writer, Michael Davis: *Cranmer's Godly Order: The Destruction of Catholicism through Liturgical Change* (1976) and *Pope John's Council* (1977), both originally published in New Rochelle, New York, by Arlington House Press.

Chapter Seven: A Deciding People

A "theology of the laity" developed in postwar Europe and structured the discussion both during the Council and during the implementation period; see Michael de la Bedoyere, *The Layman in the Church* (London: Burns & Oates, 1954); J. M. Perrin, *Forward the Layman*, trans. Katherine Gordon (Westminster, MD: Newman Press, 1956); Gerard Phillips, *The Role of the Laity in the Church*, trans. John R. Gilbert and James W. Moudry (Chicago: Fides Publishers, 1957); Jacques Leclercq, *Christians in the World*, trans. Kathleen Pond (New York: Sheed & Ward, 1961); E. H. Schillebeeckx, *The Layman in the Church, and Other Essays* (Staten Island, NY: Alba House, 1963); Yves Congar, *People in the Church: A Study for a Theology of Laity*, trans. Donald Attwater (Westminster, MD: Newman Press, 1967).

Historical studies of how the laity actualized the ideas contained in the theology are far fewer. General reflection on the people in the pews are contained within standard Catholic histories such as Jay Dolan's *The American Catholic Experience: A History from Colonial Times to the Present* (Garden City, NY: Doubleday, 1985) and James Hennesey, *American Catholics: A History of the Roman Catholic Community in the United States* (New York: Oxford University Press, 1981). A more recent survey that focuses on lay experience but does not come up with a story different from earlier scholarship is James M. O'Toole, *The Faithful: A History of Catholics in America* (Cambridge, MA: Harvard University Press, 2008).

For a more specific reflection on the new roles that Catholics undertook in their parishes, see Debra Campbell, "The Lay Ministry Explosion, 1970–," in *Transforming Parish Ministry: The Changing Roles of Catholic Clergy, Laity, and Women Religious*, ed. Jay P. Dolan et al. (New York: Crossroad, 1989), 267–280, and Virginia Sullivan Finn, "Ministerial Attitudes and Aspirations of Catholic Laywomen in the United States," in *Religious Institutions and Women's Leadership: New Roles Inside the Mainstream*, ed. Catherine Wessinger (Columbia: University of South Carolina Press, 1996), 245–268.

Women's changing involvement in the postwar parish has not been accorded the scholarly attention it deserves, either by historians of women or by historians of American Catholicism. Studies that present the Catholic women as "a problem" include Sally Cunneen, *Sex: Female; Religion: Catholic* (New York: Holt, Rinehard and Winston, 1968) and Andrew M. Greeley and Mary G. Durkin, *Angry Catholic Women: A Sociological Investigation* (Chicago: Thomas More Press, 1984). Even Mary Jo Weaver's chapter on women in the parish in *New Catholic Women: A Contemporary Challenge to Traditional Religious Authority* (San Francisco: Harper & Row, 1986) is a theoretical reflection not a historical description. There is, however, an important contribution to the history of feminist Catholics; see Mary J. Henold, *Catholic and Feminist: The Surprising History of the*

American Catholic Feminist Movement (Chapel Hill: University of North Carolina Press, 2008).

Religion rarely figures within standard histories of the modern women's movement such as Sara Evans, *Personal Politics: The Roots of Women's Liberation in the Civil Rights Movement and the New Left* (New York: Vintage Books, 1979) or Nancy Cott, *The Groundings of Modern Feminism* (New Haven, CT: Yale University Press, 1987). The exception to the absence of integrating religion into histories of the feminist movement is Ann Braude, *Transforming the Faiths of Our Fathers: Women Who Changed American Religion* (New York: Palgrave Macmillan, 2004).

On Catholic women and ordination issues, see Kelley A. Raab, *When Women Become Priests: The Catholic Women's Ordination Debate* (New York: Columbia University Press, 2000) and Joan Chittister, *Women, Ministry, and the Church* (New York: Paulist Press, 1983). For a general history of women clergy, see Carl J. Schneider and Dorothy Schneider, *In Their Own Right: The History of American Clergywomen* (New York: Crossroad, 1997), and for a sociological evaluation, see Mark Chaves, *Ordaining Women: Culture and Conflict in Religious Organizations* (Cambridge, MA: Harvard University Press, 1997).

For a negative appraisal of the impact of women in post-Vatican II Catholicism as well as Christianity in general, see Leon J. Podles, *The Church Impotent: The Feminization of Christianity* (Dallas, TX: Spence Publishing, 1999).

Studies of Catholic social teachings since the Second Vatican Council are numerous. An excellent general history is Philip S. Land, *Catholic Social Teaching: As I Have Lived, Loathed, and Loved It* (Chicago: Loyola University Press, 1994). For the period prior to the Council, see Craig R. Prentiss, *Debating God's Economy: Social Justice in America on the Eve of Vatican II* (University Park: Pennsylvania State University Press, 2008). A theological summary of the major documents is Kenneth R. Hines, ed., *Modern Catholic Social Teaching: Commentaries and Interpretations* (Washington, D.C.: Georgetown University Press, 2005). For a more conservative interpretation, see Rodger Charles, *The Social Teaching of Vatican II, Its Origin and Development: Catholic Social Ethics, an Historical and Comparative Study* (San Francisco: Ignatius Press, 1982).

My discussion of Bishop George Evans comes from Thomas J. Noel, *Colorado Catholicism and the Archdiocese of Denver, 1857–1989* (Boulder: University of Colorado Press, 1990). For other antiwar protestors, see Charles Meconis, *With Clumsy Grace: The American Catholic Left, 1961–1975* (New York: Seabury Press, 1979) and Murray Polner and Jim O'Grady, *Disarmed and Dangerous: The Radical Life and Times of Daniel and Philip Berrigan* (Boulder, CO: Westview Press, 1998). American Catholic protestors of the sixties followed in the footsteps of earlier Catholic radicals; see James Terence Fisher, *The Catholic Counterculture in America, 1933–1962* (Chapel Hill: University of North Carolina Press, 1989). Catholics also continued their role as supporters of conservative causes; see, Patrick Allit, *Catholic Intellectuals and Conservative Politics in America, 1950–1985* (Ithaca, NY: Cornell University Press, 1993) and Donald T. Critchlow, *Phyllis Schlafly and Grassroots Conservatism* (Princeton, NJ: Princeton University Press, 2005).

I relied heavily on Leslie Woodcock Tentler, *Catholics and Contraception: An American History* (Ithaca, NY: Cornell University Press, 2004) for the birth control story prior to *Humanae Vitae*. Histories of the controversy include Robert Blair Kaiser, *The Politics of Sex and Religion: A Case History in the Development of Doctrine, 1962–1984* (Kansas City, MO: Leaven Press, 1987) and Robert McClory, *Turning Point: The Inside Story of the Papal Birth Control Commission, and How* Humanae Vitae *Changed the Life of Patty Crowley and the Future of the Church* (New York: Crossroad, 1995). Charles E. Curran, *Loyal Dissent: Memoir of a Catholic Theologian* (Washington, D.C.: Georgetown University Press, 2006) reflects on his role in signing the Catholic University "statement," and his and other liberal theological reflections are contained in Charles E. Curran, ed., *Contraception: Authority and Dissent* (New York: Herder and Herder, 1969). For a fuller examination of the history of theological reflection on regulating birth, see John T. Noonan, Jr., *Contraception: A History of Its Treatment by the Catholic Theologians and Canonists* (Cambridge, MA: Harvard University Press, 1965). For Catholic John Rock's position, see his *The Time Has Come: A Catholic Doctor's Proposals to End the Battle over Birth Control* (New York: Knopf, 1963) and for an appraisal of his role in the history of reproduction medicine, see Margaret S. Marsh and Wanda Ronner, *The Fertility Doctor: John Rock and the Reproductive Revolution* (Baltimore, MD: Johns Hopkins University Press, 2008). For a recent, positive evaluation of *Humanae Vitae* that sees it as written "to assert the Church's unbroken condemnation of the use of contraception," see Janet E. Smith, *Humanae Vitae: A Generation Later* (Washington, D.C.: The Catholic University of America Press, 1991).

Based on his article, "I am a Priest, I Want to Marry" for *The Saturday Evening Post*, James Kavanaugh's *A Modern Priest Looks at His Outdated Church* (New York: Trident Press, 1967) became a best seller. Another collection of first person accounts from the era is John Anthony O'Brien, *Why Priests Leave: The Intimate Stories of Twelve Who Did* (New York: Hawthorne Books, 1969). The original studies on the priestly life were published by U.S. Catholic Conference of Bishops as Andrew M. Greeley, *The Catholic Priest in the United States: Sociological Investigations*; Eugene C. Kennedy and Victor Heckler, *The Catholic Priest in the United States: Psychological Investigations*; and John Tracy Ellis, *The Catholic Priest in the United States: Historical Investigations*. Andrew Greeley elaborated on his findings in *Priests in the United States: Reflections on a Survey* (New York: Doubleday, 1972). After fifty years, the priest crisis has been domesticated into a "priest shortage." See the demographic studies of Richard

A. Schoenherr, Lawrence Alfred Young, and Tsan-Yuang Cheng, *Full Pews and Empty Altars: Demographics of the Priest Shortage in United States Catholic Dioceses* (Madison: University of Wisconsin Press, 1993) and Richard A. Schoenherr and David Yamane, *Goodbye Father: The Celibate Male Priesthood and the Future of the Catholic Church* (New York: Oxford University Press, 2002).

For an evaluation of Pope Paul VI, see the works of Peter Hebblethwaite, *The Year of Three Popes* (London: Collins, 1978) and *Paul VI: The First Modern Pope* (New York: Paulist Press, 1993).

Chapter Eight: Legacies

Basic information on Marion County may be found in the "Images of America" book by Kevin McCarthy and Ernest Jernigan, *Ocala* (Charleston, SC: Arcadia Publishing, 2001) and on the City of Ocala Web site. Blessed Trinity Church's archival materials are overseen by Marilyn Curron. Many of their bulletins are online, and their quarterly publication, "Trinity Triangle" was particularly helpful for my discussion of their work in Africa.

The contemporary situation of American Catholicism has been documented by many studies, although most of those do not separate out the story by region. Consequently, the closing of churches and schools on the East Coast and in the Midwest belie the growth of institutional Catholicism in places like Florida. An exception to this is Jerome P. Baggett's interview-based study of Catholics in the Bay Area of northern California, *Sense of the Faithful: How American Catholics Live Their Faith* (New York: Oxford University Press, 2008). Sophisticated sociological work based on survey data is conducted by Georgetown University's Center for the Applied Research on the Apostolate (CARA) and Catholic University's Life Cycle Institute. Both of these institutes were founded after the Second Vatican Council as a response to new openness to modern, social-scientific inquiry about religious behavior. Their data has found its way into many synthetic volumes such as James M. O'Toole, *The Faithful: A History of Catholics in America* (Cambridge, MA: Harvard University Press, 2008), 266–308.

See also David Gibson, *The Coming Catholic Church: How the Faithful Are Shaping a New American Catholicism* (San Francisco: HarperCollins, 2004); William V. D'Antonio, et al., *American Catholics: Gender, Generation, and Commitment* (Walnut Creek, CA: AltaMira Press, 2001); and Peter Steinfels, *People Adrift: The Crisis of the Roman Catholic Church in America* (New York: Simon and Schuster, 2003).

American critics of the Spirit of Vatican II flourished in the nineties and after. Thomas Day skewered both sixties experimentalism and Irish American sentimentality in *Why Catholics Can't Sing: The Culture of Catholicism and the Triumph of Bad Taste* (New York: Crossroad, 1991) and the hideous "plastic surgery" (p. viii) of Vatican II design in *Where Have You Gone, Michelangelo? The Loss of Soul in Catholic Culture* (New York: Crossroad, 1993). Less humorously sarcastic but equally critical are the works by former Lutheran, Catholic priest, and journal editor Richard John Neuhaus. Before his death in 2009, Neuhaus wrote *Catholic Matters: Confusion, Controversy, and the Splendor of the Truth* (New York: Basic Books, 2006), in which he stated that the "silliest of the silly season is now past or passing" (113). George Weigel in *The Courage to Be Catholic: Crisis Reform, and the Future of the Church* (New York: Basic Books, 2002) looks forward to a "real" reform of a Church that had too long been led by liberal dissenters, who he describes as "a wrecking crew for whom nothing short of Catholicism's transformation into a kind of high-church, politically correct American 'denomination'—Catholic lite—will suffice" (3).

British Dominican and prolific writer Aidan Nichols cites the works of anthropologists (and Catholics) Mary Douglas and Victor Turner to support a return to more formal ritual. See his *Looking at the Liturgy: A Critical View of Its Contemporary Form* (San Francisco: Ignatius Press, 1996); as does British layman, David Torevell in *Losing the Sacred: Ritual, Modernity and Liturgical Reform* (New York: Continuum, 2000). The United Kingdom has provided fruitful ground for the "new liturgical movement," with a key conference occurring at Oxford in 1996. A conference volume *Beyond the Prosaic: Renewing the Liturgical Movement,* edited by Stratford Caldecott (New York Continuum, 1998) outlines the key themes of the movement. Adoremus: The Society for the Renewal of the Sacred Liturgy and the more scholarly Society for Catholic Liturgy (SCL) are two societies founded in 1995 in the United States to promote liturgical reform. The former president of SCL, Father M. Francis Mannion, has an edited collection, *Masterworks of God: Essays in Liturgical Theory and Practice* (Mundelein, IL: Hillenbrand Books, 2004) that reflects the Society's insights into ritual, art, and music. The works of theologian Hans Urs von Balthasar provides the theological foundation for many of the authors published by Ignatius Press, a company committed to post-Vatican II reform. Anglican Catherine Pickstock is also called on to provide the theoretical foundation for works like Jonathan Robinson, *The Mass and Modernity: Walking to Heaven Backwards* (San Francisco: Ignatius Press, 2005).

John F. Baldovin in *Reforming Liturgy: A Response to Critics* (Collegeville, MN: Liturgical Press, 2008) provides a summary and critical appraisal of European post-Vatican II reformers, including the influential German liturgist Klaus Gamber. Although conservatives who publish with Ignatius Press would not credit his thought with provoking an interest in rituals and devotions, Catholic theologian David Tracy's highly influential *The Analogical Imagination: Christian Theology and the Culture of Pluralism* (New York: Crossroad, 1981) stresses the importance of symbols in Christianity. Tracy's ideas were popularized and put into a sociological context in Andrew Greeley's *The Catholic Imagination* (Berkeley: University of California Press, 2001).

For biographies of Pope John Paul II, see John Cornwell, *The Pontiff in Winter: Triumph and Conflict in the Reign of John Paul II* (New York: Doubleday, 2004) and George Weigel, *Witness to Hope: The Biography of Pope John Paul II* (New York: Harper Perennial, 1999).

Joseph Ratzinger's corpus of writing is extensive. In addition to *The Spirit of the Liturgy*, see his *The Feast of Faith: Approaches to a Theology of the Liturgy* (San Francisco: Ignatius Press, 1986). For a more colloquial text, the result of Cardinal Ratzinger's conversations with Italian journalist Vittorio Messori, see *The Ratzinger Report: An Exclusive Interview on the State of the Church* (San Francisco: Ignatius Press, 1985), 119–134.

The complicated history of the relationship between Protestants, Catholics, priests, and ministers over the question of abortion has not been fully surveyed. Almost nothing has been written about the ritual and devotional dimensions of either the pro-life or the pro-choice movements. Although not a religious history, Kristin Luker, *Abortion and the Politics of Motherhood* (Berkeley: University of California Press, 1985) is helpful in understanding Catholic involvement because it utilizes oral histories. A more technical set of essays is in Timothy A. Byrnes and Mary C. Seagers, eds., *The Catholic Church and the Politics of Abortion: A View from the States* (Boulder, CO: Westview Press, 1992). Mary C. Seagers speculates on why bishops became silent on birth control but took up the abortion controversy in "The Bishops, Birth Control and Abortion Policy: 1950–1985" in her edited volume *Church Polity and American Politics: Issues in Contemporary American Catholicism* (New York: Garland Press, 1990), 215–231. D. Paul Sullins looks at who gets abortions in "Catholic/Protestant Trends on Abortion: Convergence and Polarity," in *Journal for the Scientific Study of Religion* 38 (September 1999): 354–369. For a history of various theological positions taken on abortion, see Daniel A. Dombrowski and Robert John Deltete, *A Brief, Liberal, Catholic Defense of Abortion* (Champagne-Urbana: University of Illinois Press, 2000). On pro-choice supporters in religious communities, see Tom Davis, *Sacred Work: Planned Parenthood and Its Clergy Alliances* (New Brunswick, NJ: Rutgers University Press, 2005).

The core source on foreign priests is Dean R. Hoge and Aniedi Okure, *International Priests in America* (Collegeville, MN: Liturgical Press, 2006). A more humanistic description is Laurie Goodstein's three-part series on foreign priests published in the *New York Times*, December 28, 29, and 30, 2008. The larger context of southern hemisphere Christianity is outlined in Philip Jenkins, *Next Christendom: The Coming of Global Christianity* (New York: Oxford University Press, 2002); with the role that the Second Vatican Council played delineated in

Ian Linden, *Global Catholicism: Diversity and Change since Vatican II* (New York: Columbia University Press, 2009).

During the summer of 2007, the Pew Forum on Religion and Public Life surveyed over 35,000 adults to learn about current religious beliefs and practices in the United States. What they found was that the population of American Catholics was holding steady due to immigration. Although nearly one in three Americans (31 percent) were raised as Catholics, fewer than one in four (24 percent) describe themselves as currently Catholic. It if wasn't for immigration, the Catholic population would be in decline. Currently, almost half of the Catholic population (46 percent) is foreign born; see U. S. Religious Landscape Survey, http://religions.pewforum.org/reports (accessed August 1, 2009).

Dean Hoge et al., in *Money Matters: Personal Giving in American Churches* (Louisville, KY: Westminster John Knox Press, 1996) place Catholics low on the list of denominations who gave; only Christian Scientists and Unitarian-Universalists were more tight-fisted. Topping the list were Mormons, who gave over 7 percent, and Assemblies of God, who contributed 5 percent of their income to their churches. Economist Charles Zech, who participated in the Lilly Foundation grant that produced *Money Matters*, went on to publish *Why Catholic's Don't Give: And What Can be Done About It* (Huntington, IN: Our Sunday Visitor, 2000), and another researcher, Patrick H. McNamara, wrote *Called to Be Stewards: Bringing New Life to Catholic Parishes* (Collegeville, MN: Liturgical Press, 2003). The American Catholic bishops had earlier recognized the problem and tried to correct it with *Stewardship: A Disciple's Response* (Washington, D.C.: Office for Pub. and Promotion Services, United States Catholic Conference, 1992), with follow-up resource materials in 1996. Since the late nineties, a variety of how-to books have been published on stewardship.

For a succinct summary of what sociologists have discovered about Catholic schools in the past few decades, see Gerald Rupert "Catholic Schools Post-Vatican II: A Review of Research Studies" in his *Catholic Schools: Mission, Markets and Morality* (London: Routledge, 2002), 80–96. A more in-depth overview is the result of a 1993 conference that brought together American, Irish, and British educators and scholars; see Terence McLaughlin and Bernadette O'Keeffe, *The Contemporary Catholic School: Context, Identity, and Diversity* (London: Routledge, 1996).

Although there are many "sister parishes" across the United States that partner with churches in developing countries, there are no large-scale studies on how they influence American Catholic life, promote social justice, or increase the standard of living in poor countries. A useful case study, however, of sister parishes in Haiti and Michigan is by anthropologist Tara Hefferan, *Twinning Faith Development: Catholic Parish Partnering in the US and Haiti* (Bloomfield,

CT: Kumarian Press, 2007) and "Encouraging Development 'Alternatives': Grassroots Church Partnering in the U. S. and Haiti," in *Bridging the Gaps: Faith-Based Organizations, Neoliberalism, and Development in Latin America and the Caribbean* (New York: Rowman & Littlefield, 2009), 69–82. Hefferan cites the Parish Twinning Programs of the Americas as having enabled 340 matches between churches in Haiti and North America (71). For a "how-to" guide, see Dennis P. O'Connor, *Bridges of Faith: Building a Relationship with a Sister Parish* (Cincinnati, OH: St. Anthony Messenger Press, 2007).

The concept of "twinning" began after World War II when former enemies in Europe came together as "sister cities" to promote mutual understanding and economic growth. By 1991 approximately eleven thousand sister city pairs have been formed, according to geographer Wilber Zelinsky. In general, social scientists have ignored the impact of faith-based communities on international development, although two notable studies of religious nongovernmental organizations are Erica Bornstein, *The Spirit of Development: Protestant NGOs, Morality, and Economics in Zimbabwe* (Stanford, CA: Stanford University Press, 2005) and Laurie A. Occhipinti, *Acting on Faith: Religious Development Organizations in Northwestern Argentina* (Lanham, MD: Lexington Books, 2005). In these two cases, however, professional development agencies are involved. What makes the "sister parish" movement unique is its grass-roots, decentralized, nonprofessional structure.

Research on religion and health is growing as the Baby Boom generation ages. See the excellent survey by Neal Krause, "Aging," in Helen Rose Ebaugh, ed., *Handbook for Religion and Social Institutions* (New York: Springer, 2006) as well as Klaus Warner Schaie et al., *Religious Influences on Health and Well-Being in the Elderly* (New York: Springer, 2004); Melvin A. Kimble and Susan H. McFadden, *Aging Spirituality and Religion: A Handbook* (Minneapolis, MN: Fortress Press, 2002); and Jeffrey S. Levin, ed., *Religion in Aging and Health: Theoretical Foundations and Methodological Frontiers* (Thousand Oak, CA: Sage Publications, 1994).

INDEX